Edward Lear
Vivien Noakes

Vivien Noakes is the leading authority on Edward Lear; her other work includes *Scenes from Victorian Life* and the series *For Lovers of Edward Lear*.

She has broadcast frequently and acted as adviser for the television drama about Lear by Alan Plater, *On the Edge of the Sand*, which was broadcast on BBC 2. She was guest curator for the major Edward Lear exhibition mounted by the Royal Academy in 1985.

Edward Lear was first published in 1968.

VIVIEN NOAKES

EDWARD LEAR

The Life of a Wanderer

ARIEL BOOKS

BRITISH BROADCASTING CORPORATION

The television play be Alan Plater *Edward Lear: On the Edge of the Sand* was first broadcast on BBC 2 in 1985. The part of Edward Lear was played by Robert Lang, the director was John Glenister and the producer was Michael Andrews.

Published by the
British Broadcasting Corporation
35 Marylebone High Street, London W1M 4AA

ISBN 0 563 20387 0

First published 1968 by
William Collins Sons & Co Ltd
Revised edition published by Fontana Paperbacks 1979
This edition first published 1985

Typeset by Phoenix Photosetting, Chatham
Printed in Great Britain by Mackays of Chatham Ltd

CONTENTS

To
Anya, Jonathan and Benedict

Preface

'I cannot help thinking that my life, letters and diaries would be as interesting as many that are now published,' wrote Lear in 1873, shortly before he left for a tour of India with his old servant, Giorgio Kokali, and before going he went through all his papers and letters and sorted them into bundles in case he should not return. He did come back to live another fourteen years, and when he died in San Remo he left these papers, still methodically arranged, to the trusteeship of his literary executor.

Perhaps it was the distance from England, or possibly it was Victorian discretion, but most of these carefully preserved documents of Lear's life were then apparently destroyed. Some of the letters were returned to their writers and thirty years of diaries were kept, a few small family heirlooms were sent to his nephew's children in New Zealand – but the rest is lost.

In working on this book I have drawn in particular on the diaries, now in the Houghton Library, Harvard, and the letters Lear wrote to Chichester Fortescue, Lord Carlingford, published as the *Letters* and *Later Letters of Edward Lear* and preserved now in the Somerset Record office. Of the letters he wrote to his sister Ann covering the years from 1837 to her death in 1861 no trace has been found, though these were still in existence in the 1930s in South Africa. Lear's great-great-niece who owned them had several copies made of which only one now seems to be extant, and from this typed copy I have also extensively drawn.

In the years since the publication of the first edition of this book, more material has been discovered, and the processes of reproduction of manuscript have improved. This has given me further opportunities to study both the broad sweeps and the smaller details of Lear's life, to correct errors and to be bolder in some conclusions.

'It is queer (and you would say so if you saw me) that I am the man as is making some three or four thousand people laugh in England all at one time', Lear wrote after the publication of *More Nonsense* in 1871, and part of the fascination of Lear is in discovering the tragedy of the humorous, compassionate, much-loved man he was.

Foreword

The writer of this note has made a nearly life-long study of Edward Lear, having been entranced with his writing and drawing as early as 1905, when first able to read. Later came the chance to collect and gather at Harvard University by far the largest single collection of this British poet, artist, traveller, and nonsense-inventor author.

Ever since Lear died in 1888, a thoroughly scholarly, yet eminently readable, biography has been needed. Vivien Noakes has supplied it, explained much that was hitherto unclear, and added a great deal of new information since Angus Davidson's pioneering study of 1938. She writes so understandingly, and with such deep affection, that Lear has become deservedly one of the most lovable characters in all literature. Due to her, he is assuming the well-deserved rank of a major Victorian figure.

Houghton Library, Harvard, USA.   Philip Hofer
March 1978

PART ONE

MR LEAR
1812–1848

1 Childhood
1812–1828

Edward Lear was born in Holloway on 12 May 1812.[1] He was the twentieth child of Jeremiah Lear, a London stockbroker, and his wife Ann.

It was the second year of the Regency, an age of exaggerated contrasts, of rich patronage and struggling industrial awakening. The boldness and grace of Nash's London, of the fashionable new houses built around the Regent's Park with their Grecian porticos and ostentatious stucco, contrasted sharply with the cramped poverty of the tenement houses springing up around the textile factories in the industrial towns of the north. There may have been time in more privileged circles for the young ladies to titter over the gallant officers of the militia in their scarlet tunics, and for the young and the ageing to pursue their amours in the fashion set by the royal court: in under-privileged circles a working day which could last from four in the morning until eight at night left no time for such frivolities.

But England was moving towards another age, a time of agitation and reform, and alongside the picturesque figure of the Regency buck was the dedicated, purposeful middle-class evangelist. Thomas Bowdler purified Shakespeare for the family in 1802, and in 1807 William Wilberforce succeeding in abolishing the slave trade: a frightening narrow-mindedness on the one hand, and a real sense of moral responsibility on the other, were preparing the way for Victorian England.

Lear seldom spoke of his family, and what little he said was misleading. 'My own [name]', he once told a friend, 'as I think you know is really LÖR, but my Danish grandfather picked off the two dots and pulled out the diagonal line and made the word Lear (the two dots and the line and the O representing the sound -ea). If he threw away the line and the dots only he would be called *Mr Lor*, which he didn't like'[2] – which is delightful, but quite untrue.

At the end of the seventeenth century, George Leare, the son of a butcher from Gillingham in Dorset, came up to London. He was apprenticed for seven years to a London fruiterer, and in 1692 he became a member of the Fruiterers' Company, one of the City livery companies, and a Freeman of the City of London. He never learnt to write, but within twenty years he had become Renter Warden of the Company, and was firmly established in the City. He died in 1745, and was buried in the vault of St Anne's, Westminster: it was a quiet funeral at his request, with 'only a hearse and three coaches and twelve branch candles'.

George Leare had at least seven children, and some of them were connected with a sugar-refining business which the Lear family established in the middle of the eighteenth century.[3] At this time refining was immensely profitable, for England had a monopoly of trade with the West Indies – even sugar for the Continent had to come through British ports – and refiners were opulent and respectable.

In this successful family business we find Edward's grand-father Henry Lear. The earliest mention of him is in 1744 when he was married at All Hallows, London Wall, the church of his bride, Margaret Lester. He was living then in the drab river-side parish of St Benet's, Paul's Wharf, and working in Thames Street just above London Bridge. Jeremiah, Edward's father, was born in 1757, the youngest of six children, and when he was six his father died of a sudden fever at the home to which the family had moved in Whitechapel. Margaret Lear carried on the business after her husband's death, and Jeremiah later joined her as a sugar refiner.

In 1788 he married a young Whitechapel girl, Ann Clark Skerrett – he was thirty-one and she was nineteen. Family tradition says that they eloped, though this is unlikely as the banns were called three times; but since they were married at Wanstead in Essex which was several miles from where either of them lived, and as nobody from either family was there to witness the ceremony it does look as if they did not approve of the marriage.[4] We do not know why this was, but it may have been because they came from different social backgrounds, for although Jeremiah's ancestors had been very successful they were undoubtedly 'trade', whilst Ann's family were not.

Her great-great-grandfather – John Grainger, Gentleman – lived in the hamlet of Sunnyside, five miles outside Newcastle; he had six children and the youngest was Ann's great-grandmother.

Some time after the '45 Rebellion her daughter, Ann's grand-mother, Florence Brignall Usher, came south to settle in London. When she died in 1802 she owned property in the City and in Whitechapel, which may have been where Jeremiah and Ann met. Her eldest daughter, also Florence, married an Edward Skerrett about whom we know little. He had three daughters of whom Ann was the eldest.

Jeremiah and his wife went to live in Pentonville, and here their first child, a daughter, was born on 17 January 1790, and christened Ann. In the same year he was admitted to the Fruiterers' Company, and at once became a member of the Livery.[5] By 1797 he was Renter Warden, as George Leare had been nearly a century before. Two years later he was elected Master of the Company and he left the family business to become a stockbroker.[6]

Cobbett, as he travelled round the south of England on his rural rides, came to dislike these pretentious gentlemen who had no roots in England's soil and who buried the green fields of Middlesex beneath their sprawling, status-seeking houses. Certainly a broker could become very wealthy, but he could also lose large sums of money, and as Jeremiah was now over forty and had five children to support he was taking a risk. He had some capital, for both his mother and his sister had died and left him money, and he was probably relying on his City contacts to get himself established. He chose his time well, for Stock Exchange business was expanding, and the gentle coffee-house transactions had been replaced by business-like negotiations in Sweeting's Alley. By 1802 business was so good that the brokers collected amongst themselves to build the London Stock Exchange at Capel Court in Bartholomew Lane: Jeremiah bought one £50 share in the new Exchange and was entitled to call himself a Proprietor.[7]

He prospered, and by 1806 was able to follow Cobbett's status-seekers when he moved his family to Holloway,[8] at this time a small village fashionable for wealthy City gentlemen. It was high and the air was salubrious; it was set amidst fields and woods, and there was a coach into London every half-hour. The elegant Georgian house stood on the site of an Elizabethan archery range on the corner of the Holloway Road and the Seven Sisters Road, and was called Bowman's Lodge. From the large first-floor drawing-room there was a fine view south over the countryside towards London, and one of Edward's earliest memories was of being wrapped in a blanket and held to the window so that he could see the illuminations celebrating the victory of Waterloo.

The family increased yearly, but many of them died as babies. After Ann came three Sarahs, for the Lears persisted in using a name until one of the children survived, and three Henrys. Then there was Mary, Eleanor, Jane, Olivier, Harriett, Cordelia, Frederick, Florence, Charles, Catherine, Edward, and finally a second Catherine. There were two others, a boy and a girl, but they apparently died unnamed. Perhaps it is not surprising that when their mother died in 1844 the cause of her death is given as 'general decay'.[9]

It was a large family to support, and they appear to have lived in some style. It is said that they had twelve carriages, and although this is unlikely, it does seem probable that Jeremiah was living to the limit of his income, and perhaps even beyond it. But then came the economically unsettled aftermath of the Napoleonic wars, and suddenly in 1816 Jeremiah fell a defaulter in the Stock Exchange.[10] He owed £2150 11s 1d which was then a considerable amount of money. Fortunately this related only to his dealings within the Exchange, and when a friend settled his account for him by paying the creditors 2s 6d in the £, Jeremiah was free to resume business. But all this time bills had been coming in, and he soon found himself very deeply in debt.

According to family tradition Jeremiah Lear became bankrupt and was committed to King's Bench Prison where he languished for four years. The house, the furniture and the twelve carriages were sold; the family split up, some of the children going with Mrs Lear to 'horrid New Street' where she could be near her husband. Every day she would visit him taking with her 'a full six-course dinner, with the delicacies of the season'. The girls were put out to work as governesses, and within four months four of them had died from sudden hardships.

This tradition seems to be based on truth, but is a colourful exaggeration.[11] Jeremiah Lear was never bankrupt, nor was he ever in the King's Bench Prison. Lear tells us that his father served a short prison sentence for fraud and debt, but since Jeremiah kept up his regular attendance at the Livery of the Fruiterers' Company during all this time, he cannot have been away for long.[12] Certainly the family left Holloway, but the house was not sold: instead it was let furnished to a Jewish family who 'always opened the windows in thunder storms – for the easier entrance of the Messiah, but to greater spoiling of the furniture',[13] so that brought Jeremiah capital loss as well as temporary gain. Almost certainly they split up, and those who were old enough apparently had to fend for themselves, but as there are later references to all but one of the girls, four of them could not have died, at this stage anyway.

To ease the burden on his mother, Edward was given to Ann to be looked after. He was just four, and from then on – even when they were back at Bowman's Lodge again – Mrs Lear had nothing more to do with his upbringing. He was a rather ugly, short-sighted, affectionate little boy, and he was bewildered and hurt by her unaccountable rejection of him. He understood a little of why they had had to leave Bowman's Lodge, and he seems to have blamed the encumbrance of house and possessions for his sudden misery. When he grew up he became terrified of burdening himself in the same way. Even the Yonghy-Bonghy-Bò possessed only 'Two old chairs, and half a candle, – One old jug without a handle, – ' and Mr & Mrs Discobbolos proclaimed:

> We want no knives nor forks nor chairs,
> No tables nor carpets nor household cares,
> From worry of life we've fled –
> Oh! W! X! Y! Z!
> There is no more trouble ahead,
> Sorrow or any such thing – . . .

In fact, Ann seems to have loved him very much, and to have been a kind, rather jolly little woman whose influence on Lear was profound. Her generous warmth, humour and goodness did much to balance the harm done by other aspects of his childhood. Her Christian belief was profound, but practical. 'A man's life proves his religion, more than any words can do,'[14] she would say. Here she differed from others of his sisters – particularly Mary and Harriett, whose Evangelical narrowness sometimes saddened Lear. Jollity and affection come through his letters to her, as he teases her about her spelling and her solecisms, her maidenly flirtatiousness and her fear of animals. 'Should you like me to send you a green frog by the next parcel? – or a tortoise? I won't do so unless you ask me – but perhaps you may have changed your ways of thinking about pets nowadays.'[15] It was a merriment he had learnt from her. 'Do you remember dear Fred,' she wrote to another brother, 'what I used to call you many years ago? Your constant increase in *circumference* reminds me again of the *Norfolk Biffin* – what a fine specimen of this rounded fruit you must present! ! I think I see you now how you used to run round the room after me when I compar'd you to the flat *spreading* Norfolk Apple.'[16]

Ann never married, though she loved at least one man – a Major Wilby. Another, Sir Claudius Hunter, proposed to her, but she 'did not, or would not'[17] marry him. Instead she devoted herself to Edward. She was twenty-one years older than he, and she became as nearly a mother to him as she could. 'Ever all she was to me was good,' Lear wrote after her death, '& what I should have been unless she had been my mother I dare not think.'[18]

The family was not away from Bowman's Lodge for very long.[19] Jeremiah was able to borrow £1000 from his bank to help him to get straight,[20] but when they came home again they lived very simply and there was never any money to spare. But the house was theirs once more, and it was here that Edward spent the rest of his strange and unhappy childhood.

It was a disturbing atmosphere for a child. He lived in the same house as his mother who had probably never wanted him, and his father whom he practically never saw; there were undoubtedly the usual stresses which accompany financial trouble, and despite – or because of – the twenty-one children the marriage does not seem to have been a very happy one. All his life Edward tried to avoid quarrelsome noise and arguments, and to search instead for gentleness and tranquillity.

When he was about seven the emotional strain began to show itself in sudden changes of mood with bouts of acute depression which he called 'the Morbids'. Significantly the first of these came after a rare happy evening with his father. 'The earliest of all the morbidnesses I can recollect must have been somewhere about 1819 – when my Father took me to a field near Highgate, where was a rural performance of gymnastic clowns &c. – & a band. The music was good, – at least it attracted me: – & the sunset & twilight I remember as if yesterday. And I can recollect crying half the night after all the small gaiety broke up – & also suffering for days at the memory of the past scene.'[21] He was a sad, lonely little boy grasping happiness when it came and savouring every bit of it – and broken-hearted when it had slipped beyond his grasp again.

But even earlier, when he was only five or six, had come the first attack of epilepsy – 'the Demon' as he called it. It must have been inherited, for his sister Jane was also an epileptic. 'How I remember my sister Jane's epileptic attacks, now!' he wrote in 1873, 'child as I was then, & quite unable to understand them.'[22]

His own seizures were often violent, and for a child they were terrible and frightening. The illness affected his whole life profoundly. He was fearful that one day an attack might leave him paralysed, or that the repeated assaults would destroy his mind; though he also hoped, until well into middle-age, that the disease might loosen its grip as he grew older. It was a constant threat, for sometimes he had several attacks a day. He had warning before they came on – the aura epileptica – so that he was able to get out of the way, and apparently nobody apart from his family ever realised that he was an epileptic.[23] But this perpetual secrecy forced him into isolation. Even today epilepsy is a lonely disease, and although the idea of 'demoniac possession' can now be laughed at there are still irrational lingerings of shame. In the early nineteenth century it was obscured by ignorance and old wives' tales, and one of these was that attacks could be brought on by masturbation. Lear certainly believed that there could be a connection between the two, and as an adult he constantly blamed the attacks on his lack of will power.[24] The usual threat offered to a little boy was that his penis would drop off and, like the Pobble whose toes disappeared when the scarlet flannel wrapper was taken away, Edward must sometimes have thought that he would be happier without it; the Pobble was given a feminine concoction of 'Lavendar water tinged with pink', and perhaps this was the best solution.

Doctors urged that children suffering from epilepsy should never be allowed to sleep by themselves, and it sounds as if sister Harriett was entrusted with disciplining him, for many years later Lear 'reflected on days long gone – when I was but 8 – if so many years old. And this demon oppressed me then "I not knowing" its worry & misery. Every morning in the little study when learning my lessons – : all day long: & always in the evening & at night. Nor could I have been more than 6 I think – for I remember whole years before I went to school – at 11. The strong will of sister Harriett put a short pause to the misery – but very short. How well I remember that evening! – Thus, a sorrow so inborn & ingrained so to speak, was evidently part of what I have been born to suffer – & could not have been so far avoided willed I never so much so to do.'[25]

No clinical treatment for epilepsy had yet been discovered, but a careful diet and plenty of exercise certainly helped, and it may have been to relieve the attacks that Ann and Edward went to stay in Margate. A belief in the therapeutic value of spa waters was centuries old, but the idea that sea water and sea air could also be salutary was only just becoming fashionable. 'Sea air and Sea Bathing together were nearly infallible, one or the other of them being a match for every Disorder, of the Stomach, the Lungs or the Blood,'[26] wrote Jane Austen in 1817, and she summed up the fashionable belief.

The resort was easily reached from London by the Margate hoys, small sailing boats which carried their passengers down the busy Thames and out into the estuary. It could not offer the fashionable Pump Rooms and glittering clientele of other resorts, but there was plenty to excite a small boy. Years later Edward reminded Ann of 'the hawk Mr Cox had; – & the colliers disbarking coal at the pier – & the windmills – & the chimney sweep you so *cruelly* MADE me walk round & round to be sure he was not smoking – shocking. My imperfect sight in those days – ante-spectacled – formed everything into a horror.'[27]

Ann was concerned about his health and her anxiety was justified, but her single-minded attention to him was not a good thing, and he grew up swathed by protective older sisters. Often ill and thrown back on his own resources his imagination became his plaything; but though a more boisterous boyhood would have been much better for him and a more balanced childhood would have made him a happier man, it would also have made him a different one.

It was from Ann and Sarah that he had all his early tuition. They probably taught him from one of the popular question-and-answer guidebooks – *Magnall's Questions*, or *The Child's Guide to Knowledge* – which were 'intended to awaken a spirit of laudable curiosity in young minds'. They certainly succeeded with Lear, for his soundly based but incomplete education left him always anxious to find out more. 'I am almost thanking God that I was never educated,' he wrote when he was forty-seven, 'for it seems to me that 999 of those who are so, expensively & laboriously, have lost all before they arrive at my age – & remain like Swift's Stulbruggs – cut & dry for life, making no use of their earlier=gained treasures: – whereas, I seem to be on the threshold of knowledge . . .'[28]

Ann read to him a good deal, tales of classical mythology and stories from the Bible, and while he was still small he discovered the modern poets – and particularly Byron. When Lear was born Wordsworth and Coleridge were still writing, Shelley had just been sent down from Oxford, Byron had published the first two cantos of *Childe Harold*, and Keats was apprenticed to a surgeon at Edmonton and had hardly yet discovered poetry: by the time

Lear was twelve Keats, Shelley and Byron were all dead. Byron's death affected him in an extraordinary way: 'Pale cold moon,' he wrote in 1861, 'yet now, as in 1823 – ever strangely influencing me. Do you remember the small yard & the passages at ——— in 1823, & 1824 – when I used to sit there in the cold looking at the stars, &, when I heard that Ld. Byron was dead, stupified & crying.'[29] The poet-idol, the social outcast, the figure-head of Greek independence – it was a mature hero for a boy of eleven, and it is unlikely that he knew that Byron too was an epileptic. Lear's reaction to the news from Missolonghi is like that of the fourteen-year-old Tennyson who lay numbed by the sense of finality, and carved on a sandstone rock the words 'Byron is dead'.

But the most important part of his sisters' tuition was their enjoyment of painting. Jeremiah had owned some good paintings and he must have encouraged his children's interest, for one of the downstairs rooms at Bowman's Lodge, next to Ann's room and just across the hall from the nursery, was set aside as the painting-room. To Edward it was the happiest in the house. A little of his early work has survived,[30] and it shows that he was talented in a rather precise way. Ann and Sarah taught him to paint flowers and butterflies and birds – in fact they taught him one of the social accomplishments as they themselves had learnt it.

Lear tells us that when he was eleven he went to school, but nothing at all has survived from this period. In 1822, Sarah married and went to live in Arundel. There is a tradition in the Lear family about Sarah's marriage.[31] One day, Jeremiah Lear was walking in the City when he saw a name-plate inscribed 'Jeremiah Lear'. He was intrigued, and decided to introduce himself to his namesake. The two families came to know each other, and in this Jeremiah Lear's house Sarah met her future husband, Charles Street. The second Lear family lived at Batworth Park, Lyminster, about three miles south of Arundel. There were three children, and the youngest, George Lear, was articled in 1827 to the solicitors Ellis and Blackmore of Gray's Inn. In the same year this firm took on a young clerk named Charles Dickens, and when he was writing the *Pickwick Papers* he remembered George as 'the Articled Clerk, who has paid a premium, and is an attorney in perspective, who runs a tailor's bill, receives invitations to parties, knows a family in Gower Street, and another in Tavistock Square; who goes out of town every Long Vacation to see his father, who keeps live horses innumerable; and who is, in short, the very aristocrat of clerks.'[32]

Coming from life with his sisters at Bowman's Lodge, Edward must have felt a little overwhelmed by such a worldly family.

The countryside around Arundel where Sarah lived has changed very little since then, with rounded hills and sudden scurrying streams running into the River Arun, and small stone-built villages which lie in the gentleness of the downs. Even as a boy Lear was always unusually aware of his natural surroundings and he loved the wide, peaceful landscape; the tranquillity of the hills must have come as a relief from the unhappy atmosphere at Bowman's Lodge. He was often in Sussex between 1823 and 1829, and some of his happiest memories were of those days. He made many new friends there, and the earliest of his surviving Nonsense dates from this time. He understood so well the un-happiness of life that, for him, making people happy was some-thing positive and real – and he discovered that he could make them happy by making them laugh. He was content to be thought a rather lovable oddity, '3 parts crazy – & wholly affectionate'.[33] When he was nineteen he wrote: 'My Sussex friends always say that I can do nothing like other people.'[34] This was particularly true of a family called Drewitt who lived in Peppering, a tiny village beside the River Arun. It was for one of the daughters, Eliza, that Lear wrote his earliest surviving poems.

The first of these is called 'Ode to a Chinaman'. The second,[35] which is incomplete, is called 'Miss Maniac'. It is parody, as all Lear's early Nonsense is, the sad tale of a young girl who is sent away from her father's house after the birth of an illegitimate baby. She has been deserted by the gay young buck who is the father, and as she wanders brooding on the happiness she once knew, her grief destroys her reason and she goes mad. The rhyme is intentionally bathetic and absurd, and with almost every couplet there is a drawing which completes the descent into the ridiculous. It is an immature humour, but it does bring out two characteristics of Lear's Nonsense – a combination of humour with real sadness, and an interdependence of words and pictures. It also expresses Lear's belief that happiness is a thing of the past, and the present is incomprehensibly sad.

He made other, older acquaintances in Sussex, and these influenced both his immediate and eventual careers.[36]

The grossly uneven distribution of wealth in England at this time had one particular advantage, for the rich had money to spend on beautiful things. They built themselves magnificent houses and had their gardens landscaped in the style of

Capability Brown, they filled their homes with beautiful furniture – and with pictures. This was a great age of English landscape painting, and although Constable was largely unrecognised in England, Turner found both patrons and friends in the rich. One of these was the Earl of Egremont who lived at Petworth, twelve miles north of Arundel. He was famous for the encouragement he gave to artists, and for the splendid paintings he had gathered together at his home. This was before the days of big national collections, and privately owned works of art were not generally seen by the public, so when Lear first visited Petworth in the 1820s the paintings must have excited him. Perhaps he shared some of the charming enthusiasm of the author of *British Galleries of Art*, writing in 1824: 'To those who have not already seen the princely domain at Petworth, I would fain convey such a notion of it, that, till they set out to visit it for themselves, it may thus dwell in the distance before them, like a bright spot in the land of promise.'

During one of his visits to Sussex Lear was introduced to Lord Egremont, and to the family of another of Turner's patrons, Walter Ramsden Fawkes. In 1826 he met Lord de Tabley who had founded the British Institution for the Encouragement of British Art twenty years before, and had opened his house in Hill Street to the public so that they might share his delight in the paintings he had collected – for patronage was still guided by enthusiasm and was not yet ruled by the value of investment.

In Sussex Lear found himself on the fringe of the painter's world, and during these years his childhood enjoyment of painting matured into an ambition to become a painter. He developed a lasting admiration for Turner,[37] but if he hoped to follow him and become a landscape painter he would need to go to an art school – perhaps the Royal Academy where Turner had studied and where he now occasionally taught – or at least to be financially independent whilst he taught himself how to paint.

If this had been in his mind it was suddenly quite impossible. Jeremiah Lear was now over seventy, and he had decided that it was time to retire. He had found a small house in Gravesend for himself and his wife and one of the daughters, Florence – but he was not able to make any provision for Edward whom he probably regarded as Ann's responsibility. She had apparently inherited a small annual income from her grandmother[38] so they were not destitute, though Edward always spoke melodramatically of being 'thrown out into the world without a penny', or a halfpenny, or a farthing, depending on his mood. But it did mean that any plans he may have had must be put on one side, at least for the moment. The strange, sad years of his childhood were over. 'Considering all I remember to have passed through from 6 years old to 15 – is it not wonderful I am alive? – far more to be able to feel & write,' he wrote fifty years later.[39] Now, at fifteen and a half, he had to set about earning his own living.

2 The Family of Parrots
1828–1832

Like the ancient Medes and Persians,
Always by his own exertions
    He subsisted on those hills; –
Whiles, – by teaching children spelling, –
Or at times by merely yelling, –
Or at intervals by selling
    'Propter's Nicodemus Pills.'[1]

Upper North Place, Grays Inn Road, is not a fashionable part of London, and it was here – on the top floor at No. 38 – that Ann and Edward found rooms they could afford. Then Edward started looking for work, and he began doing 'uncommon queer shop-sketches – selling them for prices varying from ninepence to four shillings: colouring prints, screens, fans; awhile making morbid disease drawings for hospitals and certain doctors of physic'.[2] Fowler, the Canadian painter who met him in about 1832, tells us that Lear's 'first attempts at earning money were made in offering his little drawings for anything he could get to stagecoach passengers in inn yards.'[3] As well as this he visited houses in Cavendish Square and St James's to teach drawing, probably through introductions from his Sussex friends.

   In fact, so little has survived from this time in his life that it is almost impossible to know what happened, but some time between 1828 and 1830 he began to earn his living by drawing birds. There was a vogue then for large, lavishly illustrated books about the new and exotic animals and birds which were being brought back to England by sailors, and by naturalists on scientific voyages of discovery. The landed gentry could go further and collect the animals themselves, and occasional wandering zebra and wild hog, or a handful of strutting peacocks were considered very à la mode. Private menageries, even on quite a big scale, were not new; Henry I had formed his own royal collection of animals at Woodstock at the beginning of the twelfth century. This was later transferred to the Tower, and in

1829 the animals were taken over by the newly formed Zoological Society of London and formed the nucleus of the Zoological Gardens which were opened in Regent's Park.

As the system for the classification of animals became established, naturalists turned their interest to the animals in their own countries, especially where there were signs of whole species being exterminated. In 1820 Audubon began on his task of drawing and cataloguing all the birds of North America before they disappeared at the slaughtering hands of the new colonists, and in England Prideaux Selby was at work on *Illustrations of British Ornithology*, a beautiful book which is now almost forgotten. It is a large book full of delightful birds with sweeping tails and impudent expressions, and set the style of lively ornithological draughtsmanship which was followed for the next fifty years. By the time Lear was sixteen he was working with Selby[4], and certainly he helped with *Illustrations of Ornithology*, by Selby and Sir William Jardine, which was published in four volumes between 1825 and 1839.

They probably met through the daughter of Turner's patron, Walter Ramsden Fawkes – a Mrs Godfrey Wentworth. Her father had been an amateur zoologist as well as a patron of the arts, and he had known Selby. Lear always spoke with gratitude of Mrs Wentworth's interest in him, and he tells us that through her he was introduced to the Zoological Society in London.[5] Mrs Wentworth may have seen Lear's talent for drawing, and decided that she would help him to get started; perhaps she knew that Selby was looking for a young assistant, or maybe she persuaded him that he could use one. It was a fortunate apprenticeship for it taught Lear to be bold and lively and imaginative in his work, encouraging characteristics which were probably already there.

In 1830 Lear decided to try a book on his own, and on 16 June he was given permission to make drawings from the parrots in the new Zoological Gardens, and at Bruton Street where some of the birds were being housed until the aviary was completed.[6] He may already have done some work at the Zoo, for the previous year a visitors' guide-book, *The Gardens of the Zoological Society Delineated*, had been published, and the drawing of the Blue and Yellow Macaws is signed E.L.[7]

Unlike earlier naturalists, Lear decided to confine himself to one family, and he chose the parrot. They were fashionable and exotic birds, and they varied from the brown-feathered Baudin's cockatoo to the brilliant red and yellow macaw. Like Audubon,

Lear never worked from a stuffed bird unless he had to, but unlike Audubon who was working with wild birds, he did not first kill the animal and draw the gradually decaying carcass; instead he drew the live, moving, screaming bird. Whilst the keeper held it he took measurements of the wing span, the length of the legs, and the size of the beak; then he made quantities of pencil studies and careful colour notes.[8] Sitting in the parrot house he was obviously regarded as something of a curiosity himself, for the visitors came and stared at him and his work, and as a change from drawing birds he would make indignant, Doyle-like sketches of the bonneted ladies and startled gentlemen who peered at him.

When the details of the drawing were worked out Lear transferred it in reverse on to a lithographic plate. In deciding to use lithography he found a process which was perfectly suited to him. With engraving or wood-engraving, which were the more usual methods of reproduction at this time, the original drawing had to be transferred to the plate or block by a professional engraver and much of the subtlety of drawing could be lost on the way. But with lithography, little extra skill was needed to transfer the drawing beyond the essential one of being able to draw at all, and this meant that Lear could carry out the whole process himself and control exactly what was printed. He took the finished plates to Charles Hullmandel, the lithographic printer in Great Marlborough Street, and in Hullmandel's studio he could look at the pulls as they came off. He made trial runs of heads alone or whole birds, and would alter anything which did not satisfy him before he drew the final plate. The prints were then coloured by hand, and he employed someone to do this under his supervision.

He called the book *Illustrations of the Family of Psittacidae, or Parrots*, and he planned to publish it for subscribers in fourteen folios priced at ten shillings each. After working hard through the late summer and autumn of 1830 the first two were ready on 1 November. They are remarkable for a boy of eighteen for they were superbly observed and confidently drawn, and they gave him an immediate reputation as an ornithological draughtsman. The next day he was nominated as an Associate of the Linnean Society;[9] he seemed to have found work which really suited him.

He worked on the parrots throughout 1831, and the drawings spilled over his rooms at Upper North Place. 'Should you come to town – I am sorry that I cannot offer you a home pro tempore,' he wrote to an acquaintance in October, 'pro trumpery indeed it

would be, if I did make any such offer – for unless you occupied the grate as a seat – I see no probability of your finding any rest consonant with the safety of my Parrots – seeing, that of the six chairs I possess – 5 are at present occupied with lithographic prints: – the whole of my exalted & delightful upper tenement in fact overflows with them, & for the last 12 months I have so moved – thought – looked at, – & existed among Parrots – that should any transmigration take place at my decease I am sure my soul would be very uncomfortable in anything but one of the Psittacidae.'[10]

In order to encourage subscribers he limited the edition to 175 copies, and the plates were destroyed after the printing. The list of subscribers was headed by Mrs Wentworth and seven members of her family, and included Lord Egremont, many leading zoologists, and the Right Hon. Lord Stanley, MP, President of the Zoological Society, from whom he had borrowed several of the birds he had drawn and who later became one of the most important men in Lear's life.

Publishing his own book was a long and costly process, especially since he worked so carefully on each drawing until he was satisfied with them all, and as the year went on he was finding it hard to keep going. 'I have pretty great difficulty in paying my monthly charges,' he wrote in October, 'for to pay colourer & printer monthly I am obstinately prepossessed – since I had rather be at the bottom of the River Thames – than be one week in debt – be it *never* so small. For me – who at the age of 14 & a half, was turned out into the world, *literally without a farthing* – & with nought to look to for a living but his own exertions, you may easily suppose this a necessary prejudice – & indeed – the tardy paying of many of my subscribers – renders it but too difficult to

procure food – & pay for publishing at once . . . I have just nine
and twenty times resolved to give up Parrots & all – & should
certainly have done so – had not my good genius with vast
reluctance just 9 and 20 times set me a going again.'[11]

A month later he received an enthusiastic letter from the
zoologist William Swainson, who had studied under Audubon
whilst he had been in England to publish *The Birds of America*.
'Sir, I received yesterday, with great pleasure the numbers of
your beautiful work. To repeat my recorded opinion of it, as a
whole, is unnecessary but there are two plates which more
especially deserve the highest praise; they are the New Holland
Palaeornis, and the red and yellow macaw. The latter is in my
estimation equal to any figure ever painted by Barraband or
Audubon, for grace of design, perspective, or anatomical
accuracy. I am so particularly pleased with these, that I should
feel much gratified by possessing a duplicate copy of each. They
will then be framed, as fit companions in my drawing room to
hang by the side of a pair by my friend Audubon.'[12]

But despite all the praise and encouragement Lear never
finished the work, and when the twelfth folio appeared in the
following April, it was the last. 'I originally intended to have
figured all the Psittacidae,' he wrote to Sir William Jardine, 'but I
stopped in time, neither will there be (from me) any letterpress.
Their one publication was a speculation which so far as it made
me known procured me employment, but in the matter of money
occasionally caused loss.'[13] Yet he had been supplementing his
income by working for other people since the middle of 1831, and
as this meant that he no longer had to rely only on the *Parrots* for
a living it does seem strange that he did not go on and complete
them – and what did he mean by, 'I stopped in time'? Though
incomplete, it was an important work, 'the first book of the kind
drawn on stone in England of so large a size, & . . . one wh. led
to all of Mr Gould's improvements – vide that gentleman's
Birds of Europe – Toucans &c – many of which the said foolish
artist drew.'[14]

A few weeks after the last folio of the *Parrots* came out Lear
had his twentieth birthday. He saw himself now as a tall, rather
ugly, bespectacled young man, and in October 1831 he drew a
self-portrait and added, '. . . this is amazingly like; add only –
that both my knees are fractured from being run over which has
made them very peculiarly crooked – that my neck is singularly
long, a most elephantine nose – & a disposition to tumble here &
there – owing to being half blind, & you may very well imagine

my tout ensemble.'[15] 'Tall, not handsome, and rather ungainly in figure, he was very agreeable and genial in manner,' Fowler recalled. 'There indeed was partly the secret of his great success in life; he was all things to all people.'[16] He felt a youthful gaucheness in society, but he had an unassuming charm and thoughtfulness which had already attracted Mrs Wentworth's attention – all through his early manhood he found that elderly women liked to help and mother him.

He does not seem to have had many young friends in London, though he frequently saw a boyhood companion from Holloway called William Nevill, and a Sussex friend called Bernard Senior who was working in a solicitor's office with George Lear, the Pickwickian clerk. Edward and Bernard Senior explored London life together, and at some point, Lear tells us, he contracted syphilis.[17]

He still went down to visit Sarah, and staying in Sussex at the end of 1829 he had experimented with writing serious poetry. Some was a pastiche of Byron praising the glories of ancient Greece, and some was more personally his, like this poem written on Bury Hill, one of the west Sussex downs which looks over the Arun valley:

> When the light dies away in a calm summer's eve
> And the sunbeams grow faint and more faint in the west
> How we love to look on till the last trace they leave
> Glows alone like a blush upon modesty's breast! —
> Lonely streak! dearer far than the glories of day
> Seems thy beauty 'mid silence and shadow enshrined, –
> More bright as its loneliness passes away –
> And leaves twilight in desolate grandeur behind! –
> So when grief has made lonely and blighted our lot,
> And her icy cold chain o'er our spirits has cast,
> Will not memory oft turn to some thrice hallowed spot,
> That shines out like a star among years that are past?
> Some dream that will wake in a desolate heart,
> Every chord into music that long has been hushed,
> Mournful echo! – soon still – for it tolls with a smart,
> That the joys which first woke it, are long ago crushed![18]

Here again was the feeling he had when he came home from visiting the clowns with his father, the realisation that happiness – which for Lear meant being surrounded contentedly by people he loved – had slipped into the past. It was a theme to which he returned frequently in his Nonsense –

Often since, in the nights of June,
We sit on the sand and watch the moon; –
She has gone to the great Gromboolian plain,
And we probably never shall meet again!
Oft, in the long still nights of June,
We sit on the rocks and watch the moon; –
— She dwells by the streams of the Chankly Bore,
And we probably never shall see her more.[19]

The beauty of the Sussex landscape haunted him in later years, so that he could scarcely let himself think of it from the pain such recollections brought. 'O Sussex! – & *what* a sunset! ! . . . "E! come passano, i dì felici!" – said I – remembering years – nearly 40 years ago! !'[20] he wrote in 1862. The view from Bury Hill is wide and beautiful, landscape to which Lear particularly responded. '. . . the vast – for it is really – vast – plain was wondrous to see,' he wrote of another view in 1869. 'Doubtless there is something in SPACE by which the mind (leastways *my* mind,) can work & expand.'[21] All his life he sought wide horizons, both the real width of his landscape drawings and the symbolic width of tolerance expressed in the landscape of his Nonsense.

At the end of 1831 Edward and Ann moved from Grays Inn Road to more pleasant and convenient rooms at No. 61 Albany Street, which runs down the eastern side of Regent's Park just a few minutes' walk from the zoo. Really he was too old to be living still with a protective older sister, and they did not always get on well now. She had known how to cope with a small child, but it must have been difficult for her to know how to treat a man of twenty, and though she remained unruffled and kind, Edward found himself getting impatient and irritable with her.

Although the *Parrots* had to come to an end there was plenty of work for Lear to do, and he found himself in demand. He illustrated the *Transactions of the Zoological Society*, *The Zoology of Captain Beechey's Voyage* and, almost certainly, *The Zoology of the Voyage of HMS Beagle*,[22] the boat on which Charles Darwin had been employed as naturalist. He did drawings for a series called the Naturalists' Library,[23] for Bell's *A History of British Quadrupeds*,[24] and he prepared for Professor Bell the lithographs for *Tortoises, Terrapins and Turtles*. He was also working for Dr Gray of the British Museum, and John Gould.

Gould, who was eight years older than Lear, was the son of a gardener at Windsor Castle. In 1827 he had been appointed taxidermist to the Zoological Society, and during the next few years he became a self-taught zoologist. In 1830 he was given a collection of a hundred or so Indian bird skins, and when he had stuffed them he decided to publish drawings of the birds. The first folios of Lear's *Parrots* were just appearing, and Gould used the same format for his book, with notes describing the zoological features of each bird. Gould planned and wrote the book himself but almost all the beautiful drawings associated with his name are the work of other people. His first book, *A Century of Birds from the Himalayan Mountains* which was published in 1831, was illustrated by his wife Elizabeth, and Lear. But Gould apparently felt that as he had paid Lear for the drawings he could claim them as his own, and there is no mention of Lear's name anywhere – indeed in later books, though he now acknowledged Lear's help in drawings, he would quite happily subscribe plates 'by J. & E. Gould' even when Lear's signature appeared in the drawing itself.[25]

The book was a great success and was much more rewarding financially than Lear's had been, and it must have been depressing for him to see Gould appropriating his work and making a profit from it. After this came *A Monograph of the Ramphastidae or Toucans* and a five-volume work called *The Birds of Europe*. One summer – probably in 1831 – Gould took Lear with him to the Continent to visit zoos there and make drawings of some of the birds. They went together to Holland, Switzerland and Germany, and it seems that in Amsterdam Lear committed himself to work for Gould until *The Birds of Europe* was finished – a decision he regretted, for although he worked with him on and off throughout the next six years it was not a happy relationship. When Gould died in 1881, Lear remembered: '... he was one I never liked really, for in spite of a certain jollity and bonhommie, he was a harsh and violent man. At the Zoological S. at 33 Bruton St – at Hullmandels – at Broad St ever the same persevering hardworking toiler in his own (ornithological,) line, – but ever as unfeeling for those about him. In the earliest phase of his bird = drawing, he owed everything to his excellent wife, & to myself, – without whose help in drawing he had done nothing.'[26]

Nevertheless, he did some very good work for Gould, particularly in *The Birds of Europe*. He was at his best when he was drawing majestic, unpretty birds like ravens and owls; he endowed them with sagacious personalities, and it is tempting to wonder if Lear found a common bond with the birds, for they too were at the mercy of unscrupulous men. '*Comme il est charmant ce monsieur avec ses beaux yeux de verre!*' a small girl said of him years later. '*Ah, que vos grandes lunettes vous donnent tout à fait l'air d'un gros hibou!*'[27]

Then in 1832 Lear was asked to do some work for a different kind of man – Lord Stanley, heir to the Earl of Derby. At his home outside Liverpool he had built up a private menagerie that was famous throughout Europe, and he asked Lear to come and stay at Knowsley and make drawings of the animals there. It was the most far-reaching invitation of Lear's life.

3 The Knowsley Menagerie
1832–1837

> Later, in his morning rambles
> He perceived the moving brambles –
>   Something square and white disclose; –
> 'Twas a First-class Railway-Ticket;
> But, on stooping down to pick it
> Off the ground, – a pea-green Cricket
>   Settled on my uncle's Nose.[1]

As his carriage rattled through the gates at Knowsley a new life was beginning for Lear. At such a moment it would be happy to think of him coming down the main avenue across the park and sweeping round to the foot of the steps leading to the main door. In fact he was probably brought to the back of the house and shown straight into the Steward's quarters, for although he had come as Lord Stanley's guest he had also come as his employee.

The Stanley family had lived at Knowsley since the fourteenth century when John de Stanley, grandfather of the 1st Earl of Derby, married Isabel Lathom, who was heiress to vast estates in the hundred of West Derby in Lancashire. The oldest part of the house dated from the thirteenth century, but the main body of it had been built and pulled down and rebuilt ever since, and most visitors found it ugly and old-fashioned and rambling. The 12th Earl had planned to rebuild the house completely, but though he abandoned this idea he did add a vast dining-room which was entered through a pair of Gothic doors which reached to the ceiling, about which General Grosvenor is reputed to have asked: 'Pray are those great doors to be opened for every pat of butter that comes into the room?'[2] But the 12th Earl needed his dining-room, for he was a warm-hearted and compulsive host, and from June until November his table was always laid for forty people – except on Mondays when he invited the Liverpool neighbourhood to come and visit him in turns, and then it could be laid for as many as a hundred guests. His first wife, Lord Stanley's mother, had deserted him for the Duke of Dorset, and after her death in 1797 he married the actress Miss Elizabeth Farren, of whom it was said that she was a lady on the stage and an actress off it. It was he who founded the Derby stakes, and he was immensely proud of his stables at Knowsley.

He was now nearly eighty, but the house was still pervaded with his spirit of welcome. 'Dear old man! his joyous temperament, and his love of society and good cheer, made his guests as happy and merry as himself,' Lady Shelley recalled. 'He constantly bantered the young ladies on their good looks, and about their lovers, which, though not always in the refined taste of modern times, so evidently proceeded from a natural *gaieté de coeur* and kindness, that no one could possibly have been offended.'[3]

Knowsley was a meeting place for the whole family, and Lord Derby's children, grandchildren and great-grandchildren would all arrive for extended visits, which delighted the old man. His exceptionally ugly sister, Lucy, had married the Rev. Geoffrey Hornby, an opportunist who accepted his wife's looks since the marriage gave him the living of Winwick, which was in the gift of the Earls of Derby and carried a stipend of £7000 a year. Their second daughter had married her cousin, Lord Stanley, and their eldest son had married Lord Stanley's sister, so the families had become very interwoven.

It was through his grandsons that the Earl heard that Lear was in the house, for he began to realise that instead of sitting with him after dinner as they had always done, they were slipping away as soon as they politely could. When he asked them why this was, they told him that the young man in the steward's room who had come to draw animals was such good company that they were going down to visit him. If he is such good company, said Lord Derby, then the young man shall come and dine upstairs with us.[4]

Fowler records a slightly different version of this story. 'His lordship had him down to his country seat, Knowsley, near Liverpool, to make certain drawings for him, and while so employed he was given into the charge of the housekeeper.' It was at about this time, on Lear's return from an early visit to Knowsley, that he and Fowler met. Shortly after their meeting, Lear had 'a renewed summons to Knowsley and he could not determine from the mode of its expression whether he was invited as a guest at his lordship's table or as that of the housekeeper. His speculation on the question was entirely free from the least shadow of pride ... Arrived at Knowsley – we had it all from himself – he took the safer part; he went below and presented himself to his old friend, but almost immediately Lord Derby was heard calling out from the head of the stairs leading to the lower regions "Mister Lear, Mister Lear, come up here." And up Lear went and from that moment took his place among the society which he was likely to find in his lordship's dining room, and which he kept with ease, all his life.'[5] In fact, only a year before going to Knowsley, Lear had confessed himself 'very little used to company or society',[6] and he must have been rather startled to find himself flung into it with a reputation for being entertaining.

Knowsley at this time was a complete little village, where meat and poultry were home-killed and vegetables and fruit home-grown. In the dairy the cows were milked and the butter churned, and on the estate beer would have been brewed, horses shod and even soap and candles made – and since Lord Derby's invitations to stay extended as well to children, servants and horses, there must sometimes have been hundreds of people on the estate.

The day for the family and their guests would start at about 9 a.m., when the housemaid or man-servant would draw back the curtains, stir the fire into life, and set out the jugs of water and the towels for the morning wash. But Lear was always an early riser, and he would have put in two or three hours' work, drawing the animals and birds in the menagerie, before breakfast at 10 a.m. He would have worked through the morning as well, whilst the gentlemen were out shooting and riding, and the ladies talked or read or wrote long letters telling their friends what the other guests wore and did and said, and passing on the scraps of gossip which had been confided to them.

Lord Derby forbade any of his guests to shoot more than five brace of partridge in one morning for he wanted them back in time to ride out with the ladies, and Lear may have joined them for the ride round the park. He certainly joined them for dinner, and he seems to have been as great a success with some of the guests as he had been with the grandsons. 'The Earl of W[ilton] has been here for some days,' he wrote to Ann, 'he is Lord W[estminster's] 2nd son, and married to Lady Mary S[tanley]. He is extremely picturesque if not handsome, and dresses in crimson and a black velvet waistcoat when he looks like a portrait by Vandyke. Miss —— says and so does Mrs —— that he is a very bad man, tho he looks so nicely. But what I like about him, is that he always asks me to drink a glass of champagne with him at dinner. I wonder why he does. But I don't much care as I like the champagne . . . I have asked why on Earth she thinks the Earl of W. always asks me to drink champagne, and she began to laugh, and said, because he knows you are a clever artist and sees you always look at him and admire him: and he is a very vain man and this pleases him, and so he asks you to take wine as a reward.'[7]

Not all Lord Derby's guests were so charmed by him. Some were 'hard & worldly critters' who 'hadn't a particle of taste, & young as I then was, I always felt that had it not been for the unvaried kindness of the Stanleys & Hornby's, they would hardly have been decently civil to the "dirty Artist" – ornithological & Landscape painter'.[8]

Others, though civil, were rich and dull, pursuing as the privilege of wealth the life-killing conventions of ennui and restraint. Such an affectation outraged Lear, who was excited by life, however great its problems. 'The uniform apathetic tone assumed by lofty society irks me *dreadfully*,' he wrote from Knowsley, 'nothing I long for half so much as to giggle heartily and to hop on one leg down the great gallery – but I dare not.'[9]

In the nursery, however, it was another matter. Here he found an exuberant enthusiasm which was the opposite of dullness, for the children could be unaffectedly merry. He entertained them with his drawings, and then 'the lines beginning, "There was an Old Man of Tobago", were suggested to me by a valued friend, as a form of verse lending itself to limitless variety for Rhymes and Pictures'.[10] The verse came from *Anecdotes and Adventures of Fifteen Gentlemen* which had been published in 1822.

To begin with, Lear drew his own illustrations to the published verses, but soon he was creating his own Nonsenses, and
his own world. From this world he removed the blandly indifferent:

> There was a young person of Kew
> Whose virtues and vices were few;
> But with blameable haste, she devoured some hot paste,
> Which destroyed that young person of Kew.

Then he disposed of the tiresomely correct:

> There was an old person of Shoreham,
> Whose habits were marked by decorum;
> He bought an Umbrella, and sate in the cellar,
> Which pleased all the people of Shoreham.

This achieved, real people were now free to indulge in amiable
excess:

> There was an Old Person of Ischia,
> Whose conduct grew friskier and friskier;
> He danced hornpipes and jigs, and ate thousands of figs,
> That lively Old Person of Ischia.

They were people whose standards were so essentially worthwhile:

> There was an old person of Bray,
> Who sang through the whole of the day
> To his ducks and his pigs, whom he fed upon figs,
> That valuable person of Bray.

Lear had found his own way of hopping on one leg down the great gallery, taking the children of the household with him.

Although there was a nursery full of children and he was meeting 'half the fine people of the day',[11] Lear sometimes felt horribly lonely. Then he would escape from the busy house and walk alone through the park. In September 1833 his father had died of a heart attack; he was seventy-six, and until a few months before his death he had been coming up to London from Gravesend for the meetings of the Livery of the Fruiterers' Company. Now Mrs Lear was on her own with Florence, who only lived four more years. Cordelia and Catherine died about this time as well. Compared with the harshness of his family's struggle, life at Knowsley must have seemed unreal.

Lear worked at Knowsley on and off between 1832 and 1837, and over a hundred of the drawings he did then are preserved still in the Library there. Some were reproduced in a book called *The Gleanings from the Menagerie and Aviary at Knowsley Hall* which was privately printed in a small edition in 1846 and soon became valuable. He was not at Knowsley all the time: he was still drawing for Gould, and did most of his work on the *Toucans* and *The Birds of Europe* during these years.

It was close, exacting work, and Lear's eyes had never been good. Now they were becoming strained and he knew that he could not go on for much longer without risking his sight altogether. In 1834 he enrolled at Sass's School of Art in Bloomsbury which prepared students for the entrance examination to the Royal Academy Schools.[12] Perhaps he hoped to go from there to the Schools, but his financial position had not altered and it would have been impossible for him to think of starting on the ten-year course.

Lear could not have been at Sass's for more than a few months, but he was obviously unsettled. That summer he went to Ireland. He travelled with Arthur Stanley, a nephew of the 1st Baron Stanley of Alderley and later Dean of Westminster, with whom Lear had often stayed to give drawing lessons. Arthur Stanley's father was visiting Dublin for a meeting of the British Association, and the two young men went over with him. Together they walked through the beautiful Wicklow mountains to Glendalough and the Seven Churches, and Lear filled a sketch-book with drawings.

The following summer he spent ten weeks in the Lake District, and by then he knew that what he wanted to paint was landscape. At the end of October he told Gould: '. . . it is impossible to tell you *how*, & *how enormously* I have enjoyed the whole Autumn. The counties of Cumberland & Westmorland are superb indeed, & tho' the weather has been miserable, yet I have contrived to walk pretty well over the whole ground, & to sketch a good deal besides.'[13] But he added, '. . . my eyes are so sadly worse, that no bird under an ostrich shall I soon be able to see to do.'

Now there was another complication. As a child Lear had had a tendency to bronchitis and asthma, and the time he had spent in the damp northern climate of Lancashire had made this worse. In 1837 his health deteriorated suddenly, and he knew that he must get away to somewhere dry and warm. Lord Stanley, who had now succeeded to the title as the 13th Earl of Derby, with his nephew Robert Hornby who had become a particular friend of Lear, offered to send him to Rome where he could recover his health and learn to paint. '. . . certainly,' Lear wrote to Ann, 'I have the kindest lot of friends any man ever had.'[14] It was a gesture of real, practical friendship, and for Lear it meant an exciting new beginning.

4 Italy
1837–1845

Lear left England at the end of July 1837. Ann travelled with him as far as Brussels where she had decided to stay until the following May. It must have been a sad parting for her as she was not to see him again for four years, and then only for snatched visits squeezed into his new and busy life. For the rest of her life she lived alone.

He did not hurry on his journey to Rome, for there was a lot to see. He wandered south through Luxembourg and Germany, stopping to draw busy street scenes in Frankfurt and strange medieval castles poised high on granite pinnacles in Bavaria, and it was September before he crossed the Alps into Italy in the gentle autumn weather.

He left his baggage in Milan, and taking only a knapsack and sketch-book set out on a walking tour of Como and Lugano. Excitedly he explored the lakes – high rock peaks climbing out of the dark blue water and thrown back into echoing reflections 'Jiggy Jaggy' below, picturesque lakeside villages with huddles of white spires and busy quays, and 'large mummy-like barrels carrying wine drawn by milk white oxen – rows of women with baskets loaded with immense logs, and Capuchin friars in quantities.'[1] The Alps at sunset were perfectly pink, the autumn woods were a blaze of glorious crimson and gold, and on the lake the boats with their red, blue and white sails looked like huge butterflies. It was not all so romantic, for the inns were cold and draughty, and they served 'mutton and goat's flesh, half putrid – garlic – and dreadfully sour wine'.[2] But the discomfort was worthwhile, and he arrived back in Milan a fortnight later with a folio full of drawings.

The journey from Milan to Florence took seven days, across the flat Lombardy Plains to Bologna and over the Apennines on the old Roman road. 'The Pass of the Apennines is quite unlike the Alps,' he told Ann, 'and as we had a most lovely day, I never enjoyed anything so much. Thick woods of oak are on every side, and the road which is very steep and winding, looks quite over all the enormous flat plain of Lombardy; – and in clear weather, – as far as the Alps. Right and left one sees tops with snow, but one only crosses the lowest part, though oxen were necessary to draw up the carriages. You may imagine how beautiful the road looked, with a string of 8 coaches being so pulled up – and all the passengers walking. So much for the loneliness of mountain passes! – at the place we lunched – 32 people – all English, sat down together.'[3]

On the seventh morning they came over the top of the mountains, and Florence lay spread below them in the wide Arno valley. It looked like the paintings by Claude Lorrain which Lear had seen at Knowsley, and was as beautiful as he had imagined. '. . . the world cannot produce anything prettier than that beautiful city,' he wrote enthusiastically to Ann, '. . . the magnificent bridges (6 close together over the Arno) – and the immense picturesque buildings of the middle ages – the clear lilac mountains all round it – the exquisite walks on every side to hills covered with villages, convents, and cypresses, where you have the whole city beneath you – the bustle of the Grand Duke's court and the fine shops – the endless churches – the Zebra Cathedral of black and white marble – the crowds of towers and steeples – all these make Florence a little Paradise in its way.'[4]

There were reports of cholera in Rome, so he decided to stay in Florence until it was safe to travel again. There was a wealth of things for him to see, '. . . the galleries – the pictures – the statues – the churches – the tombs of Michael Angelo – Dante . . . It is a hurly-burly of beauty and wonder.'[5] At once he found people he knew in the large English community, and within a day or two he had been asked to give them drawing lessons during his stay.

By the end of November sharp winds were blowing from the snows of the Apennines, and as Rome was now clear of cholera he decided to continue the journey south. He was introduced to two other artists on their way back there for the winter – one of them was William Theed, who sculpted 'Africa' on the Albert Memorial. They invited him to share their vetturino for the five-day journey, and as they rattled past the endless vineyards and olive trees of Tuscany they told him about the other artists in Rome and the life that they led there. On 3 December 1837, they crossed the wild and melancholy waste of the Campagna, and by the evening he had arrived in Rome.

Lear found rooms in Baboon Street – No. 39 Via del Babbuino – '*close* to the church and the Piazza di Spagna – The Academy – the eating and coffee houses – all the English and all the artists'.[6] There were painters and sculptors from all over Europe and from America, and with Theed to look after him and introduce him around he was soon settling happily into their routine. 'At 8 I go to the Café, where all the artists breakfast, and have 2 cups of coffee and 2 toasted rolls – for $6\frac{1}{2}d$ and then – I either see sights – make calls – draw out of doors – or, if wet – have models indoors till 4. Then most of the artists walk on the Pincian Mount, (a beautiful garden overlooking all Rome, and from which such sunsets are seen!) – and at 5 we dine very capitally at a Trattoria or eating house, immediately after which Sir W. Knighton and I walk to the Academy – whence after 2 hours we return home. This is my present routine but there are such multitudes of things to see in Rome that one does not get settled in a hurry, and bye and bye I shall get more into the way of painting more at home, for I have 2 or 3 water coloured drawings ordered already, *so I shall not starve.*'[7]

To begin with he spent most of his time just exploring the city. Christmas was coming, and everywhere there was business and bustle. The roads were choked by sleek grey cattle with enormous horns, decorated with ribbons and bells and pulling wobbling carts and waggons behind them, and the pavements were crowded with shoppers and ubiquitous priests, 'white – black – piebald – scarlet – cinnamon – purple: round hats – shovel hats – cocked hats – hoods and caps – cardinals with their 3 footmen (for cardinals *never* walk) – white friars with masks, bishops and Monsignori with lilac and red stockings – and indeed thousands on thousands of every description of religious orders.'[8]

It was quieter away from the centre of the modern city, and for hours on end he explored the ruined greatness of the Palatine Hill, the city of Romulus and the home of the Caesars, or he sat under the gentle warmth of the winter sun, drawing the tumbled, grassy ruins of Emperors' palaces and pagan temples. '. . . if you expected to see a fine collection of splendid antiques all in a bunch, you would be disappointed,' he told Ann; 'you stumble on pillars – temples – circuses – and tombs – all more or less mixed up with modern buildings . . . The arches of Titus and Constantine and Severus are the most perfect things – the Coliseum, and some of the gates – and the Pantheon – and by some lights – the melancholy and grandeur of these huge remains are very awful. But as to the *extent* of the ruins, of Rome – no one who does not see them, can form an idea; the palaces and baths of the Emperors – some filled up into convents – some covering acres of ground with masses of ancient walls – the long lines of acqueducts and tombs on the desolate and beautiful Campagna, – and (in the enormous palaces of the modern Capitol and Vatican) the thousands of busts and statues! – judge how bewildered one's noddle becomes! – for my part, I am taking things very quietly – and like better to poke about over and over again in the Forum, than to hurry with the stream of sight seers all day long.'[9]

There were quantities of English people wintering in Rome, and he found that he knew a great many of them. There were cousins of the Stanley's, and cousins of the cousins; and people like Lady Susan Percy – a niece of the Duke and Duchess of Northumberland who had each bought a copy of his *Parrots* six years before – who at once commissioned work from him and encouraged him as Mrs Wentworth had done then. Amongst the artists he found Richard Wyatt, nephew of the Georgian architect, Frederick Thrupp who later sculpted the Wordsworth bust in Westminster Abbey, John Gibson, Penry Williams and Thomas Uwins.

He was invited to grand balls and elaborate soirées, when coroneted carriages would jostle and manoeuvre for room to set down their noble occupants, but he confessed quietly to Ann: 'When I come home at night with my key I often think of Gray's Inn Road, Albany St!'[10] for amidst all the hustle he could still feel as lonely as he had sometimes felt at Knowsley.

But there was something very particular about the atmosphere in Rome which he could never have recaptured in England. Here art was an honourable and even enviable occupation, and painters were hardly looked down on at all – though one could not go too far, and they were not admitted as members of the English Club. The younger artists wandered freely into each other's studios, to talk or to criticize one another's work, and they would share models, the peasants who came into Rome for the winter months wearing their colourful costumes and who would gather at the foot of the Spanish Steps waiting to be hired. But though Hazlitt had accused the English artists in Rome of lounging and loafing, and Haydon despised the dirty habits they acquired, Lear managed to place himself between the bearded Bohemians and the English aristocracy, whose ways he was better able to understand than most of his fellow artists.

It was outside Rome on the Campagna that he found the beauty and the grandeur that he most wanted to paint. This desolate plain had once been widely populated and the people had cultivated the land for generations, but when the small farms were replaced by large estates the quality of the farming declined and the land became poorer. Then the barbarians came in succeeding waves on the city, destroying the houses and roads, pillaging the crops and the cattle, and leaving behind them a rotting wasteland into which the waters of the seven hills of

Rome drained in marshy swamps. For centuries it had been un-inhabited, with grotesque pillars and splintered roads and lines of fractured aqueducts forming a weird graveyard of industry. Foxes and tortoises and porcupines wandered freely, and beside the marshes herds of buffalo congregated. To Lear it was an uninhabited wasteland of beauty, with chunky rock shapes, gnarled olive trees and rhythmical lines of hills disappearing into wide, distant horizons. Sometimes he went further to explore the beauties of Tivoli, or the sullen, silent lake of Nemi near the Pope's summer palace: when the retreating German soldiers burnt and destroyed the treasures in the museum at Nemi in

1944, they left just a few small things untouched, and one of these is a watercolour drawing of the lake by Lear.

He was feeling well and happy, and the winter climate suited him perfectly. But the summer in Rome was dangerous, for when the sun was hot, fever-heavy air would steam off the marshes, and then it was unsafe to be within twenty miles of the city. After Easter the coaches and carriages piled with luggage would start to rumble out of the city gates, and Rome became quiet and empty.

At the beginning of May 1838 Lear left with Uwins to spend the summer in the Bay of Naples.

His first impression of Naples itself was appalling, and the whole of their short stay there was an ordeal. It was dirty and crowded and unbelievably noisy, and it seemed to gather to a climax in the Toledo, the main city street. 'If you empty all the streets of all the capitals of Europe into one – then turn in some thousand oxen, sheep, goats, monks – priests – processions – cars – mules – naked children & bare legged mariners – you may form some idea of the Toledo,' he told Ann. 'Once I walked up it – but would not again for a great deal, as I was nearly deaf & run over (almost) 20 times before I came out of it. It is a dreadful place, – yet at 8 o'clock people lounge & eat ices at every door – although the noise is like all the thunder in the world.

'At Santa Lucia – the fish market – you become so stunned & bewildered, that you don't know if you are dead or alive; it is like a horrid dream – when all the world is shrieking at you. As you pass, every woman screams out – "will you sit?" "will you drink?" "will you give me something?" "anything" "a grana?" – "Signor, Signor, Signor Water, Water Fish – Meat mussels – oysters – baskets – eggs – roses – apples – cherries?" – while every man steps before you overwhelming you with the most tremendous shouts of – "Come along Sir, – come; a boat! a boat! instantly, now, this minute, this minute! to Capri – to Vesuvius – to Sorrento – to wherever you please – a boat, boat boat boat! ! !"'[11]

'*Vedi Napoli e poi muori*,' Lear might well have thought.

They stayed only four days in Naples, then they went round the bay to the ancient Roman resort of Pozzuoli. But the sulphurous air began to bother Lear's chest and he started to cough, so they went quickly back to Naples, then climbed into the hills behind the city to search for somewhere cool and peaceful to spend the rest of the summer. They found a tiny village called Capo di Cava perched at the end of a deep valley where the only sound was the early-morning singing of the birds. 'Now what do you think I live for?' he asked Ann, 'today, for instance, we had coffee & eggs at 5 – at 12, beautiful macaroni soup, – boiled beef & mutton cutlets, strawberries, cherries, & a bottle of wine each, – & at supper, macaroni & an omelette, wine & oranges – to which you are to add lodging – & now guess? actually, for 8 carlinos is all this – which is equivalent to 2/8 of our money – daily! !'[12]

They went for long walks past tiny villages where the peasants gathered under the shade of canopies of vine, and out on to the cliff road leading down to Amalfi with views across to the Gulf of Salerno, or inland through chestnut woods busy with cuckoos and nightingales; they made expeditions to Paestum to see the Greek temples, and to Pompeii which Lear thought 'alone, worth a journey from England'.[13]

On 30 August they were in Rome again, and he was glad to be back 'for I am beginning to find, – "the rolling stone gathers no moss"'.[14] His landlady – 'the old hussy' – had decided to double the rent, so he had to look for new rooms and he found them in the Via Felice, close to the Pincian Gardens just a little out of the artists' quarter. The city was even fuller than it had been the previous winter, but for Lear this meant more work and the year rushed round into spring. 'All through the winter – (which was a very fine one, though cold,) I was over head & ears in employment,' he wrote to Gould. 'Rome was more crammed than it had been since the days of Titus – & people slept in ovens & pigstyes for want of lodgings – so that what with pupils – (of which I had numbers,) & friends – & drawings indoors and sketchings out of doors – the spring came before one knew where one was. You will lift up your hands & eyes & legs and possibly fall quite off your chair when I tell you that I was enabled to send some of my earnings to my mother & sisters & to put by 100£ besides for the use of the summer! ! !'[15]

When the summer came he went on foot to join some of the artists in a mountain village north of the city. With their help he began oil painting which he had tried unsuccessfully on his own the previous summer, but he made disappointingly slow progress, and when he returned to Rome in the autumn he told Gould: 'It takes a long while to make a painter – even with a good artist's education – but *without* one – it tries the patience of Job: – it is a great thing if one does not go backward. – Meanwhile I am extremely happy – as the hedgehog said when he rolled himself through a thistlebush.'[16]

In fact, these were the most satisfying years of Lear's life, and with Goethe he could have said: 'The first thing I did in Rome was to discover myself and to achieve a mood of balance, harmony and happiness.' He was surrounded by people with whom he could talk and work; he was painting well, despite his doubts; he had enough money; and the future was full of time and hope. Just one thing was missing, and he wrote to Gould: 'I wish to goodness I could get a wife! – You have no idea how sick I am of living alone! ! – Please make a memorandum of any lady under 28 who has a little money – can live in Rome – & knows how to cut pencils & make puddings.'[17] He never thought of women with much passion, and his ideal was a gentle companion who would look after him in a rounded, contented kind of way. As a young man he seems hardly to have considered marriage as a real possibility, partly because he knew that if he married there would be too much risk of unhappiness. He would have to break the secret of his epilepsy, and he might pass the disease on to his children and see his own horror beginning again in another child. Nor could he be sure that his wife would go on loving him – his mother had stopped loving him once and he knew that he could not go through that kind of despair and hurt again.

In 1841 he decided to spend the summer in England, for it was nearly four years since he had left and he wanted to see Ann again. 'What I shall do *in* England I have no idea,' he wrote to Gould, 'run about upon railroads – & eat beefsteaks. – I am & have been, as you have justly heard – going on very well – which is more than ever I had a right to expect, in spite of your good opinion of me: – I am very glad I took to Landscape – it suits my taste so exactly – & though I am but a mere beginner as yet – still I do hope by study & staying here to make a decent picture before I die. No early education in art – late attention, & bad eyes – are all against me – but renewed health & the assistance of more kind friends than any mortal ever had I hope will prove the heaviest side of the balance.'[18]

That summer he and Ann must have had a long talk about their future. She had kept on the rooms in Southampton Row to which they had moved together in 1835, and she was probably hoping that he would come home and settle down again. But he had written to her, '. . . you have little notion how completely an artist's paradise is Rome – and how destitute all other places would be of capacities to study or prosper. Rome is Rome; do not think about the future; let us be thankful that so far all is and has been much better than we could ever have expected.'[19] Better for him perhaps. Ann does not seem to have put any pressure on him to stay, but now that she realised he did not want to live in England again she gave up their last remnant of a home and began on an endless succession of furnished lodgings and visits to friends. When she looked forward her life must have seemed empty and very lonely.

Lear could not afford to spend the summer doing nothing, and he decided that he would publish some of his drawings of Rome. In August he went up to stay with Lord Derby, and he took lithographic stones and chalk with him to Knowsley so that he could work on them there. Since the ebullient 12th Earl had died Knowsley was much quieter, and Lear told Gould, 'my life here is monotonous enough – but such as pleases me more than all the gaiety in the world. Dear Lord Derby is surrounded by his children, grand-children & nephews & nieces & is really happy. He breakfasts with us after prayers: – then about 12 takes a drive with one of his daughters or his sons [& also] myself – he takes the greatest interest in all his grounds &c. – He dines in his own room when we lunch – but after our dinner at 7 he sits with us all the evening . . . The lot of things is immense here – birds & beasts &c. – : but I am so thorough confined by my Lithography as to have little time to see them.'[20]

From Knowsley he travelled to Scotland for a brief holiday with Robert Hornby's cousin, Phipps Hornby, but he was back in time for the autumn publication of *Views in Rome and its Environs*. This is a superb book of fresh, carefully observed drawings, rhythmically composed and confidently handled. Lear used Claude Lorrain's convention of a bundle of interest on one or both sides of the foreground framing the receding middle and far distance, and every inch has been imagined from the curling fuss of vine canopies to the dramatic mountain shapes. Tonally they are most successful, but Lear's lack of formal training sometimes lets him down. The perspective is often very odd and the figures are generally bad, for when he was drawing people his courage seemed to vanish, and it is difficult to believe that they are done by the same person who drew the bold and completely successful Nonsense figures.

At the end of 1841 Lear returned to Italy, but now he found it harder to settle back into the routine of his life there. 'Since I left

England this last time,' he told Lord Derby, 'I have not become so foreignised as before – that is – I hope I am always an *English-man*, – but I mean that my last summer's pleasures make me a bit doleful now & then ... After all, a day in England is worth a week elsewhere.'[21]

In the spring of 1842 he visited Sicily, and the following summer he travelled across central Italy, through the Abruzzi to the Adriatic coast, travels he described in the first volume of *Illustrated Excursions in Italy.* He saw 'more of that country (by knowing the Language & mixing with the people,) than any Englishman has ever yet done, near as those places are to Rome'.[22]

In May 1844 his mother died at Dover, a life-worn widow. She had had twenty-one children and seen thirteen of them die, and had plunged from genteel comfort to the verge of poverty. It is sad that we know so little about her: all we have is a drawing of a rounded and rather sympathetic woman. In the letters and diaries that have survived Lear mentions her probably no more than six times – always as 'mother' – and then only to ask Ann how she is or to say that he has been able to send her money. He never reminisces about her – either this was too painful, or he had grown to dislike the memory of her so much that he did not want to recall her – and we know nothing about her personality at all. In fairness to her it must be said that twenty-one children in twenty-four years would sap the natural affections and sense of responsibility of most women, and she had the added worry of trying to guide the family through their acute financial troubles. Perhaps if Jeremiah Lear had continued to prosper she would have supervised Edward's upbringing herself – we do not know. Certainly Lear expressed himself strongly on the worries of large families in the second part of Mr & Mrs Discobbolos, when Mr Discobbolos simply climbed down from the 'ancient runcible wall' and blew the whole family into tiny pieces.

Now that Mrs Lear was dead there was nothing to keep Ann in England, and Edward wrote asking her to come and join him in Rome, a thing he had been talking about ever since he first went there. He told her how to travel and where he would meet her, but he was just a little worried that she might let him down. 'I hope you will dress *very* nicely – (although we shall be both in deep mourning)' he said. 'You would have a capital bedroom with a fire place, for I should give you mine – and a sitting room. Your drawback would be the want of society for a few months – (for of course you would not be in the gay world;) but when you consider that the seeing Rome merely is much – and the excursions I shall take you, and perhaps the going home by Switzerland and Milan – I do not think the balance is bad. (Besides you will see *me*!) – do not forget to bring good *warm clothing*, and if you want any handsome, plain shawl or dress in Paris, (not odd looking, my dear old sister!) buy it, and keep it as a present from me. You know that I am very much known here, and live in the "highest respectability" – and so you *must not* be too dowdy. Do not forget a thick veil – for cold winds. We shall dine at home etc. – and I shall be as much with you as I can considering my great occupation and the quantity of people who come to me.'[23]

But it must all have sounded too overwhelming, and she wrote and told him that she could not manage the journey. He was disappointed, but he was planning to go back to England in the summer and he hoped that she might come back with him then. In the meanwhile he decided to spend a few weeks going over some of the Abruzzi he had missed the previous year.

In one village a drunken carabiniere demanded to know who he was, so Lear told him his name and showed him his passport 'which was one from the Foreign Office in 1837, with "Viscount Palmerston" printed thereon in large letters, "Lear" being small, and written. *"Niente vero"*, said the man of war, who seemed happy to be able to cavil, *"voi non siete Lear! siete Palmerstoni!"* "No I am not", said I, "my name's Lear." But the irascible official was not to be so easily checked, though, knowing the power of these worthies, I took care to mollify his anger as much as might be. *"Quel ch'è scritto, scritto è: dunque, ecco qua scritto Palmerstoni: – dunque siete Palmerstoni voi"*. You great fool! I thought; but I made two bows, and said placidly, "take me to the

Sott' Intendente, my dear sir, as he knows me very well."
"*Peggio*", said the angry man, "*tu! incommodare l'eccellente Signor Sott Intendente; vien, vien subito: ti tiro in carcere*".

'Some have greatness thrust upon them. In spite of all expostulations, Viscount Palmerston it was settled I should be. There was nothing to be done, so I was trotted ignominiously all down the High-Street, the *carabiniere* shouting out at everybody at door and window, "*Ho preso Palmerstoni!*"

'Luckily, Don Francesco Console was taking a walk and met us, whereon followed a scene of apologies to me, and snubbing for the military, who retreated discomforted.'[24]

In the spring of 1845 Lear met a man who became one of his closest friends, a man of sympathetic understanding with whom, in later, sadder years, he could talk. His name was Chichester Fortescue. He was twenty-two – ten years younger than Lear – he had just come down from Oxford where he had got a first in Classics and won the Chancellor's English Prize. Now he was touring Europe before following his father into a parliamentary career. He was a quiet, self-questioning man who never felt really at home in political life, though under Gladstone he was to become Lord Privy Seal and later President of the Council. He was happy in the less formal company of painters and writers, and he liked Lear at once. Lear certainly enjoyed his company, for in Fortescue he found his two favourite virtues – sensibility and enthusiasm: Rome was new, the artist's life exciting and the older man splendid company. 'I like very much what I have seen of Lear,' he wrote a few days after they had met, 'he is a good, clever, agreeable man – very friendly and *getonable* with.'[25] They went sketching together on the Campagna, they visited Tivoli, and Fortescue wrote in his diary: 'Lear a delightful companion, full of *nonsense*, puns, riddles, everything in the shape of fun, and *brimming* with intense appreciation of nature as well as history. I don't know when I have met any one to whom I took so great a liking.'[26] Here was another person, like his Sussex friends, with whom Lear could indulge in absurdities and nonsense, and his letters to Fortescue over the next forty years make delightful reading.

In April he left Rome to spend the summer in England. 'Lear came to say goodbye just before dinner – he has gone by diligence to Civita Vecchia,' Fortescue wrote in his diary. 'I have enjoyed his society immensely, and am very sorry he is gone. We seemed to suit each other capitally, and became friends in no time. Among other qualifications, he is one of those men of real feeling it is so delightful to meet in this cold-hearted world.'[27] He had discovered the essence of Lear.

5 A Queen and a Revolution 1845–1848

Most of the best-loved children's songs and tales were made up without any idea of publication. Charles Dodgson told the story of *Alice in Wonderland* to three little sisters as he rowed them down the river from Oxford one dreamy afternoon in June, Beatrix Potter wrote *Peter Rabbit* for a small friend who was ill in bed, and Hugh Lofting created *Doctor Dolittle* in the trenches of Flanders for his children at home. And so it was with *A Book of Nonsense*, for it was not until 1845 that Lear decided to publish the 'Nonsenses' that had so delighted the children at Knowsley.

Many people now find it hard to understand why *A Book of Nonsense* should have been so popular, and they remember that as children they did not particularly enjoy it. Since Lear the limerick has become a vehicle of wit, and later creations are much more clever than his. But Lear's intention was not wit: it was something which at that time was far more important. Today we are used to the benign, kindly personalities of characters like Mole, Winnie the Pooh and Paddington who are so often foolish in the happiest way. A hundred and fifty years ago most writers for small children disliked folly of any kind.

In 1762, Rousseau wrote a book about a boy called Emile, who was brought up by a system of 'natural education'.[1] He was to discover the world by his own experience. He would never be forced to do what he did not want to do, but too late he would realise that because of his own laziness he had missed what was best. If he wished he could lose his temper, but if he did so he would be treated as though he were ill. The stories he would hear would be about the world around him, for there was no point in telling him tales of fairyland. In England Maria Edgeworth became the great missionary of natural education, though Rousseau's genuine ideas of self-discovery became a little buried at her hands, for the situation was always arranged so that the good child made the wise and true decision and was raised to yet higher virtue, whilst the bad child sank deeper and deeper, becoming an object of pity to the rest of the visionary world. When Evangelical Christians added their ideas of virtue and wickedness, the terror of the moral tale had reached its peak. 'Babies do not want to hear about babies,' Samuel Johnson had written: 'they like to be told of giants and castles and of something which can stretch their little minds.' But what children wanted did not matter – it was what would do them the most good that was important, and in the first part of the nineteenth century the realms of giants and castles were shut to all but a few lucky children.

Of course, it was not all so bleak. The terrible tales of the brothers Grimm appeared in English in 1824, and Hans Andersen's stories were published in London in 1846, the same year as Lear's nonsense. There was a rich inheritance of nursery rhymes, and occasional books without a high moral tone slipped through like *The Butterfly's Ball*, published in 1807.[2] In 1821 the first known book of limericks appeared,[3] *The History of Sixteen Wonderful Old Women*, and in the following year came *Anecdotes and Adventures of Fifteen Gentlemen*, the book which had inspired Lear. Some of these early limericks were soon popular in the nursery, but the books themselves had none of Lear's lasting success. What Lear did, and the reason why his book made so much impact, was that he came down firmly on the side of real children. At Knowsley he had seen that apathy denied life, but so also did the improving tale, for it disclaimed children as they were in favour as children as they ought to be. In his rhymes Lear disposed of the irreproachable:

> There was an old man of Hong Kong,
> Who never did anything wrong;
> He lay on his back, with his head in a sack,
> That innocuous old man of Hong Kong.

He even suggested that virtue did not always bring rewards:

> There was an Old Person of Cadiz,
> Who was always polite to all ladies;
> But in handing his daughter, he fell into the water,
> Which drowned that Old Person of Cadiz.

Some of his heroes are vain and others are greedy, and one even runs away with a thief. Some are sad and some are provoking, and a few are quite shockingly weak willed – though if they have not the strength of character to see a thing through, they have instead a handsome honesty:

There was a Young Lady of Clare,
Who was sadly pursued by a bear;
When she found she was tired, she abruptly expired,
That unfortunate Lady of Clare.

Unlike the virtuous heroes of the moral tales they are on the children's side, for Lear still remembered how it had felt to be a child. He wanted to make them happy – society would do its best to make them good. 'My dear child, I'm sure we shall be allowed to laugh in Heaven!'[4] he said to a little girl many years later.

The same affectionate abandon is found in the drawings. Children's book illustrations then were generally either rather stilted woodcuts, or elaborate, often very charming, drawings – but the illustrations to the limericks are fresh and clear and almost crude in their simplicity. They are the work of a professional natural-history draughtsman who knows what he is about, and running through them all is a sense of movement – the arms are flung spontaneously back like birds in flight and the legs stride out or stand poised expectantly on tip-toe as if they are going to be spun round like a child's top. There is none of the genteel decorum which was thought so proper but instead, like children, the Old Men and Women are hardly ever still and nobody minds at all.[5]

The book's popularity extended beyond the nursery, though as much for its verse form as for its content, and we are told that it 'originated quite a new class of prose rhymes that for a good twelvemonth were the rage in all societies'.[6]

We do not know why Lear decided to publish the Nonsenses at this point, for as always when he came back to England he no longer needed to write letters and it is difficult for us to discover what was going on. Perhaps his friends persuaded him to publish them so that other people's children could share their enjoyment. Possibly he was hoping to make some money to pay towards the expense of coming home.

This was certainly the motive for another book on which he was working in 1845. This was a book about the Abruzzi describing his journeys there the two previous summers, and it was illustrated with large lithographic plates.

In the autumn he was at Knowsley working on the drawings, but there were so many friends to see that he found it difficult to get much done, and before the winter began he came back to London where there were fewer distractions. Ann was living at this time in Richmond, so he took rooms on his own at 27 Duke

Street, St James's. There he settled down to write the text of the Abruzzi book and finish the thirty lithographs and forty vignettes. Then he had the long task of writing round asking people if they would subscribe. The proofs of the Nonsense book had to be checked, and this was published first, on 10 February 1846.

There were altogether seventy-two limericks in two volumes selling at 3s 6d each, and they were published by Thomas McLean who had published *Views in Rome* in 1841. It was called *A Book of Nonsense* by Derry down Derry, and on the title page there was a rhyme:

> There was an Old Derry down Derry,
> Who loved to see little folks merry;
> So he made them a book, and with laughter they shook
> At the fun of that Derry down Derry.

There was no mention of Lear's name anywhere, although anyone buying a copy of the second volume of *Illustrated Excursions in Italy* later in the year might have guessed the secret, for on the last page there was an unlikely advertisement for *A Book of Nonsense*. It was the convention at that time for children's books to be published anonymously, but Lear was proud of his work and in the third edition of 1861 his name was printed firmly on the title-page.

The first volume of *Illustrated Excursions in Italy* was published in April. It was dedicated to the Earl of Derby and, like Lear's earlier books, was extravagantly illustrated and expensively priced at four guineas. It is a beautiful book, and his enjoyment and excitement in discovering every new sight and sound make it very good reading. And its publication had a worthy outcome, for Lear was summoned by Queen Victoria who had seen the book and so admired it that she wanted Lear to give her lessons in drawing.

The twenty-seven-year-old Queen was having a very busy summer. Her fifth child, Princess Helena, was born on 25 May, and just a month later Peel's administration was toppled. The Whigs were returned to power under Lord Russell, and within a few weeks Palmerston, the new Foreign Secretary, created an international crisis by upsetting the arrangement which the Queen herself had made with the French over the marriage of Queen Isabella of Spain.

She had gone down to stay at Osborne, which was then being rebuilt, and it was there that Lear began the course of twelve lessons. The Queen recorded them in her diary:

15 July 1846. Osborne. 'Had a drawing lesson from Mr Lear, who sketched before me and teaches remarkably well, in landscape painting in water colours . . .'

16 July 1846. Osborne. 'Copied one of Mr Lear's drawings and had my lesson downstairs, with him. He was very pleased with my drawing and very encouraging about it . . .'

17 July 1846. Osborne. 'I had another lesson with Mr Lear, who much praised my 2nd copy. Later in the afternoon I went out and saw a beautiful sketch he has done of the new house . . .'

18 July 1846. Osborne. 'After luncheon had a drawing lesson, and am, I hope, improving . . .'[7]

Lear wrote down the details of his stay at Osborne, but all that has survived is one memory which he recalled after the Prince's death in 1861. 'Prince Albert showed me all the model of the House, (then being built only,) & particularly a Terrace, saying – "This is what I like to think of – because *when we are old*, we shall hope to walk up & down this Terrace with our children grown up into men & women."'[8]

At the end of July Queen Victoria returned to London and the lessons were resumed at Buckingham Palace. It was probably here that two embarrassing incidents occurred which Lear liked to recall.[9] He was accustomed now to mixing with earls and viscounts, but he had no experience of the finer points of Court etiquette – though he did know that he enjoyed standing on the rug in front of the fire warming his coat tails. Each time he took up this position facing the Queen, the attendant Lord-in-Waiting invited him to see something on the far side of the room. The charade was repeated several times and no one explained what was going on. It was only later that Lear realised that a subject must not stand with his back to the fire in the presence of his monarch.

But Queen Victoria had apparently taken a liking to her drawing master, and she decided to show him some of her bijou treasures which were kept in display cases. Lear was delighted with what he saw, and exclaimed exuberantly: 'Oh! where *did* you get all these beautiful things?' Calmly Her Majesty replied: 'I inherited them, Mr Lear.'

The twelfth and last lesson was on 6 August, and a few days later a second volume of *Illustrated Excursions in Italy* was published. This was a book similar to *Views in Rome and its Environs*, with drawings of places rarely seen by tourists, like Sermoneta and Ardea.

By coincidence, in the same year as the publication of *A Book of Nonsense*, the result of Lear's other activities at Knowsley appeared, for Lord Derby decided to reproduce some of his drawings in *The Gleanings from the Menagerie and Aviary at Knowsley Hall*.

And so it had really been a remarkable year. He had been drawing master to the Queen, and had seen the publication of a book of Nonsense, a travel book, a volume of landscape drawings and one of natural-history illustrations. It was almost a microcosm of his working life, and – characteristically – he made only £100 profit.

Ann still could not be persuaded to come to Rome. Lear stayed in England until the beginning of December 1846, then he packed his things and left for Italy.

He had been away from Rome for nearly two years, and his friends were delighted to see him. 'Everybody exclaims at my well-looks and says I have come back half as big again as I went,' he told Ann. '. . . I have hardly time to write, so many people are calling to congratulate me on my return.'[10]

When the first flurry was over he settled down to his routine of painting and walking and dining out, but after his unexpected success in London it all seemed rather tame. He had not been forgotten in England, though. He had presented to the Queen the drawings that he had done at Osborne and she had had one of them engraved. 'I had nearly forgotten to tell you a piece of honour which has happened to me,' he told Ann within a few sentences of starting a letter to her, 'namely, that one of the Queen's Ladies in Waiting who is here, has delivered to me a little print engraved from one of my drawings – of Osborne House, – at Her Majesty's desire. This is one trait of many that have come under my notice that Queen Victoria has a good memory for any little condescension and kindness. I am really quite pleased with my little engraving, and shall have it placed in a good frame as soon as I can get one made; – you need not however, tell the incident to everybody; – for it would look like boasting upon my part, who have done little enough to deserve so gratifying a notice.'[11]

In fact he was rather worried about appearing to do too well, for he was starting on a busy winter with a lot of work, and he told Ann: 'I have so much more to do than I merit by my actual place in artistic repute, that such success may give rise to complaints from those who are more skilful & yet have little to do.'[12]

Yet it was not going to be an easy year financially. The paintings were small and the journey out with large packets and trunks had been expensive. 'I reckon that I may get £100 – or perhaps £120 this year, & that is what I certainly cannot save much out of. You must remember that I work only up to May – & that the summer does not count. Still, that is far cheaper than I could live for in London, where £300 does not seem an overplus. – We must therefore be grateful on account of my publications – whatever trouble they gave me – (& what is done without trouble?) – for through them I laid by a whole £100. And when we consider that eyesight is not of long duration – laying by now is really a necessary duty.'[13]

He had begun to think that he might settle down once more in England. Ten years before, Rome had given him a thrilling introduction to a completely new way of life, but in those years he had matured and changed whilst life amongst the English there had scarcely altered. The winter visitors, kind though many of them were, went monotonously on asking the same questions, making the same bright remarks, and what had once seemed so vital now appeared horribly dull. He had to be realistic though. Living was cheaper in Italy, and as long as there were English people in Rome there was always a sale for his paintings. And though the city might look 'filthier and duller than ever after England',[14] the country around was still beautiful and the climate usually perfect. But that winter was one of the worst of the century: long, dark days with pouring rain and so little light that he could hardly see to paint, gave way to intense cold and heavy snow which kept him snared indoors and unable to get the exercise he needed to keep off attacks of epilepsy.

In March he wrote to Ann, 'I do not now consider myself *settled* here ... please God I will return & live some time in England, I hope to be more comfortable in London – when I trust you will live with me. We shall be very cosy & antique. I shall be 40 – or 41 – you – 60 or 61. We must have an old cat, & some china; – & so we shall go on smoothly.' But, in case he should find himself tied down, he added: 'My dear Ann, this is all nonsense – but you must see I'm half asleep – so that's my apology.'[15]

In the end the decision of whether or not he should stay was made for him. For many years Italy had been grumbling with discontent. The people wanted a united country but their struggle was going to be a hard one, for they had first to over-throw the autocratic rulers of the existing Italian states who had strong reactionary forces under their command. By the end of 1846 the atmosphere had become so unsettled that many English people decided not to risk spending the winter in Italy, and they went no further than the south coast of France.

But Lear was not going to leave before he had to. He wanted to see the rest of Italy whilst it was still possible for travellers to move freely. He had not yet been either to the north-east coast round Venice or to the north-west round La Spezia, nor had he seen the foot of Italy. Since he wanted to revisit Sicily, he decided to go south first. When Fortescue wrote saying that he might join him in Naples in mid-August to walk with him in Calabria, Lear decided to spend the early summer in Sicily, returning to Naples in time to meet Fortescue there. Meanwhile, a friend of a friend in Rome, a man called John Proby, decided to go with him on the first part of the tour. Proby had come to Italy to study painting, and during the dreadful winter of 1846–7 he had contracted Roman fever. Now he felt better he wanted to do some walking and drawing, though it is doubtful if he realised how whole-heartedly Lear went about his sketching tours.

Lear left at the end of April 1847 and travelled down to Naples. From there he caught a steamer to Palermo where Proby met him, and on 11 May they set out together.

They soon found the island hot, dirty and poor. In Calatafimi, where they stopped first, they could buy nothing but bread full of aniseed, and broad beans which they boiled and ate for the next six days. But, though he preferred to be comfortable and well fed, it was what he had come to see that interested Lear, and for the next month they were out each morning before the sun came up, walking and drawing until the last of the daylight had gone. They travelled right round the island, and visited the temple of Hera at Segesta, and the six temples at Agrigento, both busy towns in the centuries when Sicily had been ruled by the Greeks; they explored the honeycomb of cave dwellings in the valley of Ipsica which had been the home of the most ancient Sicilian settlers, and they spent a night in a castle beside the wild and romantic southern seashore.

On 8 June Lear and Proby reached Syracuse, once 'the largest of Greek cities, and the most splendid of all capitals'.[16] It had stood for nearly two thousand years before being overrun by the Saracens who levelled it to the ground: now the old quarries had been made into cool green gardens heavy with flowers, and the trees were filled with nightingales. A new city had been built, and they were glad to rest there for a few days, for throughout rural Sicily the living conditions had been terrible. Worst of all had been the food. There was almost no meat, nor any fresh fruit or vegetables, which was surprising for as they travelled they had passed acres of cultivated fields. Because of the extreme heat the peasants kept just enough for themselves each day, and by early morning the rest had been sent into the big towns to be sold. 'Milk, do you want? The goats are driven in from the country at *sunrise*, are milked in the street, & off they go again; if then you do not run about with a milk jug, no hope of milk – for 2 hours turns it sour. Oil, vinegar, salt, pepper – matters collected, or grown by richer people – are either consumed in small quantities by each household or exported altogether. Fish? If much is taken *at sunrise*, the happy catchers eat it, & there is none for the passer by at noon; if they catch less – so much less the chance for you. Eggs? You cannot make a hen lay when you please, & the morning produce of the hen roost is all gone by noon. Meat? – This is rarely killed & as it were *by subscription*, everybody taking a part & cooking it directly or it would be bad very soon . . .'[17]

From Catania, north of Syracuse, they set out to climb sulphurous Mount Etna, an experience Lear did not enjoy. They were back in Palermo again on the eve of the festival of Santa Rosalia. There was a week of music and fireworks and crowds, and Lear found the noise and bustle very trying. In fact both he and Proby were feeling thoroughly low: when he planned his lengthy itineraries for travel he never realised that being constantly on the move, eating badly and sleeping in primitive inns, being up before dawn and working till dusk, could leave him run down and exhausted. Whilst he was still young he could recover quickly, but later he would travel until he was unable to go on for one more day, yet it never occurred to him that he was just very tired. Lear always enjoyed walking – it was the most certain way of keeping off attacks of epilepsy – and he found the world a happier place when he was outside and on the move. It was the shuffling around, the uncertainty of whether they would find somewhere to stay or where they would be able to get a meal, that bothered him. For Proby it was even more exhausting, for he had only just recovered from his illness and he had never travelled in this way before. 'I am sorry my companion, as his health improves, *does not* in temper,' Lear told Ann; 'he is sadly imperious & contradictory at times which is rather trying.'[18]

When they crossed back to Naples they heard that Fortescue had gone back to England to take up a seat in Parliament, and as Lear and Proby had now settled their difficulties they set off again together. Travelling on foot, they engaged a muleteer to look after their baggage. He spoke in a strong southern dialect which they could hardly understand, but to Lear's delight he finished every incomprehensible sentence with the refrain 'Díghi Dóghi Dà' – surely the inspiration for the Yonghy-Bonghy-Bò.

Like the Abruzzi, Calabria was uncharted, and there were very few roads and practically no inns, so they had to travel from day to day relying for their accommodation on the letters of introduction that Lear had been given. It was after they had been staying in an inn for the night that Lear overheard two young Englishmen talking. 'I say, Dick,' one of them asked, 'do you know who that fellow is that we were talking to last night?' 'No,' replied the other. 'Why, he's nothing but a d———d dirty landscape-painter,' a title that Lear adopted as his own: 'Edward Lear, Dirty Landscape Painter' he called himself henceforth.[19]

They decided that their best plan was to travel up the eastern side of the peninsula close to the mountains, and when they heard of anything exciting they could turn off this track and explore. Their hosts were happily hospitable, indeed often too much so. Thrown into confusion by the sudden arrival of unknown foreigners carrying letters of introduction, and wondering what two Englishmen could possibly want in their impoverished corner of the world, they would set about preparing a meal fit for travellers from a wealthy land. Whilst Lear and Proby sat and talked with their host, answering endless questions about the modern wonders of England, the animals were killed in the yard and then lengthily cooked, 'till you are reduced (ere it comes) to a state of torture and despair, in the protracted struggle between hunger, Morpheus and civility'.[20] And the meals, when they did arrive, were not always easy to eat. 'At one time a dish was exhibited full of roasted squirrels, adorned by funghi of wonderful shapes and colours; at another, there were relays of most surprising birds: among which my former ornithological studies caused me to recognise a few corvine mandibles, whose appearance was not altogether in strict accordance with the culinary arrangements of polite society.'[21] Whilst they ate, a man stood beside the table, 'and in order to dissipate the flies, which at this season are a legion, flapped a long flapper of feathers, Laputa-wise, close to our faces. No sooner did we begin to speak than whizz – flick – down came the flapper, so as to render conversation a rather difficult effort.'[22]

When they reached the south again a few weeks later they found that the atmosphere had changed. The people were no longer so friendly, indeed they seemed nervous and strained and pressed them with questions – had they seen anything unusual, had they heard anything? They knew now that the revolution might break out at any moment, but there were still places that Lear wanted to see. Whilst Proby went for a few days across to Messina, he made a short dash on his own down to Melito on the southernmost tip of Italy. He had a letter to one of the families there, but though they made him welcome he soon realised that they were fidgety and worried. The atmosphere became really fraught when two or three gunshots were heard, but as nothing more happened they gathered nervously for dinner. As they were eating a man came in from Montebello, one of the villages further north. There was some nervous whispering, and then his host suddenly shouted: '"The Revolution has already begun." . . . sobs and groans and clamour followed, and the moaning hostess, after weeping frantically, fell into a violent fit, and was carried out, the party breaking up in the most admired disorder, after a display, at least so it appeared to me, of feelings in which fear and dismay greatly predominated over hope or boldness'.[23]

Lear left the next day to meet Proby in Reggio. It was one o'clock in the morning when he reached the city. 'How strange was that scene! All the quiet town was brilliantly lighted up, and every house illuminated; no women or children were visible, but troops of men, by twenties and thirties, all armed, and preceded by bands of music and banners inscribed, "Viva Pio IX", or "Viva la Constituzione", were parading the high street from end to end.

'"*Cosa x'è stata*, Ciccio?" said I.

'"*O non vedette*," said the unhappy muleteer, with a suppressed groan. "*O non vedete? é una rivoluzione! Díghi, dóghi, dà!*"

'No one took the least notice of us as we passed along, and we soon arrived at Giordano's Hotel. The doors were barred, nor could I readily gain admittance; at length the waiter appeared, but he was uproariously drunk.

'"Is Signor P—— arrived by the boat from Messina?" said I.

'"*O che barca! O che Messina! O che bella rivoluzione! Ai! ao! Orra birra burra – ba!*" was the reply.

'"Fetch me the keys of my room," said I; "I want to get at my roba – "

'"*O che chiavi! O che camera! O che roba! ai, ai!*"

'"But where are the keys?" I repeated.

'"*Non ci son più chiavi*," screamed the excited cameriere; "*non ci sono più passaporti, non ci sono più Ré – più legge – più giudici – più niente – no x'è altro che l'amore la libertà – l'amicizia, e la constituzione – eccovi le chiavi – ai! o-o-o-o-o-orra birra bà!!*"' ['There are no more keys, there are no more passports, no more kings, no more laws, no more judges, no more nothing! Nothing but love and liberty, friendship and the constitution.']²⁴

Throughout the night people came into Reggio, mostly young men from the mountains, gathering with banners and guns and swords and musical instruments. At the moment it was a rather strange charade, but this might change and Lear was worried to find that Proby had not arrived. Next morning he persuaded a very reluctant boatman to row him across to Messina. Fighting had already broken out there, and he found Proby waiting anxiously in the hotel unable to get a boat to the mainland. Two days later they boarded a steamer en route from Malta to Naples. It was a sadly abrupt ending to a happy tour, and they were worried that the families with whom they had stayed might now be under suspicion for having entertained strangers. 'Gloom, gloom, overshadows the memory of a tour so agreeably begun',²⁵ wrote Lear in his journal as they left Calabria behind.

As they now had time to spare, they spent three weeks in the Kingdom of Naples. They reached Rome on 14 October 1847 and there they parted. Lear had been with Proby for five months, and he told Ann: 'I shall be exceedingly sorry to lose him, as he is a most excellent creature, & if ever he was cross as I unluckily told you, I am sure it was more than half my own fault.'[26] Proby died in 1858 when he was thirty-five, and his sister believed that he never recovered from his months of hardship travelling with Lear.

For Lear it was a busy winter. Rome was still safe, and he stayed there until the end of March working on the summer's drawings. He had twice-weekly open days in his studio, where you make think of me as being very busy with explorers'.[27] He dined out frequently, but all the time he was preoccupied about what he should do next. 'I am in a disturbidious state,' he wrote to Fortescue, 'along of my being undecided as to how I shall go on with art – knowing that figure drawing is that which I know least of & yet is the "crown and roof of things" ... whether I stop here to draw figure, – or whether to go to Apulia & Calabria, or wherever I Archipela go (V.A. Archipelago – P. Archipelawent, PP. Archipelagone) or whatever I do – I strongly long to go to Egypt for the next winter as ever is – if so be as I can find a sufficiency of tin to allow of my passing 4 or 5 months there. I am quite crazy about Memphis & On & Isis & crocodiles & opthalmia & nubians – and simooms & sorcerers, & sphingidae. – Seriously – the contemplation of Egypt must fill the mind – the artistic mind I mean – with great food for the rumination of long years. I have a strong wish also to see Syria – & Asia Minor & all sorts of grisogonous places – but – but – who can tell ... You see therefore in how noxious a state of know-nothingatallaboutwhatoneisgoingtodo-ness I am in. – Yet this is clear: – the days of possible Lotus=eating are diminishing – & by the time I am 40 I would fain be in England once more.'[28] So, whatever he decided to do, he would not be returning at once. He told Ann, 'you know how greatly my illustrated works have conduced both to make me known, & towards my little saving, – so that, the more I am able to store up against English residence, the better. However, I am moving snail fashion, by degrees, & this is probably my last settled winter in Rome.'[29]

He began to pack his things and send them back to England. In February he met Thomas Baring who, as the Earl of Northbrook, was later appointed Viceroy of India and who became another of Lear's closest friends. '... he is an extremely luminous & amiable brick, & I like him very much,' Lear told Fortescue who had arranged the meeting, '& I suppose he likes me or he wouldn't take the trouble of knocking me up as he does considering the lot of people he might take to instead.'[30]

Then, in the early spring, a new acquaintance, a man called Bowen who was President of the University of Corfu, invited Lear to come and stay on the island. It would be a perfect place to begin his exploration of Greece. He spent March clearing his possessions and tidying up his business in Rome. It was more than ten years since he had first come there, but he had no time to feel sad. The revolution in Calabria had been a flurry which died out, but by the beginning of 1848 something more forceful was building up. Early in the year there were riots in Lombardy, and in the middle of March Milan and Venice burst into rebellion. The port of Ancona was closed, and as Lear travelled down to Naples to board a boat for Corfu soldiers were gathering along the roads. He was glad to leave Italy behind him.

6 The Mediterranean 1848

The boat taking Lear to Corfu wandered on its journey, and they stopped at Malta for a week. It was a happy and busy few days, for in the English community he found old friends who entertained him and showed him the small rocky island. But the scenery was terribly disappointing: 'I could not live at Malta,' he wrote, 'there is hardly a bit of green on the whole island – a hot sand stone, walls, & bright white houses are all you can see from the highest places, excepting little stupid trees here & there like rubbishy tufts of black worsted. The harbours are very interesting, but I don't love water well enough to be always boating – nor can I draw ships well enough to portray such scenes characteristically. The street scenery – so white, so bright, so clean, so balconied, is really beautiful – but there the charm ends.'[1]

From Malta he crossed the stormy Ionian Sea to Patras, passing Missolonghi where Byron had died, and as they came into the shelter of the mainland the storm dropped. Then in the calm moonlight they cruised between the Ionian islands and the rocky Grecian coast. Just before dawn on 19 April 1848, they anchored in the beautiful bay of Corfu – Prospero's Cell.

After landing, Lear went straight up to the university to find Bowen, but heard that he had left a few days earlier to visit the other Ionian islands. Lear decided to follow him on the next boat, and for two weeks he explored Zante and Cephalonia and Ulysses's little kingdom of Ithaca. He was back in Corfu on 10 May.

Corfu is a luxuriant and peaceful island. In the spring it is carpeted with millions of flowers, and in the summer it bends under the weight of dark green olives; tiny white convents perch by the pellucid blue sea, and from the shores the land climbs up into mountains and the peak of Pantokrator. At first Lear was so astonished by its loveliness that he just walked without stopping to draw. 'I wish I could give you any idea of the beauty of this island,' he told Ann, 'it is really a Paradise.'[2] 'The extreme gardeny verdure – the fine olives, cypresses, almonds, & oranges, make the landscape so rich – & the Albanian mountains are wonderfully fine. All the villages seem clean & white, with here & there a palm overtopping them. The women wear duck, black or blue, with a red handkerchief about the head; the men – the lower orders that is, mostly red caps – & duck full Turkish trousers. Here & there you see an Albanian all red & white – with a full white petticoat like a doll's – & a sheepskin over his shoulder. Then you meet some of the priests – who wear flowing black robes & beards. Mixed with them are the English soldiers & naval officers, & the upper class of Corfiotes who dress as we do; so that the mixture is very picturesque.'[3]

He had been there less than three weeks when he met Sir Stratford Canning, the British Ambassador in Turkey, whom he had known in Rome. He and Lady Canning were on their way to Constantinople, and they invited Lear to join them as their guest. They were spending a week in Athens on the way, so he would be able to see something of Greece whilst enjoying all the privileges of the ambassador's party.

The ambassador's man-of-war sailed out of Corfu harbour on the afternoon of 30 May. Two days later they crossed the isthmus of Corinth on horseback, and on the evening of 2 June they were in Athens.

Lear was up very early the next morning, for he wanted to see as much as he could. '... surely never was anything so magnificent as Athens!' he exclaimed to Ann, 'far more than I could have had any idea of. The beauty of the temples I well knew from endless drawings – but the immense sweep of plain with exquisitely formed mountains down to the sea – & the manner in which that huge mass of rock – the Acropolis – stands above the modern town with its glittering white marble ruins against the deep blue sky is quite beyond my expectations. The town is all new – but the poorer part of it, what with awnings, & bazaars & figures of all possible kinds is most picturesque.'[4]

In the afternoon the whole party went to the Acropolis, 'really the most astonishing monument of a great people I have yet seen. Poor old scrubby Rome sinks into nothing by the side of such beautiful magnificence ... I wish you could see the temple of the Parthenon, or the Acropolis by sunset – I really never saw anything so wonderful. Most of the columns being rusty with age the whole mass becomes like gold & ivory – & the polished white marble pavement is literally blue from the reflection of the sky. You walk about in a wilderness of broken columns – friezes etc. etc. Owls, the bird of Minerva, are extremely common, & come & sit very near me when I draw.'[5]

In Athens Lear met another friend whom he had known in Italy, a young man called Charles Church whose uncle, Sir Richard Church, had commanded the Greek forces in the War of Independence against Turkish domination. There were almost too many opportunities at once, for now Lear had the chance of travelling round part of Greece with Charles Church, and as he could not speak any modern Greek at this time he would have both a guide and interpreter in his friend. The ambassadorial party would have to go on without him, but he could follow them by boat later.

First he spent two weeks in Athens drawing as much as he could, and then they hired horses and set out north-east across the foothills of Pentelicon towards Marathon. The tour started badly for Lear, for on the first day his horse slipped and he sprained his shoulder. 'This is the way of travelling,' he told Ann. 'We hire a man who undertakes to do *everything* for a certain sum a day; he finds us horses & has others for our baggage, & for his cooking utensils & for provisions & for beds: we were in all 7 horses. We start at sunrise after a good breakfast of coffee and eggs – & we travel till 10. Then we halt at some village, or near a fountain, & a tent is pitched, & in about 2 hours a most capital dinner – soup & 3 courses – is set forth! ! – so you see there is not much hardship. Then we go on till at dusk we reach some village when any house does for our night's dwelling – for little iron bedsteads with mattresses are put up directly, & on these a large muslin bag tied to the ceiling, into which I creep by a hole which is tied up directly I am in it, so that no creature gets in & one sleeps soundly in a room full of vermin. I thought I should have laughed all night long the first time I crept into this strange bag, but soon grew used to it. In the morning – all is packed up & off we go again . . .

'All the great towns – except 3 or 4 – are *quite* new – having been destroyed by either Turks or Greeks, or both over & over again, in the last war. They are built on no plan & look very mean & scattered. From Chalcis we made a tour of a week all over Euboea; no such beautiful scenery can be found anywhere as the forests: you ride for days & days through whispering woods of bright green pine, – the odour of which is delightful & the branches are full of bright blue rollers. It is more like a very magnificent English park than anything else I can compare it to.

The peasants – few as they are, are the most obliging simple creatures. The men wear a plain tunic, but the women dress very prettily. They bind the head with a yellow handkerchief; but plait the long hair, & then tie it on to still longer plaits of silk or horse hair till it ends in bunches of silk with silver tags; in some villages they string cowries shells all down these long tails, which are confined by a girdle . . .

'From Euboea we crossed to Lamia – or Leitun as the Turks called it; the last town of the Turkish frontier, & very Turkey in its appearance. I wish you could see it. The strangest feature of the place is the *immense* number of storks it contains. Every house has one or more, some 8 or 10 nests, & the minarets – (now only ruins) & other ruined houses are all alive with them. The clatter they make with their bills is most curious, & makes you fancy all the town are playing at backgammon. From Lamia we came to the celebrated pass of Thermopylae, where the few Spartans withstood so many Persians.'[6]

At Thebes he was suddenly taken ill, and had to be carried back to Athens 'by 4 horses on an Indiarubber bed'.[7] He had not felt really well since his fall, but the illness was brought on by an insect bite followed by an overdose of sun. In fact he probably had malaria, for the fever recurred over the next few years and was treated with quinine. Lying quietly in Athens he began to recover, and had 'books, jelly, porter, & visits continual from all the English residents'.[8] He told Ann, 'I have made many drawings of great value – & hope my time & money are well spent in ensuring me a stock of classical subjects for future paintings.'[9] He was annoyed to have missed seeing Delphi, but by the end of July he was well enough to think again of going on to Turkey.

He spent most of the voyage lying in his cabin, but as they steamed into Constantinople at sunrise on 1 August he climbed on to the deck to watch the city slide past. 'Certainly – no city is so wonderfully beautiful when you approach it – it was far beyond my idea,' he told Ann: 'I think the perpetual change as the steamer moves on, of ruined walls, immense domes – brilliantly white minarets – & all mixed with such magnificent cypress, pine, & plane foliage is truly wonderful.'[10]

The Embassy was a few miles farther on in Therapia, and as soon as he arrived Lear went straight to bed. Lady Canning was 'as kind as 70 mothers',[11] and fed him broth and chicken, tea and thin slices of bread and butter, and within a fortnight he was walking in the Palace gardens. But then the fever returned and he was in bed once more, and lying there looking out over a monotonous tow path he began to think again of the future. 'What to do my dear Fortescue when I return to England ! ! ? ? ¿- ¿¡- (expressive of indelible doubt, wonder, & ignorance). *London* must be the place – & then comes the choice of 2 lines: – society – & half day's work – pretty pictures – petitmaître praise boundless – frequented studio – &c. &c. – wound up with vexation of spirit as age comes on that talents have been thrown away. – or – *hard study* beginning at the root of the matter – the human figure – which to master alone would enable me to carry out the views & feelings of Landscape I know to exist within me.

Alas! if real art is a *student*, I know no more than a child – an infant – a foetus: – how could I – I have had myself to thank for all education – & a vortex of society hath eaten my time. – So you see I must choose one or other – & with my many friends it will go hard at 36 to retire – please God I live – for 8 or 10 years – *but* – if I did – *wouldn't* the "Lears" sell in your grandchildren's time!'[12]

He could have gone on for years leading what he saw as a dilettante artist's life, although this would probably have been more difficult in London than in Rome. Many landscape painters, including Claude Lorrain whose work he so much admired, had employed other artists to paint in their figures, but Lear was unusually interested in the peasants and their strange and often beautiful costumes, and he wanted to be able to draw them for himself. As well as this he needed to satisfy his artistic conscience, and this he could not do if he pandered to *petit maître* praise – although it is arguable that the kind of topographical landscape work that Lear liked to do was best suited to just this kind of patronage. Now he was thinking of going right back to the beginning and working through the training that he had never had. At thirty-six he was perhaps fortunate to be free of responsibilities so that he could consider doing this. Few men of his age would have been prepared to start again, but despite his humility he was realistic enough to recognise the value of his work.

He had a little money saved, but even so he would find it hard to support himself throughout the lengthy training. There was just one possibility though, for in his letters to Ann he frequently referred to a Mrs Warner, who was a friend of the Lear family. For years now she had hinted that Edward was featured in her will, and she was very wealthy and rather aged.

Gradually he began to feel really better, and as he lay in bed recovering he wanted more than thin bread and butter. 'Hunger! did you ever have a fever?' he asked Fortescue. 'No consideration of morality or sentiment or fear of punishmt. would prevent my devouring any small child who entered this room now. I have eaten everything in it but a wax-candle & a bad lemon.'[13]

On 28 August he took his first proper walk, through the quiet of a Ramadan day. The month of fasting was just ending, and the ambassador's party had been invited to Constantinople the following day to see the Sultan's procession to and from the Mosque of Santa Sophia and the ceremony of 'foot kissing' in the Seraglio. It was a brilliant, spectacular, hours-long affair with Pashas and Generals, incense and music, feathers and diamonds, an exotic and exciting introduction to eastern custom. 'I can't tell when I have passed so delightful & novel a day,' Lear wrote to Ann later, '& after a long illness, one is so thankful for a change.'[14]

Now that he was feeling better he wanted to make up the time he had lost. The next morning he returned to Constantinople to explore the city on his own. He crammed every moment of the next seven days. He saw the mosques and the ancient cypress-clad burial grounds, he sat in a boat to draw the minaretted skyline and he crossed to Scutari and back, he visited the sacred place of Ayoub where Mahomet's standard-bearer lies buried, and he poked through the stalls of the Stamboul bazaar for dress lengths of silk to send home to Ann. In fact, he was so absorbed and excited with all there was to see that his health improved in a great rush, and when he returned to the Embassy late at night on 8 September everybody was amazed at how well he was looking.

Lear's idea now was to visit Mount Athos with Church, then go on to spend the rest of the year in Greece. In Constantinople he had engaged a servant to accompany him, and on 9 September they embarked together for Salonika. Church planned to join them in Mount Athos, but when Lear landed at Salonika he found the city isolated because of cholera, and Mount Athos closed to all travellers. The only road out of the city still open went north-west into Macedonia, and as there was now no chance of meeting up with Church, Lear decided to leave by this route and travel right across Greece to Albania then down the isolated western coast. It would be a more difficult journey than any he had yet undertaken.

They went first through Turkey, and from the beginning he found the customs weird and difficult. There were no tables or chairs and it was uncomfortable sitting always on the floor. But the Turks were understanding: 'they never stare or wonder at anything; you are not bored by any questions, and I am satisfied that if you chose to take your tea while suspended by your feet from the ceiling, not a word would be said, or a sign of amazement betrayed.'[15]

By mid-September they were in Monastir on the border of Illyria and Macedonia. It was a beautiful place, and Lear settled down eagerly to draw. Then he discovered how difficult it was going to be to work in this primitive Islamic country where drawing was believed to be devil's work. 'I cannot but think – will matters grow worse as I advance into Albania?' he wrote in his journal, 'for all the passers-by having inspected my sketching, frown, or look ugly, and many say, "Shaitán," which means, Devil; at length one quietly wrenches my book away and shutting it up returns it to me, saying, "Yok, Yok!" [No, No!] so as numbers are against me, I bow and retire. Next, I essay to draw on one of the bridges, but a gloomy sentinel comes and bullies me off directly, indicating by signs that my profane occupation is by no means to be tolerated.'[16]

From Monastir they crossed the central mountain plateau and reached Scutari in Albania on 21 October. Then they turned south along the coast. Because this part of the country was so little known, Lear took on a local guide called Anastásio to

show them the route and to arrange some kind of accommodation for each night's stay. 'I give much more trouble than
ordinary travellers,' Lear told Ann. 'For instance, instead of sitting or lying down quietly after a long day's ride, I require him to
get me a man from the Agà or Bey, or Pasha of the town to
accompany me to some place whence I may sketch, so that his
life is much troubled by my making the most of every hour.'[17]

At Durazzo he already had a letter of introduction to the Bey,
a boy of sixteen. Neither could understand a word the other said,
so conversation was impossible, but Lear liked the lonely, sad
young man and wanted to see him smile, 'so I drew for him – &
amused him immensely by drawing a steam carriage & saying –
rattle-attle-attle-attle-attle – & a ship-steamer – saying
wishwashsquishsquash – at which the poor boy laughed
immensely'.[18]

Travelling south on the road to Dukadhes the scenery was
awesome in its bleak grandeur. 'At the highest part of the pass a
most singular scene opens. The spectator seems on the edge of a
high wall, from the brink of which giddy elevation he looks down
into a fearfully profound basin, at the roots of the mountain.
Above its eastern and southern enclosures rises the giant snow-
clad Tchika in all its immensity, while at his very feet, in a deep,
dark green pit of wood and garden, lies the town or village of
Dukadhes, its houses scattered like milk-white dice along the
banks of a wide torrent, which finds its way to the gulf between
the hill he stands on, and the high western ridge dividing the
valleys from the sea.

'To this strange place, perhaps one of the most secluded in
Europe, I began to descend, and as we slowly proceeded, halted
more than once to sketch and contemplate. Shut out as it stood
by iron walls of mountain, surrounded by sternest features of
savage scenery, rock and chasm, precipice and torrent, a more
fearful prospect, and more chilling to the very blood I never
beheld – so gloomy and severe – so unredeemed by any beauty
or cheerfulness.'[19]

In contrast to the landscape, the hospitality was warm and
expansive. Lear's stay was made the excuse for a celebration in
the village. Two gypsies were called in to play, and he was
treated to an Albanian musical evening.

'At first the entertainment was rather slow. The gipsies had
two guitars, but they only tinkled them with a preparatory
coquettishness; till another friend dropping in with a third
mandolino, a pleasing discord was by degrees created, and

increased to a pitch of excitement that seemed to promise brilliant things for the evening's festivities. Anastásio, also, catching the melodious infection, led the performers by his own everlasting Greek refrain – sung at the full power of a tremendous voice, and joined in by all present in the first circle – for now, many more than the chorus had entered the room, remaining seated or standing behind, and the whole formed, in the flickering light of the wood torches, one of the most strange scenes imaginable . . . As the musical excitement increased, so did the audience begin to keep time with their bodies, which this people, even when squatted, move with the most curious flexibility.

'Presently, the fun grew fast and furious, and at length the father of the song – the hideous idol-gipsy – became animated in the grandest degree; he sang and shrieked the strangest minor airs with incredible accompaniments, tearing and twangling the guitar with great skill, and energy enough to break it into bits. Everything he sang seemed to delight his audience, which at times was moved to shouts of laughter, at others almost to tears. He bowed backwards and forwards till his head nearly touched the ground, and waved from side to side like a poplar in a gale. He screamed – he howled – he went through long recitatives, and spoke prose with inconceivable rapidity; and all the while his auditors bowed and rocked to and fro as if participating in every idea and expression . . .

'The last performance I can remember to have attended to, appeared to be received as a *capo d'opera*: each verse ended by spinning itself out into a chain of rapid little Bos, ending in chorus thus: "Bo, bo-bo-bo, BO! – bo, bobobo, BO!" – and every verse was more loudly joined in than its predecessor, till at the conclusion of the last verse, when the unearthly idol-gipsy snatched off and waved his cap in the air – his shining head was closely shaved, except one glossy raven tress three feet in length, the very rafters rang again to the frantic harmony – "BO, bo-bo-bo, bo-bo-bo, bo-bo-bo, bobobo, BO!" – the last "BO!" uttered like a pistol-shot, and followed by an unanimous yell.

'Fatigue is so good a preparation for rest, that after this savage mirth had gone on for two or three hours, I fell fast asleep, and heard no more that night.'[20]

Next morning the gaiety was gone. The sombre village was dripping with rain, and he was glad to get away on the last stretch of the journey south. He reached Yannina at the beginning of November 1848, with 219 drawings and a diary of a strange and exciting tour. In 1851 he published *Journals of a Landscape Painter in Albania &c*, a book dominated by descriptions of the landscape just as the places themselves had been dominated by the gaunt, majestic scenery.

Now it was winter and he was loath to exchange the Mediterranean sun for the damp gloom of London. When John Cross, whom he had known at Knowsley, invited him to travel as his guest in Egypt and Palestine, Lear accepted eagerly.

7 Franklin Lushington
1848–1849

Cairo was astonishing. Everywhere was noise and colour, busy Arab traders shouting their strange Oriental wares, hidden black-draped women, Copts and Ethiopians, donkeys, camels, mosques and minarets, exotic bright-plumed birds and brilliant oleanders.

Lear had nearly missed coming altogether, for quarantine and winter storms had delayed him in Greece and he arrived in Malta to find that Cross had gone on without him. Now he reached Cairo just as Cross was preparing to leave for Mount Sinai, but he put off going so that they could spend a week discovering the city and visiting the sphinx and pyramids. On 6 February they set out on camels for Mount Sinai, but the next day 'the weather changed frightfully – torrents of rain fell – & the wind was *most terrible* – & I caught a severe cold, & was extremely unwell. Now I reflected maturely, that if, as is frequently the case – all March should be thus rainy – how should I get on? *Tent* travelling is not like my doings in Albania or Turkey or Greece – where you can always reach a Khan, & *dry your clothes by a fire* . . . Thinking also how very very serious it would be were I laid up when 10 or 12 days from assistance – what great anxiety & hinderance it would cause my dear friend, & what risk I ran of fever – I at last decided it would be more kind to him to leave him.'[1]

What Lear really wanted to do was to go back to Greece, for he had an idea of publishing a really comprehensive book. 'I cannot but think that Greece has been most imperfectly illustrated,' he told Fortescue. '. . . the vast yet beautifully simple sweeping lines of the hills have hardly been represented I fancy – nor the primitive dry foregrounds of Elgin marble peasants &c. What do you think of a huge work (if I can *do* all Greece –) of the Morea & alltogether?'[2]

From Alexandria he boarded a boat for Malta, and on 3 March he sailed for Patras. He wrote to Ann: 'My companion is Mr F.

Lushington – the government secretary's brother at Malta, a very amiable & talented man – to travel with whom is a great advantage to me as well as pleasure.'[3] This was the first mention of the man who was to become Lear's closest friend.

Lushington was several years younger than Lear. He had been at Rugby under Dr Arnold, then went up to Trinity College, Cambridge, where he got a First in Classics, won the Chancellor's gold medal, and was elected Fellow of his College. One of his brothers, Edmund, was Professor of Greek at Glasgow University, and another, Henry, the Chief Secretary to the Government in Malta, had been one of the select society of Apostles at Cambridge with Tennyson and Arthur Hallam.

With Henry, Franklin published three books of verse. *Points of War*, which was published in 1854, was inspired by the fighting in the Crimea, and expressed the view that though war is bad an ignoble peace is worse. It went into two editions and was followed in 1855 by *Battle Pieces*. The third volume, *Joint Compositions*, is undated and talks about reforms at home:

> They say the land is over-full –
> With wealth like this to crown the soil –
> The bloated city sucks it in;
> And they who neither plough nor spin
> Take all the fruits of toil.

> Why should the idle eat? 'tis well
> That English tempers suffer long,
> And yet it makes a plain man wroth,
> When evil laws that pamper sloth,
> Insult the poor they wrong.[4]

and on hanging:

> . . . oh age of boasted power,
> Of conquered land and sea –
> Ask yet a nobler birth from time –
> Be humble still – or find for crime
> A worthier remedy.[5]

Lear's friendship with Lushington later became fired with such intensity on Lear's side that he had deep unhappiness in store, but there was no hint of this now as they left together for what were probably the happiest few weeks of Lear's life.

They landed at Patras on 9 March, and travelled south into the Morea, a land rich in the history of centuries. On the hills of

Arcadia the shepherds worshipped Pan, and it is traditionally the region of rustic contentment and a perfect place to be happy. In fact for most of the year it is a barren, unfriendly countryside, and the gentle happiness of the poets' Arcady is a lie. But now the hills were indulgent, for it was spring. Day after day they walked and drew – the temple of Apollo at Bassae, Sparta, Argos, Mycenae – the days were too short for all the happiness that had to be crowded into them. The countryside was green, and the occasional showers only helped to bring out the profusion of flowers. 'No one can form any idea of what the spring is in Greece – ; it is all very well to say that there is a mile of bright scarlet ground, then half a mile of blue or pale pink – but it is difficult for you to realise that the whole earth is like a rich Turkey carpet. As for Lushington & I, equally fond of flowers, we gather them all day like children, & when we have stuck our hats & coats & horses all over with them – it is time to throw them away, & get a new set.'[6]

They crossed from Corinth to Athens then travelled up through Attica to Thebes where Lear had been taken ill in 1848. From there they went to Parnassus and Delphi and on to Patras where they parted. '... we got here yesterday at noon,' Lear wrote to Ann from Patras, 'after the most delightful 6 weeks' tour I ever made; everything has been so very fortunate & pleasant that the time has gone by a great deal too quickly, & Mr Lushington has been so constantly the most merry and kind travelling companion that I am very sorry he is obliged to return to England.'[7]

Left on his own Lear went north to Yannina and over the Metsovo Pass to the Vale of Tempe and Mount Olympus. He passed through beautiful countryside, but its splendour made him feel strangely sad: 'A keen sense of every kind of beauty, is ... if given in the extreme – always more or less a sorrow to its owner, – tho' productive of good to others,'[8] he once said, and even as a boy this had disturbed him: 'What a mingling of sadness & admiration of landscape botheringly will persist in existing,' he wrote. 'All the unsought morbid feelings – (certainly unsought – for I knew not what even the meaning of morbid was in those days,) of past years crop up at once – such as the Hornsey fields & Highgate archway, & the sad large Thorn tree at Holloway about 1819 – or 1820 ... the Mill at Arundel, or Peppering in 1824 or 5 – the heights above Plymouth in 1836–37 – the Godesburg – 1837 – Civitella 1839 & Nemi – all were with me at once. How far is it right or wise to get rid of & crush the morbids altogether? – I can't tell. Yet I have tried & do try to do so – tho' I crush a good deal else with them.'[9]

The gentle unhurriedness of nature, peaceful blues and greens, the absence of strife – these were on the side of man. He had known this on the Campagna and in Greece, and again later in Corfu, when he wrote: 'This is everywhere a flood of gold & green & blue. This, & the breeze, blowing freshly now & then, remind me of days in many lands before *that* knowledge came which tells us we have so little, & so much conjecture. On Swiss, & Como hills in 1837 – in the first years of Roman & Amalfi life /38, /9 – the long Civitella sojourns – 1839–40 – Abruzzi 43–44 – Sicily & Greece, 47, 48/49. – I do not now suppose that kind of happiness can ever come back but by unexpected & unsought snatches; so I do not strive after it, nor mourn that I cannot have it.'[10]

He was still unable to get to Mount Athos, and had to resign himself to missing the Holy Mountain. In fact there was much he had not seen, but when he boarded the boat to take him back to England he was going home to settle down. The days of Lotus-eating were over.

PART TWO

SLOPES OF MYRTLE
1849–1869

8 Pre-Raphaelite
1849–1853

Mrs Warner's legacy was perfectly timed, for shortly after his return to England at the beginning of June 1849 Lear heard that she had left him £500. The rest of her fortune of nearly £50,000 she had bequeathed to perpetual widows. 'I thought, directly I heard of this matter, that I would instantly marry one of the 30 viddies,' Lear told Fortescue prudently, 'only then it occurred to me that she wouldn't be a viddy any more if I married her.'[1] But for the first time in his life he had a little capital, and could go ahead with his plans.

He wanted to go to the Royal Academy Schools. The foundation of the Academy in 1768, and in particular its first President, Sir Joshua Reynolds, had done something very special for painting in England, for with the granting of the Royal Charter artists became gentlemen. Reynolds had been in Rome between 1750 and 1752 studying the work of Raphael and Michelangelo, and he believed that a revival in British art would only come through a study of great masters of the past. By copying what was good in them and rejecting what was bad, the students would learn from the experience of earlier generations, and could then go on to develop their own style. They would need a very thorough knowledge of their technique, and the course at the RA was spread over ten years, incidentally giving an atmosphere of refined leisure. After devoting three years to drawing and to a study of human anatomy from the antique, they moved into the Preliminary School of Painting where they learnt to handle paint. It was only in the final stage of their training in the Upper School of Painting that they were allowed to work from the living model. For History Painters the subject matter was either biblical or classical, and as this was the age of neo-classicism in England, Reynolds's approach gave painting an intellectual – and not merely artisan – status. But by the end of the eighteenth century Pope had given way to the Romantic poets, and the classical revival had been absorbed. The new thinkers were finding their truth in Nature, but at the Academy the teaching of Reynolds was still rigidly followed and was becoming increasingly academic and remote. The landscape painters had moved on, and whilst most Academicians turned out turgic academic studies in brown, Turner's paintings were singing with a brilliance of colour which burned to a white heat.

In 1843, Ruskin published the first volume of *Modern Painters*, in which he championed the brilliance of Turner and preached a return to the study of Nature itself, and in the Summer Exhibition of 1849 – the year of Lear's return to London – three strangely new paintings were hung, fresh in colour and medieval in concept, and each was inscribed mysteriously with the initials P.R.B.

Despite the criticism, the RA Schools were unrivalled in London and it was not easy to get a place there. Lear's experience might help him, but his age – for he was thirty-seven – would not. They would be selecting students in January and he had until then to prepare the drawings, from the antique of course, which he had to submit. He enrolled again at Sass's, the school in Bloomsbury which prepared students for the Academy and where he had been fifteen years before.

The term did not begin until September, and during the late summer he wandered from one country house to another. He went down to Maidstone to visit Lushington at his home, Park House, but the atmosphere was heavy and subdued and instead of the abandoned youth who had travelled with him in Greece he found a silent, inturned man.

Another house Lear visited was of course Knowsley, and from there he wrote to Fortescue: 'My dear old friends Mr Hornby & Lord Derby I found just as ever – though 72 – & 75 – & every day has caused fresh shaking of hands with old friends . . . Certainly English people do go on with friendship just where they left off – as you go on with a book at the page you last read. – So you see – barring the queer climate – I have been intensely happy, & if one were morbidly inclined, one would think that like old Dives one was enjoying all one's good things here below!'[2]

But the good things had to end, and by mid-September he was in London ready for the new term. He had taken a five-year lease on rooms at No. 17, Stratford Place, a cul-de-sac running north from Oxford Street where some of the three-storey Georgian houses still stand. We do not know whether he and Ann discussed the possibility of their living together, but the following spring Mary Lear wrote to her brother Frederick:

'Dear Ann has been very unsteady in her habits this last Summer! – She compares herself to *"Thistle down"* – blown here & there – but She will shortly be settled in a family at the West End.'[3] '. . . so good, & yet so unable to be my companion,'[4] Lear wrote of Ann in 1858, and despite the earlier talk of 'an old cat, & some china', they continued to live apart.

During the next three months Lear prepared his drawings for the Academy. At the beginning of January 1850 he sent his work to the selectors and on the 16th he heard that he had been accepted. He was delighted, and yet a little worried, when he wrote to Fortescue to tell him the news:

Dear Fortescue,

What fun! – pretty little dear – ! – he got into the Academy – he did! – Yes – so he did.

You will be pleased to hear that the R. Academy have sate on my drawing from the antique, and that I am a 'probationer' – & on my trial till April, when the 3 drawings I have to make will be again sate on – & I shall be admitted for 10 years as a student – or – rejected. – *Vedermo quale sarò.*

I tried with 51 – little boys – & 19 of us were admitted. And now I go with a large book and a piece of chalk to school every day like a good little boy.

Your's affectionately,
Edward Lear[5]

It must have been difficult to have been surrounded by students twenty years younger than himself, but they probably thought of him as rather special, for here was a man who had travelled

widely and had published three books about his journeys, who had illustrated numerous works of natural history and was the author of the famous *Book of Nonsense* – a man, moreover, who had been drawing master to the Queen.

Practically nothing has survived from Lear's time at the RA Schools, and we do not know how he reacted to this strange interlude. We do know that he was accepted as a student after the three months' probationary period on 26 April, but it is doubtful that he ever intended to stay the full course, for he would have been nearly fifty when he finished. It seems probable that he stayed for a year. In this time he would have done a great deal of drawing from the antique and learned something about the human form, but he would have had no tuition in oil painting.

He was finding London life expensive, and to supplement his diminishing capital he published in 1851 the *Journals of a Landscape Painter in Albania &c.* It was an immediate success. 'I receive *heaps* and *loads* of compliments & congratulations about the book,'[6] he wrote.

It was at about this time that Lear was introduced to Tennyson. They met at the Lushingtons' home, Park House. In 1841 the poet's family had moved to Boxley, a village two miles from Park House, and the following year his sister, Cecilia, was married to Edmund Lushington – their epithalamium forms the epilogue to *In Memoriam*. When Lear met Tennyson the poet was just over forty. The previous year, 1850, had been an important one for him, for he had published *In Memoriam*, he had been made Poet Laureate, and he was married at last to Emily Sellwood. Lear sent Emily Tennyson two volumes of his travel books as a late wedding present. 'I intended long ago to have done a series of little landscapes illustrative of some of the Poems,' he said in the covering letter, 'but a thousand things have stepped in between me & my wishes . . . There have been but few weeks or days within the last 8 years, that I have not been more or less in the habit of remembering or reading Tennyson's poetry, & the amount of pleasure derived by me from them has been quite beyond reckoning.'[7] Emily too was enthusiastic as she wrote back: 'Very often shall we delight ourselves by looking upon those beautiful drawings, which give one, as Alfred said of one in particular, something in the glory of nature herself looking upon them.'[8] In fact, so impressed was Tennyson that he wrote the lines, 'To E.L. on his Travels in Greece.'

Whilst Lear was at the Academy, the dissatisfaction that some young painters felt with its principles of painting became a public issue. A few weeks before the Summer Exhibition of 1850 the meaning of the letters P.R.B. became known, and the Pre-Raphaelite Brotherhood became a controversial part of the Victorian art scene.

The Brotherhood was the creation of three young men of unusual talent and utterly different temperament. It is extraordinary that they came together at all, and yet their very differences meant that each contributed something to the movement. John Millais – attractive and charming, yet not entirely likeable – had been encouraged to paint by enthusiastic parents who had brought him from Jersey to London so that he could study drawing. When he went to the RA Schools at the age of eleven he was the youngest student they had ever had, and when he left at seventeen he won the Royal Academy Gold Medal. William Holman Hunt was plain, puritanical, and rather self-consciously intense: he had to fight his father for permission to study art, and had worked for four years in a City office before going to the RA Schools in 1844. The third man, Dante Gabriel Rossetti, imposing and strange, was born into a house where culture seemed intuitive. His father had escaped from Italy in 1824 when King Ferdinand of Naples, whom he had openly opposed, came to power, and when Dante Gabriel was born was Professor of Italian Literature at King's College in the Strand.

Their aims were to have genuine ideas which they sought to express well, and to study nature itself. Instead of painting on to a half-tone which absorbed the light, they used a white canvas which reflected the light and pushed it back through the paint giving a brilliance to the colour. They did not deny the work of earlier painters, providing it was 'direct and serious and heart-felt', and they continued taking subjects from the Bible. But they discovered the little known poetry of Keats, and found new sub-jects in the medievalism of Isabella and La Belle Dame sans Merci. Rossetti, the true son of a revolutionary, suggested a secret brotherhood, esoteric and dedicated to its beliefs, which they modelled on the German Nazarene painters of fifty years before, and when Collinson, Woolner, Stephens and William Michael Rossetti were invited to join, the Brotherhood numbered seven.

The first paintings exhibited with the mysterious letters P.R.B. had aroused a certain inquisitive interest, but nothing more. But now the Academicians realised that one of their brightest young painters was questioning the very foundation of the Academy. Whilst a lesser painter could be ignored – in fact the work of Hunt and Rossetti was scarcely mentioned – the new Millais could not. The critics saw in his work a rejection of the values which they had been content to endorse, and their response was entirely predictable. They were voraciously insult-ing. Speaking of Millais's gentle, and to modern eyes, senti-mentalised painting of 'Christ in the House of His Parents', Dickens warned the public that they must expect to see 'the lowest depths of what is mean, repulsive and revolting',[9] and – whatever one may think of the painting – his notice published in *Household Words* must be one of the saddest pieces of un-informed bigotry a great writer ever wrote. Perhaps it did offend against their ideas of the Holy Family, and certainly there were cries of 'blasphemy', but in the following year the same tone of criticism met Millais's 'The Return of the Dove to the Ark', which was not, even then, a subject about which the public would have felt with passion.

This time Ruskin was persuaded to take up their cause in *The Times*, and after this the Brotherhood became more respectable. During the winter of 1851 Millais worked on his painting of 'A Huguenot', a deliberate concession to public taste, and by the middle of 1852 the fervour of the Brotherhood as a group had been spent.

The Summer Exhibition was held then in the National Gallery, and Lear, who was studying in the Schools tucked away behind the Gallery, could watch the developing controversy. In fact, he had a picture in the Academy himself for the first time that year, a painting of Claude Lorrain's house on the Tiber. He had no particular sympathy for the subjects which the Pre-Raphaelites chose, for his ambition was always and only to be a landscape painter, but they did seem to embody some of his own ideals. A close study of nature was essential to him and had been one reason for the extraordinary success of his ornithological paintings, and he had admired freshness of colour in Turner's work.

It is unlikely that Lear stayed at the Academy beyond the end of 1850. In November of that year he was corresponding with Lord Stanley about a painting for Lord Derby. It was to be a view of the Acropolis at harvest time, and Lear intended to apply what he had been learning. '. . . groups of figures are as *natural*, as they are picturesque in themselves,' he wrote, '& indispensable to a good foreground in a large subject.'[10] However, he was soon forced to realise the limitations of his knowledge, and in the following March he was writing to Lord Derby: 'The time is to be sunrise or a little after, & I have avoided many figures as solitude & quiet are the prevaling [sic] feelings on that side of Athens.'[11]

During the early months of 1851, the damp and cold were bothering him so much that he was confined indoors. London always oppressed him with its 'dazzly dirty dimmy slippery streets',[12] and its light 'so narrowed & contracted & small'.[13] It was then a city with 'an endless roar of traffic, under an opaque sky and a steady drift of smuts, sending up, according to season, fountains of mud or whirlwinds of dust, straw, and paper',[14] an unpleasant contrast to wide Grecian valleys and Albanian hills. 'I never can apply to remembering how hours of sedentary life make me boil over when I get away – a steam=force which is let off by walking, but bursts out in rage & violence if it has no natural outlet,'[15] he wrote later, for without exercise his epilepsy was always worse.

By June, his painting of Athens was finished. But then came sudden news. '. . . he had been very busy – engaged for several Months in painting a large Picture for the Earl,' Ann wrote to Frederick's wife, 'and had just finished it and was going down with it to Knowsley (the Earl's Country Seat) to pay a visit there of a few weeks – when the family wrote to tell him of the Earl's death.'[16] His old patron, the 13th Earl, was dead. 'O Lord! o Lord! how fondly I used to suppose that if ever I lived to 40 I should become like unto an iron pot without feeling & quite hard!' he wrote to Emily Tennyson. 'I'm sorry to say I ain't at all: – the more my misery.'[17]

'Overworked and unwell & unable to bear the disquiet of London',[18] he decided to escape to Devon for a few weeks. But it was wet, he was isolated, and he felt worse than ever. 'I don't improve as I wish,' he told Fortescue sadly, 'which added to the rain prevents "happiness and tranquility". It is true I don't *expect* to improve, because I am aware of my peculiar incapacities for art, mental & physical: – but that don't mend the matter – anymore than the knowledge that he is to be always blind delights a man whose eye is poked out. The great secret of my constant hard work is, to prevent my going back, – or at best, standing quite still. – I certainly did improve *last* year a little – but I ain't sure if Lydford & the rain & the cows won't have made me go back, *this* year. However, I did it all for the best, as the old sow said when she sate on her little pigs.'[19]

In August Lushington came down, and they went for a walking tour through Cornwall, but when Lear was depressed he could be an extraordinarily bad companion, and it was a disaster. What he needed was some real instruction and encouragement in his work. He had come back to England enthusiastic and wanting to make real use of this chance, but now he was beginning to drift. He began to talk about going to a nightly academy to draw from life. Not only figure drawing worried him, but also his inadequate knowledge of how to use oil paint. When he tried to make considered paintings from the sketches he had brought back from Greece and Palestine, he realised that he simply did not know how to go about them.

Then one day in the summer of 1852, Robert Martineau, whose picture 'Kit's Writing Lesson' painted that year hangs now in the Tate, brought Holman Hunt to Lear's studio at Stratford Place. Lear was nervous and Hunt remembered that he 'overflowed with geniality, and at the same time betrayed anxiety as we turned over the drawings'.[20] Hunt saw that the sketches were not detailed enough as reference for large oil paintings, and his Pre-Raphaelite principles were a little shocked to think of Lear working only from drawings. The obvious thing was for Lear to find countryside which resembled what he was painting, and then he could study the scene direct from nature. The painting of the 'Quarries of Syracuse', for instance, included limestone rocks and fig trees, and both these could be found in England. He was about to go down to Fairlight, in the hills above Hastings, to work on his painting of 'The Strayed Sheep', and he suggested that Lear might like to go with him and he could show him what he meant.

Lear accepted the offer excitedly, and it was arranged that he would go there first to find somewhere for them to stay. A few days later he wrote to Hunt telling him that he had found Clive Vale Farm, which was rather poky but otherwise ideal. Hunt told him to go ahead and take it, and then came a strange letter from Lear. It was unwise, he wrote, for them to be too impulsive. Living so close might strain their friendship, and he suggested that they should have separate parts of the house and meet only at mealtimes. He was still guarded when Hunt arrived a few days later with William Rossetti, who had come to spend the first week with them. In exchange for lessons in painting Lear was to teach Hunt Italian, and Rossetti's presence that first evening proved a blessing, for he and Lear chatted to one another in Italian. By the end of dinner Lear was no longer strained. 'Now I had intended to go to my own room,' he told them, 'but, if you do not mind, I'll bring down some of my drawings and pen them out here, so that we may all be together.'[21] The suggestion of separate rooms could then become a joke, and he explained to Hunt – most unsatisfactorily – that he had been frightened that he might be a lover of bulldogs and would arrive at the farm bringing two of these detestable pets.

No more explanations were given, but perhaps it is worth noting that this was the only time, except when he was travelling, that Lear risked living closely with someone else, and that not one of these friends apparently ever realised that he was an epileptic. He had warning of the attacks, but he had to be sure of the arrangements, and to know that he could have the privacy he needed. He must have been satisfied that his secret would be kept, for there was no more mention of separate rooms.

For the first ten days Lear went with Hunt to watch him paint, and then he decided to try on his own. It was a short apprenticeship, and Hunt, writing to F. G. Stephens, was most uncomplimentary: 'Lear is a very nice fellow but much too old to live with always – he is about 40. I am being drilled in Italian by him and in return I am letting him see me paint, which from his productions I confess myself unable to feel is a very great advantage.'[22]

Fortunately, his disdain did not come through to Lear, nor was it apparently seriously intended, and the two men enjoyed one another's company. They lived primitively, and after their evening meal would settle down and talk whilst Lear penned out his drawings or made notes about Hunt's technique, particularly his use of colour, in *Ye Booke of Hunte*. They probably discussed the 'narrow & illiberal' RA, for Lear's disabusement with the Academy began at this time. Hunt enjoyed listening to Lear's accounts of his travels, and they planned one day to explore Palestine together. They discussed Tennyson's poetry, and, prompted by this, Lear's thoughts went back to his earlier idea of illustrating the poet's work. From Clive Vale Farm he wrote to Emily Tennyson: 'I have latterly extracted & placed in a sort of order all the lines which convey to me in the most decided manner his genius for the perception of the beautiful in land-scape ... My desire has been to show that Alfred Tennyson's poetry (with regard to scenes –) is as real & exquisite as it is relatively to higher & deeper matters: – that his descriptions of certain spots are as positively true as if drawn from the places themselves, & that his words have the power of calling up images as distinct & correct as if they were written from those images, instead of giving rise to them.'[23] But, though he frequently had lines of Tennyson's verse in mind as he painted, Lear was unable to carry his plans forward for many years. Meanwhile, he asked the poet down to pass 'a rural Sunday' with them. 'There is a cliff on purpose to smoke on – & nobody near,'[24] he wrote, enticingly. Sadly, the poet did not accept.

Other friends did come. Millais spent a day with them, the first time that Lear had met him. Martineau lived nearby in Hastings, and William Rossetti came to stay again, this time helping Lear to correct the proofs of his *Journal of a Landscape Painter in Southern Calabria* which was published that autumn.

During the months that Hunt and Lear lived together, a deep and lifelong friendship grew. It had none of the emotional charge of Lear's relationship with Lushington, nor – despite the letter to Stephens – any of the condescension which later marred his relationship with Fortescue for a time. They respected each other and had much in common: 'He is very plain & uneducated, except by his own exertions',[25] Lear said of Hunt that summer, and he might have been speaking of himself. It was a symbiotic relationship – Hunt could give Lear help with his painting, and Lear was able to implant in Hunt some of his own love of poetry and music: 'I am indebted to you for the amount of culture that I have got since the time I first met you,'[26] Hunt told him, many years later.

Lear never aspired to being a Pre-Raphaelite Brother, but he

did feel himself qualified to be called a Son. He christened Holman Hunt 'Daddy', and Millais and Woolner were then his Uncles. 'Daddy Hunt's head would cut up sufficient for 10 men, & his heart for 200 at least. God bless him.'[27]

In the late autumn Hunt returned to London. Lear felt that these three months had been the most valuable of his whole stay in England, and after they parted he sent Hunt a copy of his Nonsense to show his gratitude. 'I really cannot help again expressing my thanks to you for the progress I have made this autumn,' he wrote in the covering letter. 'The Reggio, and the Venosa are both done and in frames, – (except that the latter will have to benefit by some of your remarx when we meet –) and I hardly believe I did them. I am now beginning to have perfect faith in the means employed, and if the Thermopylae turns out right I am a P.R.B. for ever. Indeed, in no case, shall I ever return to the old style.'[28]

Lear stayed on to work on the fig tree in his painting of Syracuse, for he had discovered a perfect tree in the garden of Frederick North, the Member of Parliament for Hastings. Whilst he was working there, Lear took rooms with the gardener. He wanted to paint jackdaws perched in the tree, and had brought with him a stuffed bird which he wired on to the branches in different positions, with a delightful disregard for strict Pre-Raphaelite principles.

Frederick North had two daughters who soon became Lear's friends. The older girl, Catherine, later married John Addington Symonds. Whilst he was at Hastings Lear stated firmly and a little sadly what his own views on marriage had become. 'No my dear Fortescue,' he wrote, '*I* don't mean to marry. never. – *you* should – but there's time enough yet for you – 6 or 8 years perhaps. In my case – I should paint less & less well – & the thought of annual infants would drive me wild. If I attain to 65 – & have an "establishm'" with lots of spoons &c. to offer – I *may* chain myself: – but surely not before. – And alas! & seriously – when I look around my acquaintance – & few men have more, or know more intimately, do I see a majority of happy pairs? No – I don't. Single – I may have few pleasures – but married – many risks & miseries are semi-certainly in waiting – nor till the plot is played out can it be said that evils are not at hand . . .

'In one sense I am growing very indifferent to the running out of the sands of life. Years are making me see matters with totally different eyes than I formerly saw with: – but at the same time I am far more cheerful. I only wish I could dub & scrub myself into what I wish to be, & what I might be I fear if I took proper pains. – But *chi sa*? How much will be allowed for *nature*, & early impressions, & iron early tuition? – Looking back, I sometimes wonder I am even what I am. I often wonder & wonder how I have made so many certainly real friends as I have. Sometimes 6 or 8 of the kindest letters in the world come together, & the effect is rather humiliating tho' not to my peculiar idio-syncracy.'[29]

Frederick North's younger daughter, Marianne, later travelled over the world making the drawings of plants which now fill the North Gallery at Kew Gardens. She liked to go and watch Lear painting, and remembered how he would 'wander into our sitting-room through the windows at dusk when his work was over, sit down to the piano, and sing Tennyson's songs for hours, composing as he went on, and picking out the accompaniments by ear, putting the greatest expression and passion into the most sentimental words. He often set me laughing; then he would say I was not worthy of them, and would continue the intense pathos of expression and gravity of face, while he substituted Hey Diddle Diddle, the Cat and the Fiddle, or some other non-sensical words to the same air.'[30] Lear had no musical training and could neither read nor write music, but he was a popular after-dinner entertainer. In 1853 he published some of his set-tings of Tennyson's poems, including his own sad favourite, 'Tears, Idle Tears'. His were the only settings that Tennyson himself liked, 'they seem to throw a diaphanous veil over the words – nothing more,'[31] he said, and after hearing 'Home They Brought the Warrior Dead', Archbishop Tait exclaimed, 'Sir, you ought to have half the Laureateship.'[32] 'You are the only person whose singing could make me cry whether I would or not,'[33] Lady Waldegrave told him, and perhaps this was the response he sought. Listeners who responded without emotion were less appreciative. 'Edward Lear, a charming man and author of the well-known *Book of Nonsense*, could hardly be called a musician,' wrote one, 'but being good at "vamping" he sat down to the piano and hummed rather than sang two of Tennyson's songs to tunes of his own composing. It was a clever performance; but the really musical people there were quite surprised at the eulogistic terms in which Tennyson spoke of the compositions. I cannot help thinking, however, that it was regard for the man rather than the music which caused this unexpected outburst of praise.'[34]

He had intended to return to London in January, but when the ceiling in the London house fell down he decided to stay on until the winter was over. He wanted to submit his new paintings to the two big London exhibitions – at the British Institution and the Royal Academy – and needed to have them finished early in the new year. Working alone he quickly became disheartened, and he wrote to Emily Tennyson, 'It is a sad evil with me that I *think* I can do so much more than I ever *can* do: & that I have so little faith in my powers of improvement. Whether I shall ever see myself in a fair groove of continuous improvement is very doubtful now.'[35] He needed Hunt's constant advice to help him over the difficulties in his painting, for he never really understood what he was doing well enough to analyse what was wrong. '... if you cannot tell me how the shadows of the blessed jackdaws will fall I don't know what I shall do,' he wrote despairingly to him, 'also the shadows of the 3 blox of stone are too similar in color, – but I don't know how to change them. Altogether I foresee the possibility of this picture being a failure & remaining unfinished, unless you can help me out of the mess. – It has been so completely impossible even to *see* nature lately – much more to paint from it, that the poor beast of painting has not had fair play. This however by no means weakens my faith as to the proper way of painting – had I been really able to follow it out.'[36]

He was back in London by the end of February in new rooms at 65 Oxford Terrace. The sale of a painting to Richard Bethell, later Lord Westbury, helped him over the move. He had left the Academy by now, and was getting most, possibly all, of his tuition from Hunt. There was still much for him to learn, but the climate had started to worry him again. He was torn between a desire to go through and master the technique of oil painting with Hunt's help, and a hankering to be on the move again to somewhere where the sun shone.

The acceptance of his picture of the 'Mountains of Thermopylae' by the British Institution in the spring of 1853 gave him new encouragement, for it was widely praised. 'Lear has a picture at the B.I. which is capital,' Stephens told Woolner; 'he delights to acknowledge his obligations to Hunt for instruction while they were staying at Fairlight together. He goes everywhere saying that Hunt taught him all he knows and he has improved wonderfully.'[37]

Sending-in day for the RA was in April, and his magnum opus – the five-foot-long painting of 'The Quarries of Syracuse' – must be ready in time for this. But his sister Sarah and her husband had decided to leave England to go and live in New Zealand, and Lear was working well on his painting when he had to put it to one side and help Sarah with her preparations. He fretted over the valuable time which was slipping away, and when he was able to get back to it he had lost the flow. Disappointed, he again asked Hunt for help, and it was ready – but not as he had wished it – in time.

Despite his misgivings, the painting was accepted, and within a few weeks had been bought by Henry Lygon, heir to the Earl of Beauchamp, who chose it as his Art Union Prize. 'Dear Daddy,' Lear wrote when he heard the news, 'The Syracuse *is* sold, for £250 – thanks my boy to you. Tell Millais – and W. Rosetti from me. – I am now going out – to hop on one leg all the way to Hastings.'[38]

In March, Lord Derby asked him to do a painting of Windsor Castle, a partner to the painting of the Acropolis commissioned by his father. At the beginning of July Lear left for Windsor but, working there completely alone, his world became black. The weather was bad and this made painting according to his new discipline very difficult. 'The sky is always beastly blueblack, & I have sent for no end of tubes of that ingredient: – & during this week the sun has shone twice,' he told Hunt. 'It is therefore utterly impossible to do this view on a strictly P.R.B. principle, – for supposing a tree is black one minute – the next it's yellow, & the 3^d green: so that were I to finish any one part the whole 8 feet would be all spots – a sort of Leopard Landscape. I must therefore – *if ever* there is sun again, (toward evening,) make out the shadows grossly and work away as I can. All the distance also is blue, gray & black – dark & light – by fits, – & the castle which should be in strong light & shade has been for 2 days jet black – 2 more scumbled gray without an iota of detail, & the remaining 2 days wholly invisible. The difficulty of the whole thing disgusts me immensely, the more that as it is to be a portrait I can give way to no remedies of imagination.'[39]

He was finding problems with the foreground reminiscent of those he had encountered in the Athens picture, only the subjects were different. 'In order to make the foreground as good as I could,' he wrote to Lord Derby from Lewes, 'I have been trying all sorts of ways to paint sheep of a good size. First, I went to a friend the Rector of Gt. Berkhamsted – but his sheep were so wild I could do nothing, & being caught, made so great a noise that my friend became nervous, & I was obliged to go away, lest he should preach from Samuel's question about the bleating of sheep in his ears.

'Then I went to Hastings, but though I made many small drawings, I could not find good South Down Sheep near enough, or otherwise available to be painted large on so large a canvass.

'Lastly, I came here: – but infinite obstacles owing to the size of the picture, the shearing of the sheep, the growth of the lambs &c &c &c &c &c &c, have at last worn me out utterly, & therefore I shall give up all idea of doing the sheep *as large* as I intended, & confine myself to a simple foreground of green, with distant sheep: – of which I have meanwhile made several studies.'[40] In a letter to Holman Hunt he confided his final decision on the matter: 'The sheep here are all lame, & entirely driven away. So I shall put in a drove on Apes from the Zoological Society.'[41]

Later in the year he was in Leicestershire making studies of rocks for a painting of the temple of Bassae. As he struggled on with his Pre-Raphaelite methods, he wrote to Holman Hunt: 'Sir Joshua Reynolds used to use a large basin of Asphaltum, & as he walked about the room, it used to drop on the floor.'[42] 'I got oak boughs indoors, but did no good by so doing . . . If I could only get the *leaves* done, & one little bit of fern, I could get the branches & rocks easily. But the leaves are falling fast . . . Lord! how I wish I could go back to sloshing & Asphaltism.'[43]

Winter with its damp and fogs was coming on again, and he wrote to Emily Tennyson, 'I am turning over in every way some mode of leaving this loathsome climate & getting a living for the remainder of my life, even if as a shoeblack, so I could see the sun. Perhaps I may go & fight the Russians – perhaps go to

Australia. But stay here I *won't*, to be demoralised by years of mud & fog & gnats and rheumatism & small beer and stupid boors and coalfires and choleramorbusses and income taxes and calvinists and steel forks and humbugs and midnight atmospheres all the year round – I have had enough of it, & forthwith I am growing moustaches in sign of going elsewhere.'[44]

He decided to go on the trip to Egypt and Palestine which he and Hunt had talked about in the evenings at Clive Vale Farm. Hunt could not leave at once as he was working on his painting of 'The Light of the World'. In fact, when he looked at the 'decayed returned prodigals and flourishing fatted calves',[45] he wondered if it was wise for him to leave England at all. For Lear there was no choice, for his health had become so bad that he could not wait. 'You will be sorry to learn that my lungs & throat are so much worse that I am going off at once to see the "Palms & Temples of the South",' he told Emily Tennyson. '. . . I wish I could see you, but I shall wait to see my friends with comfort in heaven – for in England is none for me.'[46]

He had been home for four and a half years, and later 'rejoiced at my slavy labours at anatomy in 1849–50 – for small progress as I made – I can make somewhat like figures now – & never could before'.[47] On the whole it had been a disappointing time. He had committed himself to years of drawing from the antique, an impossible task for a man of his age with his painting experience. If he had gone to a smaller art school, one less bound by tradition – possibly even the night school he had talked about – where he could have concentrated on figure drawing, he might have learnt what he needed in one or two years. But maybe it was not just figure drawing that he had in mind when he came home. Perhaps he felt that to qualify for acceptance as a serious painter he must have studied at the Schools where almost all the major British painters of his day had at some time been students. Perhaps too he had a hankering to fulfil a boyhood ambition by going through the training that he had been cheated of then.

Sadly, for it was the end of a hopeful dream, he boarded the *SS Indus* on 6 December 1853, and sailed for Alexandria.

9 The Morbids
1853–1855

As Lear's boat steamed south into the Mediterranean he began to soak up the warmth of the sun. He was usually a bad sailor and it was late in the year, but the weather in the Bay of Biscay had been perfect and for the first time in his life he was really enjoying being on a boat. There were about 150 'merry & agreeable' passengers, most of them on their way out to India.

At Gibraltar there was time to make a quick dash ashore to see the Alameda and the public gardens, and then they settled back to a gentle cruise along the North African coast. To pass the time they ate breakfast at 9, luncheon at 12, dinner at 4, tea at 7, and supper at 9.30. The rest of the time they played cards and games, and worked up an appetite for the next meal by walking round the deck. Each evening after supper they sat out in the warm moonlight chatting and listening to music; with the ladies in their evening gowns the deck looked like 'a great sea drawing room'[1] – colourful gaiety a few feet from the quiet rushing of the black sea as the boat cut through the water.

They stopped briefly at Malta which looked 'pretty & sunny & gay',[2] and perhaps Lear thought of his meeting there with Lushington nearly five years before.

Cairo seemed even more bustling and colourful than it had been five years earlier. From his hotel room he looked out over a garden of high palms and green acacia trees filled with doves and kites and crested hoopoes: this was what he had missed in London where there was nothing to satisfy his feeling for rich, colourful beauty. Thomas Seddon, one of the painters on the fringe of the Pre-Raphaelite movement, was there, and he told his brother: 'I have been very glad of Lear's arrival, both because his advice as an experienced traveller has been very useful, and also because I have been able to consult him about the pictures I think of painting. He says that I have become accustomed to the language and habits of the people, and have settled down to work, in much shorter time than most persons, so my conscience is at ease.'[3]

Lear's own conscience was not so easy. He really had meant to settle in England and not start wandering again, and he kept feeling that he must justify his journey to Ann. 'Of this I am sure,' he wrote to her, 'that had I persisted in remaining in England, my lungs would not have recovered again. So you see I am *taking it easy*, & regarding my EXILE, as a medicinal & necessary remedy.'[4]

He dithered for a few days, uncertain whether to travel up the Nile alone or stay in Cairo with Seddon, painting and learning Arabic until Hunt arrived. Then he was invited to join a party which was leaving just after Christmas, and he decided to go with them. 'We start – (don't laugh!) 4 boats together, & 3 more go before, & 5 or 6 follow after! ! ! – so that it is a regular English company,' he told Ann. She must have been particularly anxious as he then began lengthy reassurances: 'Our Dragoman, Khaleel, is a *well known*, & *most respectable* person, & I hope you will think of me as being *quite among friends*, and also enjoying myself in seeing the wonderful temples I have so long desired to see. I wish you to know also that I promise you *not* to go into *any pits*, or *caves*; for I hate dust & mummies & dark holes. – *I will take the greatest care of myself in every way*.'[5]

They travelled up the Nile at a leisurely pace, dropping anchor each night. By the end of the first week they had reached Minyeh. 'So far, it is a magnificent river, with endless villages – *hundreds* & *hundreds* on its banks, all fringed with palms, & reflected in the water; – the usual accompaniments of buffaloes, camels, etc. abound, but the multitude of birds it is utterly impossible to describe, – geese, pelicans, plovers, eagles, hawkes, cranes, herons, hoopoes, doves, pigeons, king fishers & many others. The most beautiful feature is the number of boats, which look like giant moths, – & sometimes there is a fleet of 20 or 30 in sight at once.'[6]

The colour astonished him most. It was so clear and brilliant that he found it impossible to paint it, and when he went back to Egypt thirteen years later the first thing he realised was that his pictures of the Nile were drained of colour. If he could have used oils he would have been able to get more brilliance from glazes of pure paint, but oils dried almost as soon as he squeezed them on to the palette, and he had to do his best with more restricted water colour.

He was surrounded by English people, yet he felt terribly lonely – a thing he had scarcely been aware of when he was

travelling by himself in the isolated mountains of Albania. He had an extraordinary way of exploring and savouring every little bit of what he saw, from the majesty of the scenery to the eccentricities of his companions, but he found nobody with whom he could share his excitement. Whenever he could he walked on his own along the river bank. 'This morning I have had a delicious walk – through never ending corn fields,' he wrote just after they had left Girga; 'at times the ground was all blue & gray with *clouds* of pigeons; & the most beautiful little plovers & kingfishers hop just before my feet. But what pleased me very much, was to find a real vulgar old English *toad*! waddling in the field!'[7]

They travelled as far south as Aswan and the first cataract, and some of the party went on into Nubia as far as Wadi Halfa. Lear did not join them because he wanted plenty of time to explore Philae, the beautiful little oasis of ancient temples and palm trees, the home of Isis, sister-bride of Osiris. Philae is an island, and as their boat was moored upstream they could not return to it each night. Instead they took luggage and beds and cooking things and set themselves up in the Temple of Isis. Every day parties were arriving or leaving, and as there were always three or four boatloads of English people they had a dinner party each evening, with music on the Temple terrace.

He stayed there for ten happy days. 'It is impossible to describe the place to you,' he told Ann, 'any further than by saying it is more like a real *fairy island* than anything else I can compare it to. It is very small, & was formerly all covered with temples, of which the ruins of 5 or 6 now only remain. The great T. of Isis, on the terrace of which I now am writing, is so extremely wonderful that no words can give the least idea of it. The Nile is divided here into several channels, by other rocky islands, & beyond you see the desert & the great granite hills of Assouan.'[8]

On 8 February he began on the return journey, and a week later the boat reached Luxor. Here he spent ten more days exploring Karnak where he felt 'like a cheese mite among such giants',[9] the ruined temples at Thebes and the tombs in the Valley of the Kings. It was all more magnificent than Philae, but less drawable.

The rest of the journey, down stream for hundreds of miles, became very tedious. The wind kept dropping completely, and they had to heave-to for days at a time. When he reached Cairo on 16 March 1854 he had been away for ten weeks, and had grown a bushy beard. 'You will be happy to hear that I shall come home with a beard like Henry 8th,'[10] he warned Ann. He had had other beards on his travels, but had shaved them off when he reached home. This one stayed on, compensating for other losses, for 'I hope to be quite bald some day, & then I shall paint my noddle in blue & pink stripes, like an Oronooko Indian's – & all further trouble will be saved.'[11]

'Cairo seems like home once more. – So many friends are here,'[12] he wrote. One of them was Holman Hunt who had finished his painting and had decided to come. Lear wanted to go on with him to Jerusalem, but the Nile trip had been expensive and Palestine must wait.

He reached London at the end of April, pleased with his collection of Egyptian drawings, which 'refute the proverb, "Ex Nile, nihil fit."'[13] He was feeling well, and Lord Derby's picture, which had seemed such an impossible burden the previous autumn, was finished within a few weeks. His mind was filled now with plans for visiting Palestine, and he engaged an Arab to teach him Arabic in preparation for the tour. But the climate soon began to tell again. 'For a fortnight I was quite knocked up by cold East winds,' he told Hunt in July, 'but now it is rheumatism & gloom & cloud & mud & beastliness.'[14]

He wanted to try another winter in England, though, for once he made the decision to live abroad for half the year he was going to find it much more difficult to become established as a serious painter. If he could be really fit before the cold weather came, he might be able to get through the winter without trouble. There was talk of his going with Lushington for a walking tour of the Pyrenees, but then Lushington was sent to Malta to bring back his sister who was ill. Perhaps this was as well, for Lushington had changed completely since their carefree spring in Greece. Instead Lear decided to have a proper look at Switzerland which he had only passed through on his way to Italy, and Bernard Senior – who had changed his name to Bernard Husey Hunt – arranged to go with him for part of the time.

Lear left London on 1 August 1854 and waited for Husey Hunt at Thun, resting beside the lake and wallowing in the clear, clean air. In mid-August they set out together to walk over the Bernese Alps and across the Rhône Valley to Piedmulera, a few miles from Lake Maggiore. Then they turned west along the valley of Anzasca to the foot of Monte Rosa and up through Saas and the Stalden Pass to Zermatt. There Hunt left him, and Lear went north on his own to Interlaken. He had planned to cover Switzerland systematically, but it was getting cold and he decided not to stay any longer. He had enjoyed the trip and the scenery had been wonderful, but somehow he was not enthralled by the beauty of the Alps as he had been by the wide Grecian landscape or the tumble-down splendour of parts of Italy.

Lear seemed to look for two things in scenery – associations with the ancient past, and tranquillity – neither of which he found in Switzerland. Horizontals and verticals in landscape give a sense of peaceful harmony, and in most of Lear's work there is a recession into wide horizons. But in Swiss scenery the shapes clash diagonally, and the feeling of grand beauty combines with a fearful severity. 'I can hardly tell why I so much wished to see the Alps,' he wrote to Holman Hunt in Jerusalem – 'partly because (perhaps) I was tired of hearing them talked of without having seen them. Now that I have done so, I feel I was right in coming, as there is so much of the astonishing and majestic in Swiss scenery that no Landscape painter who wishes his mind to open to the admiration & comprehension of *all kinds* of nature, should pass through life without seeing this country.'[15]

He returned to England at the beginning of October to face the worst winter he had ever known. London was bitterly cold and damp and dirty. His asthma was bad, and from the middle of January until the middle of May he went out only once. 'I now imitate the conduct of marmots, dormice, truffles, tortoises & other hybernating things with the utmost strictness until summertime comes,'[16] he wrote to a friend.

Tied indoors with short, dark days and only spluttering dim gas light to work by he felt unbearably depressed, and he had to put away the large painting of Bassae on which he had started working again. Instead he painted £5 'potboilers' which he hoped would help to pay his bills. In February, the publisher of his Albanian and Calabrian books became bankrupt though, as Lear told Hunt, 'as I got nothing before I can't get less now – so that makes no difference'.[17] Friends came to visit him, and on 18 March Fortescue wrote in his diary: 'B'fast with poor Lear, whom I am v. fond of. He hardly goes out, so delicate in lungs.'[18]

For four months he lived a half-life, knowing that he could not struggle through another English winter. The lease on his rooms ran out at the end of the year; from now on he must winter abroad and concentrate on sending work back to the big exhibitions where he might still make his name known. Living abroad would make it more difficult for him to become established, and his decision was a step towards the chronic uncertainty which he was to know for the rest of his life. It meant also that he would belong nowhere – to his friends in London he would be someone who lived abroad and came home for the summer months, and on the continent he would be just another of the winter visitors. Wandering, which had begun as a necessity and become an enjoyment, was now forced upon him as an exile.

It seemed to him that year that life was going on around him, and that he was scarcely involved. In June he went to the stag party which Wilkie Collins gave for Millais before he left for Scotland to marry Effie Ruskin, and afterwards he wrote sadly to Tennyson: 'I feel woundily like a spectator, – all through my life – of what goes on amongst those I know: – very little an actor. David's particular Pelican in the Wilderness was a fool to what I have been all my days, whether in a crowd or not.'[19]

The gloomy weather had started him on a stream of introspection which he seemed unable to shake off. He felt that he needed the kind of sympathetic understanding that Alfred Tennyson's gentle wife Emily could give, and he thought of spending the summer months near their new home at Farringford on the Isle of Wight. 'Do you think there is a Pharmouse or a Nin somewhere near you, where there would be a big room looking to the North? – so that I could paint in it quietly, & come & see you & Mrs Tennyson promiscuously?' he asked Alfred – 'I know what you would say, or are saying – "come to us". – But that *wouldn't* do: – the botherations of 6 feet paintings & all the conbotherations of artists' ways *do not*, & *will not* dovetail with country houses in Anglosaxnland; – I have tried the matter well – & know it to be so. Utter idleness gets possession of me body & soul in that atmosphere: – afterwards, remorse ... If one were but a chimney pot, or a pipkin, or a mackerel, or anything respectable & consistent there would be some comfort; but the years go by without making the use of one's faculties one ought to do, & so I feel disgusted I do.'[20]

In fact it is very unlikely that the Tennysons would have welcomed him that summer. In June Alfred was in Oxford receiving the honorary degree of DCL, and in July he was faced with an onslaught of criticism when he published *Maud*. 'If an author pipe of adultery, fornication, murder and suicide, set him down as the practiser of those crimes,' wrote one critic, to which Tennyson replied with dignity: 'Adulterer I may be, fornicator I may be, murderer I may be, suicide I am not yet.'[21]

Instead, Lear spent the summer of 1855 moving around. During July and August he was at Eastbourne where the Lushingtons were spending the summer. Henry Lushington had been taken suddenly ill in Malta, and Lear probably felt that he could be of some help to the family. 'As Frank's friend you could not, I am sure, be in any place where you could so much wish to be,'[22] Emily Tennyson wrote to him, but the Lushingtons disagreed. As they waited for news their silence and gloom were even more oppressive than usual, and they made it quite plain that Lear was not only superfluous but a downright nuisance. He left, deeply hurt by the way they had treated him. '... they do understand you and are at heart grateful and sympathising though the gift of utterance is except on rare occasions denied them,'[23] Emily Tennyson encouraged him, and when Henry died early in August, she wrote: 'I have a dim sad feeling we must help each other, those who at all understand each other & love each other.'[24] For the next few months she gave him the only encouragement he had.

Emily alone understood what he felt for Lushington, and she comforted him as she might have done a young boy in love for the first time. More than anyone she realised the depth of his craving for affection, though one wonders if she understood the nature of his feelings at that time. Her response seems almost naïve, but it was warm and heartfelt, and Lear came to adore her.

To help him over his loneliness she confided her own feelings of isolation when Alfred left her alone at Farringford: 'What right have I to feel so sad who have so unspeakably much to make me cheerful even when he is away,' she wrote at the end of August; 'a love tried by all the changes & chances of a more than five years marriage and tried only to prove its unimagined worth more & more ... Dear Mr Lear why do I say all this to you but from a feeling you are not to be always "alone" & you must now sympathise prophetically with me.'[25]

In October she invited both Lear and Lushington to stay. 'I must tell you what hard work is in store for you at Farringford,' she wrote to Lear. 'Not only are you to be sofa to my shyness & Frank's silence but you are to be yourself wellest and freshest and happiest.'[26] She seemed to be planning to divert his affections somewhere more promising, for one evening she invited some friends and included in the party a bright young woman called Miss Cotton. After dinner Emily asked Lear to play some of his settings of Alfred's poems, and the effect on one side was as she had hoped. 'I am afraid you will not believe me when I tell you what a hero of romance you are ...' she wrote ingenuously after he had left. 'How Miss Cotton was found all pale after a sleepless night how her companion came and poured into my ear a mighty river of thanks and praises and admiration.'[27]

But Lear was not interested. 'Alack! for Miss Cotton!' he wrote, '... and all admirers. But we all know about the beautiful blue glass jar – which was only a white one after all, only there was blue water inside it.'[28] He had spent a wonderful few days at Farringford, and when he left he wrote a long letter to Emily: 'According to the morbid nature of the animal, I even complain sometimes that such rare flashes of light as such visits are to me, make the path darker after they are over: – a bright blue & green landscape with purple hills, & winding rivers, & unexplored forests, and airy downs, & trees & birds, & all sorts of calm repose, – exchanged for a dull dark plain horizonless, pathless, & covered with cloud above, while beneath are brambles & weariness.

'I really do believe that I enjoy hardly any one thing on earth while it is present: – always looking back, or frettingly peering into the dim beyond. – With all this, I may say to you & Alfred, that the 3 or 4 days of the 16th–20th October/55, – were the best I have passed for many a long day. – If I live to grow old, & can hope to exist in England, I *should* like to be somewhere near you in one's later days. I wish sometimes you could settle near Park House. Then I might have a room in Boxley, & moon cripply cripply about those hills, & sometimes see by turns Hallam & Lionel's children, & Frank's grandchildren, & so slide pleasantly out of life. Alfred, by that time would have written endlessly, & there would be 6 or 8 thick green volumes of poems. I – possibly, – should be in the workhouse, but I know you would all come & see me.'[29]

Now it was November, and he must make his plans for the winter. Earlier in the year Lushington had been offered the post of Judge to the Supreme Court of Justice in the Ionian Islands. He would be living in Corfu, and Lear had always promised himself that he would return to that beautiful little island. After the doubts and distress of the summer, he must have asked himself if he was really wise to think of a future with Lushington. Perhaps it seemed such a wonderful opportunity to combine winter sunshine and companionship that he did not stop and think if it could ever work. As he prepared to leave London he was looking forward to 'a new beginning of life'.[30]

Fortescue wrote him a cheerful note before he left, wishing him well. Lear had stayed with him earlier in the autumn, and Fortescue had written then in his diary: 'He spoke to me more of himself & his secret feelings than he has ever done – showed me a good deal of his great & self-tormenting sensitiveness.'[31] But he never knew the real torment that was going on in Lear's mind – the thwarted, frustrated, impossible love that he had for Lushington.

On 21 November 1855 the two men sailed from Dover.

10 Corfu
1855–1857

The journey across Europe to Trieste took a week. In Prague the snow began to fall, and when they reached Vienna the bright moonlight shone on to a cold, white city. The Alpine railway zig-zagged its way up and up and over the Semmering Pass, and then they dropped down to the Adriatic coast. 'Nothing can be so kind & thoughtful as my dear friend all the way,' Lear wrote reassuringly to Ann; '– making me take food when I did not care to leave the carriage, by buying cakes or bread & bringing them to me, & saving me all the trouble possible, although he, from being my mere travelling companion in 1848–9, has now risen to one of the very highest places of the land at the age of 33 – . But he is as wonderfully good & even tempered, as he is learned & wise.'[1]

On 3 December they reached Corfu, traditionally Homer's island of Scheria. In the centuries after the age of Greek heroes and gods, Corfu had passed from one ruler to another, for its position close to the rocky mainland of Albania guarded the important sea route between Greece and Italy. At the end of the eighteenth century all the Ionian islands were held by the French, but in 1814 they were ceded to the British after the defeat of Napoleon. During their fifty years of rule the British became much disliked, more by just being there than for anything they did, for in the islands they were benign imperialists and did much to improve conditions for the Corfiotes. Their own way of life revolved round the wives of the officials and was typical of so many nineteenth-century imperial courts. There were balls and dinners and petty intrigues, interminable evenings of cards and gay little picnic excursions. Most of the English had no idea of the beauty of their island, just as in Rome so few of them had explored the beauties of the Campagna.

Lushington went to stay with Bowen until his own house was ready, but there was no room there for Lear. However, he saw a fair amount of Lushington during the next few days: they dined together, and went to look at houses, and Lear found himself some expensive but pleasant rooms overlooking the harbour. But as the new judge, Lushington was an important and sought-after man, and soon he was too busy meeting people and settling into his work to have time for anything else. If Lear had been happy this probably would not have worried him unduly. Of course he was lonely, but it was quite reasonable for Lushington to be single-mindedly absorbed in his new work. As it was he became acutely and morbidly depressed.

Ever since his return to England in 1849 things had started to go wrong. He had already mastered his best work, the fresh, uncluttered water-colour drawings which are now coming into their own. If he had taken a thorough course in life drawing he could have begun again with increased powers. Instead, he had tied himself to years of working from marble statues and plaster casts, and had left the Academy dissatisfied with both himself and his work. Then he had turned to the new painters, and was deceived into thinking that the Pre-Raphaelite approach had much in common with his own.

Lear's best work was essentially *petit maître*, and he would have thrived in the atmosphere of personal patronage which he had seen as a boy, but which had died with men like Fawkes and de Tabley. Now reputations were made in large, mixed exhibitions, and his paintings could not compete with the elaborately conceived compositions which were usually the centre of attention. So he began painting canvases seven or nine feet long.[2] But what excited him could best be expressed with spontaneity, and lost a good deal when it was put down on a large, slowly worked canvas. Indeed, in painting landscape at all he was working in the wrong age to achieve popular success, for what the public wanted now were narrative paintings like 'The Order of Release' and 'Derby Day'.

The outcome of all this was that few people wanted his work. In Rome there had always been a sale for his paintings, and some years had been extraordinarily good, but that kind of success depended on his being known, however small the community that knew him.

Perhaps this was one reason why he now turned with such emotional craving to Lushington – if nobody wanted his work at least someone might want him. If Lushington had loved and encouraged him, theirs might have developed into a full homosexual relationship. As it was, Lear probably only partly realised his homosexuality, though in the deeper layers of his mind there

was conflict as he fought to suppress it, a conflict which contributed to his constant state of restlessness and depression. He
was not a philandering homosexual as some writers have believed him to be. His search was not for physical love, but for
someone who would want him as a person in the way that his
parents had not wanted him as a child.[3] Through his sensibility
and charm he was sought after as a friend, and he loved to be
with children because they liked him and showed it. But what he
was searching for, and never found, was real spiritual involve-
ment with another person.

Beyond even this was the terrible unhappiness of forty years,
the constant epileptic attacks which still came as often as twenty
times a month, marked in his diary by sad little crosses, and
which he now had to accept would never go – and the bewildering memories of his childhood. Usually he could tuck
these away into an undisturbed corner of his mind where they
were gradually covered by comforting layers of dust, but when a
new unhappiness found its way into that corner the dust was
suddenly shaken off and the monster of memory was there.

Today we would say that Lear was on the verge of a nervous
breakdown. What he knew was that he was so unhappy he could
do nothing. For hours he walked up and down his room with
tears streaming down his face. If he tried to sleep he just lay
looking up at the ceiling. Nobody called, nothing happened, and
day after day it rained.

He told Ann what was going on, though she had little enough
to make her life happy and he was careful not to upset her. But
he did ask her to write each week instead of fortnightly, even if
only a few lines. 'I will also write every week, & your letters will
be, I fear, at present, the only thing I have to look for. £2.10.0 or
£3 will be the utmost expense of this – even if it went on for a
year, but you must let me pay this, & I know you will.'[4]

Gradually the crisis passed. The weather improved and he
began to get out. People started to visit him and even to buy his
work, and on 26 January 1856 he wrote excitedly: 'On Monday,
there was a regular burst of people into my rooms, & they ran
away with £28 of little drawings! ! So, allowing for frames, I have
cleared 23 – by the morning's work! – & several of the people
who came wished for other views – so that it really *does* seem as if
one were going to get a comfortable living after all.'[5] He could
even suggest rather sheepishly to Ann that there was not really
enough news to fill a letter every week.

In fact, he soon found himself becoming fashionable on the

island. 'We have found him a most agreeable person – and a great addition to our society, and we all like him very much – especially Lady Young, who has taken to sketching with great ardour,'[6] the High Commissioner wrote to Fortescue, and 'goodnatured vulgar roaring helter-skelter'.[7] Lady Young bought three of his drawings. The other ladies followed suit, and back came the familiar feeling of being a big fish 'in this very little fish pond of a place'[8] – the very thing he had turned his back on five years earlier, but which was after all essential to him.

He was invited to dinners, and to balls at the palace, and Lushington told Emily Tennyson: 'Lear having for the first month he was here asserted that he hated music more than anything in the world, has now become the most admired musician in Corfu – a very much more natural position for him to occupy than that of a music-hater.'[9]

Then at the beginning of February he received a tempting offer. There was a plan to open an art department in the university of Corfu, and he was invited to become its first director. He would have a salary of £100 a year, a free house and four months' holiday. In return he would be responsible for the administration of the school, and would have to give lessons in drawing and lectures in Italian. But he would be a civil servant responsible to the Government, and this would mean no more independence – and even though that independence was risky, Lear valued it. As well as this, he would not have time to get on with his own work, and it would mean the end of his ambitions as a painter – so he wrote and declined the offer, hoping that he had been wise.

During his terrible winter depression he had had one encouraging thought – there was still time for him to paint the superb picture which would catch the public imagination and establish him as a painter. At the beginning of April he sent to England for two large canvases so that he could get to work on a painting for the 1857 Summer Exhibition. Then he began to explore the island for the best view. This was an enjoyable task, for it was spring and 'lo! – all the hedges & trees have said to each other – "bless us! – here is April the 10th there is no time to lose" & out they have all come in full leaf most wonderfully! – & as for flowers, things have now reached their utmost, & I suppose there is now no more possible room for any more ... There is hardly any green left since an immense crop of marigolds, geraniums, orchises, irises, & cannonilla have come out. The hills are positively an immense crop of geraniums all gold colour – & in the olive woods, the large white heath looks like snow, & the pale lilac asphodels in such profusion as to seem like a sort of pale veil over all the ground. The hedges are *absolutely* pink, & in fact the whole thing is almost absurd from its very oddity.'[10]

There was some beautiful scenery to choose from, with the land climbing from the lowlands of the south through gentle undulations to the mountains in the north. In the end he chose the view from above the village of Ascension, a sweeping vista over the top of receding olive groves to the rocky peninsula and the Citadel of Corfu, with the sea and the snow-topped mountains of Albania beyond.

Whilst he waited for the canvases to arrive he worked on drawings that had been commissioned, and every day before breakfast he had a Greek lesson. 'It will be good fun when I can understand Greek well,' he wrote to Ann, 'as I can then get many things more as the natives do, than after the extravagant English modes.'[11]

At the beginning of April he found new rooms which were bigger and lighter, and as he had more space he decided to take on a servant – a man who would be valet, housemaid and cook.

He chose a Suliot – Suliot guards had ridden with Byron in the last days before he died – called Giorgio Kokali, who stayed with him for twenty-seven years, went with him on all his travels, and became the tempestuous companion of his old age.

Now that Lushington had settled into his job they were seeing more of each other again, and at the end of April they went to explore the coast of Corfu in Lushington's little yacht, *Midge*. But for Lear it was a 'screwy & bumpy & squashy' agony. 'I have come to the conclusion yachting does not suit me at all,' he wrote from the safety of a little bay on the western coast of the island: 'all the week has gone without my having done one single thing of any sort, & the nuisance of knocking one's head, & being in a cramped cabin is not repaid by any society in the world. I really believe the liking for yachts is merely a fashion, just as many women will bear the utmost pain in lacing rather than not appear in the mode.'[12]

He began to make friends of his own, though there were not many people there who shared his interests. Generally they were absorbed in Court palaver, and even though they liked his drawings they did not take him very seriously. The wives would sometimes be seized with the sudden whimsy of coming to visit him as he worked, and when he was drawing out of doors he could hardly stop them. Then the quiet olive groves would fill with horses and their gay, chattering riders, though fortunately they did not enjoy being in one place for too long and they would leave as suddenly as they had come. But amongst all the bubbling and superficial wives and daughters he found two young women whose company he could enjoy. Their father was Italian, their mother was English and a relation of the Lancashire Hornbys. The girls' names were Helena and Madeleine Cortazzi, and Lear found himself fascinated by Helena. 'She knows every word of In Memoriam, & indeed all Alfred's poems – & has translated many into Italian, & set many to music,'[13] he told Emily Tennyson whose heart must have warmed at his news. Corfu society did not share Lear's enthusiasm for Helena Cortazzi, who 'with her complete knowledge of Italian French & Greek, her poetry & magnificent music, but withal her simple & retiring quiet, – is not thought half as much of as that large Miss A.Z. who can only talk English & dance polkas'.[14] With Holman Hunt he was really enthusiastic: 'Do you know I am half in love?' he confided. 'There are two *awful* sisters here (I call the house Castle Dangerous) English, but brought up here – & so simple and good! – & so full of poetry & good taste, & grace, & all the nettings whereby men are netted – I begin to feel I must either run for it, or rush into extremes – and as neither they nor I have money, am not I a fool for thinking about it? Yet sometimes at 43 I cannot help believing that half & half life will get too wearisome to bear ere long. The older is my alarm, – but the younger is the prettier – o Papa! What a blasted old ass your son is.'[15]

Could marriage be the answer to his dreadful loneliness? He had found someone who could enjoy the things that he found important in life, and who was feminine without being fluffy. But marriage and a home still meant danger and almost certain unhappiness, and he did not seriously consider it. 'Bless me – even if I could afford it, I am not sure that marriage would be a safe risk:' he wrote to Ann, 'if one could only unmarry again if it didn't suit! – only one couldn't!'[16]

He decided not to go back to England that summer, and arranged for two oil paintings in London to be sent in for the Academy. They were both accepted, but were hung over the door in the miniature room where they could hardly be seen. Holman Hunt's picture of 'The Scapegoat' was also in, and received much derisive comment. Even Lear, who was such an admirer of Hunt's work, was doubtful about the result. 'I agree with you in not liking the subject,' he confessed to Ann, 'but, where the skill & genius which Hunt possesses is so immeasurably in advance of that of the mass of painters, we must take what we can get.'[17]

In June and July he was at Ascension making drawings for his big picture, but the heat and the flies made work difficult. 'Strange,' he wrote to Ann, 'that what to me is always painful & disagreeable work – painting – should in a couple of months create a work which not only gives pleasure to its possessor at present but may continue to do so to hundreds of others for a century or more! – a very unfair division of happiness I think.'[18] When he returned to Corfu the canvases still had not arrived. Lushington was about to cross to Albania in *Midge* for a few days' holiday, and Lear decided that whilst he was waiting he would go over with him and have a third try at getting to Mount Athos.

He at once realised the difference in travelling through Albania and Greece since his last visit. At the start of the Crimean War the British had moved in to preserve the country's neutrality, and as most towns now had a British Consul he hardly needed the beds and cooking things he had brought. '. . . as I sit in a beautiful room in the English Consul's house here [Larissa], with sofas all round the walls, matting on the floor, & painted ceilings, & look out on a little court yard where 2 tame cranes are walking up & down – I cannot but think how much easier it is to travel in these parts now than it was in 1848.'[19]

They went straight across the mainland without stopping, but when they got to Katerina on the east coast they found that there was a local fiesta and no one would take them over to Salonika. They had to wait for two days and were running out of food: '... we began to speculate how Giorgio should cook the large blue jelly fish that the sea threw up. We found 2 small crabs also – & I proposed – as there were blackberries all about, to boil the jelly fish with blackberry sauce, and roast the crabs with rhum & bread crumbs – a triumph of cookery not reserved for us – for at last boats began to come, & horses appeared over the hills by scores.'[20]

This sounds reminiscent of another of Lear's feasts:

'... if we may take the liberty of inquiring, on what do you chiefly subsist?'

'Mainly on Oyster-patties,' said the Blue-Bottle-Fly, 'and, when these are scarce, on Raspberry Vinegar and Russian leather boiled down to a jelly.'

'How delicious!' said Guy.

To which Lionel added, 'Huzz!' and all the Blue-Bottle-Flies said, 'Buzz!'[21]

From Salonika they walked fifty miles overland and crossed the isthmus cut by King Xerxes – the X of Lear's nonsense alphabets – when he led the invading Persian armies into Greece. A pair of wooded gates marked the beginning of the monks' territory, and when they had come through these Lear was at last on Mount Athos.[22]

This strange place points forty miles into the Aegean Sea, and is covered in dense forests of beech and oak and ilex trees which fall away into deep, wooded ravines, and tumble down cliffs and crags into the sea. On its southern tip is the great high peak of the holy mountain whose white marble summit glows at sunset like a lighted torch which can be seen from Mount Olympus and the Plain of Troy. It was the seat of Greek gods long before Olympus, and was called Athos after Poseidon's son. It had originally been part of central Thrace, but one day Athos, in a fit of fury against his father, picked it up and hurled it at him into the sea. The ancients tried to smooth out the quarrel by dedicating it to Poseidon, but they heard rumblings of heavenly discontent and quickly rededicated it to Zeus.

And so it became a holy mountain to the pagans, until one day in AD 49 when the Virgin Mary was invited by Lazarus, then Bishop of Kitium in Cyprus, to come and visit him. He arranged for a boat to collect her, but on the journey back to Cyprus it strayed from its course, and when they sighted land it was Athos that they had found. The boat anchored in a little bay, and the Virgin looked long and silently at the mountain. Then she said: 'This mountain is holy ground. Let it now be my portion. Here let me remain.' As she stepped ashore there was a terrible crash and the pagan idols and statues crumbled to the ground: the whole population was baptised, and Mount Athos became a holy Christian domain. But the Virgin was jealous of her rights, and refused to allow female creatures on to the peninsula, so that no woman, nor any cows nor chickens may go to Mount Athos.

By the Middle Ages it was the home of isolated hermits, and the first monastic foundation was established during the tenth century. From then until the fall of Constantinople more and more monasteries were built. There was a moment of crisis in this period of fruitful expansion when it was discovered that the Vlach shepherds, who supplied the monasteries with milk and wool, were also supplying them with the services of their wives and daughters. Strict measures were taken and the situation was retrieved, but not before half the monks had left with the shepherds.

In 1430 Salonika was captured by the invading Turks, and the monks of the Holy Mountain submitted voluntarily to Turkish rule. Islamic tradition forbids the pillage of property voluntarily surrendered, so the Byzantine treasures of Athos remained intact and the Christians were allowed to keep their methods and places of worship.

Lear and Giorgio made their way up the tortuous rock path which wound through the dense woods. That evening they reached Kariess, the capital where the Holy Synod of twenty monks, appointed annually from each of the twenty ruling monasteries, administers the domestic affairs of the mountain. Lear went first to the 'head of the Holy Mountain', the leader osthe twenty. 'He made me a tolerably civil welcome – for I had letters from consuls – bishops etc. – & gave me some supper – & a bed; first of all, they bring you a tray – some sort of sweets, & a glass of spirit; (oh! dear! – what a lot of sweets & rhum have I taken in that Holy Mountain!) then coffee . . . Next morning the Synod of 20 were assembled – & I was put at the head of the room, while my letters were read; a circular was then given to me, to present to all the convents as I chose – & in the afternoon I began my tour . . .'[23]

The monks of Athos live to pray. Soon after midnight the wooden clappers of the semandron rouse them for the first service which continues until dawn, and throughout the day they repeat prayers and intone the name of Christ. But Lear preferred the idea of attaining sanctity through other people, and he could not begin to share their philosophy. Soon he was feeling 'oppressed with this atmosphere of falsehood and ignorance . . . I do not say – hypocrisy; – but I say falsehood, because I am positive that living alone – banishing all women whom God has made to be our equals & companions, – passing life in everlasting repetition of formal prayers – in fact – turning God's will & works upside down – I say this is falsehood – though it may be ignorance as well.'[24]

The grandeur of the scenery was wonderful though, and for three weeks he was walking and drawing, climbing through the thick lush woods and scrambling up rocky paths, discovering energies he had not had for years.

Then, only a few days after they had started, he realised that Giorgio was ill. They were staying in the dirty little monastery of Philotheo where all they could get to eat was bad bread and salty cheese. He knew that if they remained there Giorgio would only get worse, so he left his servant and rode on to Gran Lavra, the largest and most ancient of the monasteries, where he arranged a bed for him. They had a dreadful journey there on mules, but once in the monastery Giorgio gradually recovered, and whilst his servant lay there getting back his strength Lear filled the time 'drawing it all round; poking about the sea shore or into the hermitages among the half witted old filthy Caloyeri; or watched the Tom cats in the galleries; or talked Greek with Melchisedek & Anthemos – smoking 5 pipes a day . . .'[25]

At the very tip of the peninsula he found the tiny monastery of St Nilo perched on the cliff: '. . . that was the queerest & saddest spot I ever beheld!' he told Ann. '2 old men lived there – neither more than half witted; they gave me a dry fish & water melon, – but only said these words all the time I was there – "are you a Christian?" – hundreds of times over and over.'[26]

When Giorgio was fit enough they moved on again along the western side of the mountain, visiting all the twenty principal monasteries and many of the smaller ones. The collection of drawings Lear was making would be unique and valuable in England, and he planned to publish them with the journal he had kept of the tour. But he was anxious now to be finished: 'oh Holy Mountain! what have I not suffered to get drawings of you!'[27] he wrote, and to Fortescue he explained: 'The worst was the food & the filth, which were uneasy to bear. But however wondrous & picturesque the [ex]terior and interior of the monasteries – & however abundantly & exquisitely glorious & stupendous the scenery of the mountain, I would not go again to the Ἁγιος Ὀρος for any money, so gloomy – so shockingly unnatural – so lonely – so lying – so unatonably odious seems to me all the atmosphere of such monkery. That half of our species which is natural to every man to cherish & love best – ignored prohibited & abhorred – all life spent in everlasting repetition of monotonous prayers – no sympathy with one's fellowbeans of any nation class or age – the name of Christ on every garment & at every tongues end, but his maxims trodden under foot – God's world & will turned upside down, maimed & caricatured: – if this I say be Xtianity – let Xtianity be rooted out as soon as possible. More pleasing in the sight of the Almighty I really believe, & more like what Jesus Christ intended man to become – is an honest Turk with 6 wives, or a Jew working hard to feed his little old clo' babbies – than these muttering, miserable, muttonhating, manavoiding, misogynic, morose, & merriment= marring, monotoning, many-Mulemaking, mocking, mournful, mincedfish & marmalade masticating Monx. Poor old pigs! – Yet one or two were kind enough in their way – dirty as they were: but it is not them, – it is their system I rail at.'[28]

A few months later, he thought he had discovered the remedy: 'As soon as Parliament meets,' he wrote to Fortescue, the Member for Louth, 'move that all Sidney Herbert's distressed needlewomen be sent out at once to Mount Athos! – By this dodge all the 5000 monks young & old will be vanquished – : distressed needlebabies will ultimately awake the echoes of ancient Acte, & the whole fabric of Monkery, not to say of the Gk church will fall down crash & for ever. N.B. let the needle-women be all landed at once – 4000 at least, on the south *east* side of the peninsular, & make a rush for the nearest monastery: that subdued – all the rest will speedily follow.'[29]

He decided not to make the return journey across the mainland of Greece, and instead went by boat from Salonika. He had to wait for a few days in the Dardanelles, and he was able to go quickly to see the plain of Troy. He would have liked to linger there, but he wanted to get back to Corfu to begin on the large painting so that it would be finished in time for the Academy.

It had been a successful trip, and he told Fortescue: 'I have gained a g^t amount of health bodily and mentle, to my great satisfaction & I hope thankfulness – & I also trust to the benefit obliquely of many of my felly creaturs who will hereafter peeroose my jurnles, and admyer my pigchers.'[30]

On Lear's first night back in Corfu there was a violent earth tremor, and his house was badly damaged. This gave him an excuse to move into rooms which were vacant next door to Lushington on the Condi Terrace. 'Condi Terrace is the "west-end" of Corfu & we are all more or less swells as lives in it,' he told Fortescue. He had a 'stewjew 30 feet long: 3 windys all a lookin to the North East – whereby the light is always perfect.'[31] It might have seemed rather unwise to be so near Lushington, for only a few days earlier Lear had told Emily Tennyson, 'The impetuosity of my nature however cannot always be controlled & we have had one or two sad antagonisms – tho we are perhaps better friends afterwards: but our natures are so different, & he is so changed since I first knew him, while I have remained so absurdly the same – (I mean, he has become 70 – & I have stuck at 20 or any boy=age all through my life –) that I feel convinced we are best when not with each other.'[32]

It was as if he knew what was wise, but could not act on it. A part of him was realistic, but then he let himself believe that one day they would be as happy together as they had been during that spring in Greece. That happiness had been real, and it could not just disappear. He did not realise that what Lushington had enjoyed then had been a free abandonment to life which he had never known before and which he certainly never knew again. Because he loved beautiful things so completely Lear had been part of Lushington's happiness, but in a sense he had been incidental – a background to Lushington's first real look at beauty. For Lear it had been the other way round. Though eventually his relationship with Lushington became the most valuable of all his friendships, this time had not yet come. 'You ask about the price of his drawings – meaning water colour I suppose,' Lushington wrote to Emily Tennyson that summer. 'He has been making some very beautiful & careful watercolour drawings of various views in Corfu for 12£ a piece . . . Nevertheless I should say, don't waste your monies on them – How can you afford it, with 7000£ to pay, & the whole house to patch up? and Hallam's school expenses growing a frightfully near prospect.'[33]

Now Lear settled into his new rooms and went busily to work. He laid in the drawing on his big canvas, and painted several local views to get some quick money to reimburse him after the expenses of his trip. In the evenings, when the light had gone, he penned out the drawings he had made on Mount Athos. He was pleased with some of the work he was doing, but was quickly disheartened with his lack of real progress. 'Dear me – I wish I could paint faster & better & had 20 pairs of hands, not to speak of an elephant's trunk to pick up any brushes when they fall down,'[34] he lamented to Ann, and to Holman Hunt he wrote: 'O dear me I wish I had gone to the Academy when you did – & had been working with you ever since! Coming so late as I did to the light of any kind of truth in painting – when my habits of life were already but too much formed, & my eyes & hands less than ever able to execute what I desired to do, I was never very likely to turn out much of a painter. Moroever, my topographical, & varied interests as to different countries – my split=application by my musical – ornithological – & other tastes – have all combined to bother & retard me – society being by no means the least of the pull=backs.'[35]

He missed the artistic companionship he had had in Rome and London, for there was nobody in 'this rustymustyfustydustybustycrusty Corfu'[36] with whom he could discuss his work, or indeed anything. The eccentricities of an artist's life were a barrier, for Lear liked to go to bed at about the time their elaborate dinners began so that he could be up before 4 a.m. and out working before the day grew hot and misty. Nor could they be sure of their reception if they came to call: 'I was obliged to send away Mrs & the 2 Miss Cortazzi,' he told Ann, 'as to stop in a sky is to spoil all; a circumstance which all Corfu will be sure to hear of directly, & I never the last of.'[37] The incompatibility of the demands of a painter's life with the obligations of friendship was a problem Lear never resolved, though the companionship of friends was something he both needed and enjoyed.

But though he lacked friends he had many acquaintances and was often invited out. Now that he had Giorgio to cook for him he could entertain in return, generously yet cheaply, as he told Ann: 'Soup, Ma'am, fish, Ma'am, a beefsteak pudding, Ma'am, woodcock & apple pie, Ma'am; & all very nicely done; all which sounds expensive, but isn't – because all the large dish of fish cost 5d, & the woodcock are 3d a piece just now! It does not appear to me that I ought to do otherwise than live what is called sociably & comfortably as far as I can, though an artist's life, if he has no capital – must always have its uncertainties & difficulties from month to month. So much however, of the artist's capacity & strength for going onward depends on his ordinary comforts, that if he were to live wholly alone drinking water & eating barley bread, – the money he would save by such a diet would be over-balanced by the depression which would soon prevent his getting any money at all.'[38] It was a low level of extravagance, indeed his dinners were described by a friend as 'very Præraphaelite ... very minute'.[39] Even so it sometimes worried him. 'I feel so very selfish & thoughtless to be living in comfort without adding to that of others,'[40] he wrote to Ann in November, enclosing £5 for her and £10 for his sister Mary, a typical act of generosity which he frequently extended beyond his family.

As the winter of 1856 came on, he felt the gloom of last year returning. Bad weather, and daylight that was too dark to paint by, turned him in on himself and he began to brood. Gradually the sense of desperation returned. What he needed now was someone who would gentle him out of his depression by en-couraging him and turning his thoughts out instead of in, keep-ing his mind free of the endless re-enacting of old sadnesses and hurts which he could forget when he filled his mind with happier, more constructive thoughts. He became so throttled by unhappiness that he had to put away the large painting until he could think clearly again. 'O dear! I find Corfu very like a prison I do,'[41] he told Ann, but the impenetrable prison was in his own mind. 'I am older than Babylon in many ways,' he lamented. 'I wish sometimes I grew hard & old at heart – it would, I fancy – save a deal of bother – but perhaps its all for the best.'[42]

Just after Christmas he spent a few days in Albania with Lushington, and though it rained most of the time the change did him good. He enjoyed the 'solitary quiet of nature' just across the water from the fuss and flurry of garrison life, for he sometimes felt that the people and the ridiculous life they seemed to enjoy destroyed the beauty of Corfu. '. . . what a place this might be if there were any good people to give it a twist!' he told Ann. 'As it is – a more disorganised fiddlefaddle Poodly-pumpkin place never was . . . at the Palace they are active – dancing & rushing about pauselessly & continually. I suspect Lady Young would not be happy in Heaven if she did not get up an immense ball & land & water picnics, among the angels. It is sadly frivolous work – this life for "amusement" & that only.'[43]

Of course, when spring began to reawaken the island he felt better at once – 'we are all sunshine & anemones & clear skies & asphodels & little green frogs just as usual,'[44] he wrote with relief. The world was better, and the Corfu painting was the finest he had yet done. He had come on so well with his daily Greek lessons that he could read the New Testament in old and modern Greek, fulfilling a long-standing ambition and renewing his desire to see the holy places in Palestine which he had missed. Clowes, a friend from Knowsley days, had written suggesting that they might travel there together, but then he could not get away. Instead, on 1 May, Lear wrote to Fortescue: 'I am coming to England as fast as I can – having taken a red-boom at Hansens 16. Upper Seymour Street, Squortman Pare, – and also a rorkwoom or Stew-jew – at 15 Stratford Place. My big picture is in a mess, & without Holman Hunts help I cant get on with it – though it is done as to what must necessarily be done here, – & requires but 2 months of cropping & thought. Pray heaven I may sell it. – I bring to England my drawings of Athos – I hope – for publication. Also – sketches of Corfu for separate lithogrofigging, & sale here. Also one or two paintings to finish. Why are you coming say you – ? – because I can't stay here any longer – without seeing friends & having some communion of heart & spirit – with one who should have been this to me – I have none. And I cant bear it. And I want to see my sister. And also another sister who is going to N. Zealand – before she goes. And some Canadian cousins. And *you*. And my dear Daddy Holman Hunt: – & other people. – So I'm off . . . *What a talk* we will have!'[45]

11 The Holy Land
1857–1858

Lear was in England by the end of May 1857, and at once began on a busy round of visits: 'Mr Lear is in town but I have not yet been able to see him,' Woolner wrote to Emily Tennyson; 'he is so very busy and says he ought to go to 756 places on every evening.'[1]

Despite this, Lear worked hard to complete the Corfu picture, and at the beginning of August he wrote jubilantly to Ann:

> Dear Ann,
> At half past one o'clock THE CORFU PICTURE WAS SOLD – TO
> W. EVANS ESQ. M.P.
> FOR 500 GUINEAS,
> HURRAH!
>
> Your affect., Grandfather
> Edward Lear.[2]

So speedy a sale at a good price delighted Lear, and reassured him that there was a public for his work.

A few days later he left London for Nuneham in Oxfordshire, the home of Mr Harcourt and his wife, Lady Waldegrave. In the spring of 1850, Fortescue had been walking down Piccadilly when an open carriage passed him. Riding inside were an elderly man and a beautiful young woman. She was Lady Waldegrave, daughter of the famous tenor Charles Braham, and widow of both John Waldegrave and his younger brother George, the 7th Earl. She had inherited both their fortunes and now, at twenty-nine, was married to the dull and elderly Mr Harcourt.[8] Fortescue arranged to be introduced to her, and before long he was desperately in love. Within the limits of propriety she encouraged her young suitor with coquettish tête-à-têtes, and he filled his diary with descriptions of what she said, how she looked, and exactly what she wore. He was a frequent guest at Lady Waldegrave's homes – Carlton Gardens, Strawberry Hill, Dudbrook or Nuneham – and sometimes Lear was invited to join the party. He found them kind, but rather patronising. 'Lear came today,' Fortescue wrote in his diary on 8 August. 'I am glad Lady W likes him so much. He has sold his Corfu to Evans M.P. for 500 guineas – poor old boy. When I told Mr H it gave him greatly increased respect for L.'[4]

Nevertheless he enjoyed his stay. 'At Nuneham there was only a small & friendly party,' he told Ann, 'though a very merry one, – & the dancing did me a great deal of good.'[5] And the visit was fruitful, for Lady Waldegrave commissioned two paintings of Palestine if he should go there in the spring. The trip began to look possible now, for the sale of the Corfu painting had cleared his debts and left him with £100. The visit to Nuneham also gave him what he most needed, an opportunity to talk at last with Fortescue, who wrote in his diary: 'I have sat with old Lear both nights, he in low spirits, longing for "sympathy", which means a woman, specially a wife.'[6] Before they went back to London he invited Lear to go with him to Ireland and stay for six weeks at his home in Ardee.

Lear spent a busy fortnight in London, and they left for Dublin at the end of August. The party at Ardee was very quiet – just Lear, Fortescue, his aunt Mrs Ruxton who was a widow of 85, and an aged governess. It was Lear's ideal of 'talk & music & domesticity, – which you know are in my way'.[7] He was given a room where he could paint during the day whilst Fortescue saw to his business on the estate.

But he had not gone there to work, and the times he looked forward to were the evenings when he could go with Fortescue for long walks through the beautiful green Irish countryside. Then he would unburden the weight of loneliness which he had been bearing for so long. He talked endlessly about Lushington, though Fortescue did not see the meaning of what Lear told him and saw more significance in his mention of Helena Cortazzi.

Whilst Lear was at Ardee his dear friend Robert Hornby died. It was he who, with Lord Stanley, had sent Lear to Rome in 1837, but we know little of this important friendship, for nothing has survived. '. . . he was my oldest & kindest friend in the world,' Lear wrote to Ann when he heard the news, 'and I cannot replace him.'[8] As thousands of other Victorians had done he fingered through *In Memoriam*. One night he and Fortescue sat up until the small hours to read the poem right through – this was the 'consistent kindness & reciprocity' he had been yearning for.

He stayed in Ireland until the beginning of October, then crossed back to Liverpool and spent a few days at Knowsley.

From there he travelled across to Manchester to see his painting of 'The Quarries of Syracuse' in the International Exhibition, then went on to London.

By now it was well into October and he had done none of the things he had planned to do. He had not published the Athos drawings nor had engravings made of his Corfu drawings. Instead he had spent the time with Fortescue – amd that, after all, was why he had come.

He dreaded the return to Corfu, for during the summer the Cortazzi family had left and he would be even lonelier than before. He stayed on in England until the middle of November when he knew he must get away south. 'Come back soon well & happy,'[9] wrote Emily Tennyson, and Lear must have echoed her wish.

Back in Corfu he was soon choked by the feeling of stagnation, and he wrote in desperation to Fortescue: 'My dear Chichester, I do not know how I shall bear it – being an ass: – & if you don't write & if others don't write, – I really can't tell what I shall do. –

'Just figure to yourself the conditions of a place where you never have any breadth or extent of intellectual society, & yet cannot have any peace or quiet! – Suppose yourself living in Piccadilly, we will say – taking a place with a long surface, – from Coventry St. to Knightsbridge say. – And suppose that line your constant & only egress & ingress to & from the country – & that by little & little you come to know all & every of the persons in all the houses, & meet them always & everywhere, & were thought a brute & queer if you didn't know everybody more or less! – Wouldn't you wish every one of them, except a few, – at the bottom of the sea? – Then you live in a house, one of the best here it is true – where you hear everything from top to bottom – : a piano on each side, above & below, maddens you: & you can neither study nor think, nor even swear properly by reason of the proximity of the neighbours. I assure you, a more rotten, dead, stupid place than this existeth not . . . L. is just as ever: perfectly calm – & although doubtless intending to be kind, – is as ever, more & more indifferent & passive to all but his own routine of life. I vow I never felt more shockingly alone than the 2 or 3 evenings I have staid in.

'Yet all that must be conquered if fighting can do it. – Yet at times, I have half thoughts of – I hardly know what. The constant walking & noise overhead prevents my application to any sort of work, & it is only from 6 to 8 in the morning that I can attend really to anything . . . And then, if I can't sleep, my whole system seems to turn into pins cayenne-pepper & vinegar & I suffer hideously. – You see I have no means of carrying off my irritation: others have horses, – or boats, [in short]: I have only walking – and that is beginning to be impossible alone. – I could not go to church to-day – : I felt I should make faces at everybody – so I read some Greek of St John – wishing for you to read it with – some Robinson's *Palestine*, some *Jane Eyre*, – some Burton's *Mecca*, – some *Friends in Council*, – some Shakespeare, some *Vingt ans après*, – some Leake's *Topography* – some Rabelais, – some Tennyson, – some Gardiner Wilkinson, – some Grote, some Ruskin – & all in half an hour. O! doesn't "he take it out of me" in a raging worry? – Just this moment I think – I *must* have a piano: that may do me good. – But then I remember Miss Henderson over my head has one, & plays jocular jigs continually. Then what the devil can I do? Buy a Baboon & a parrot & let them rush about the room? . . .

'I still hold to going to Palestine if possible . . . Sometimes I think I must begin another big picture – as I want something to gnash & grind my teeth on. – If Helena Cortazzi had been here – it would have been useless to think of avoiding asking her to marry me, even had I never so little trust in the wisdom of such a step . . .'[10]

But had she been there he would not have done so. The few amorous sentiments Lear expressed towards unattached women faded when he was actually with them and they were no longer safely unattainable.

The next few months were, as he had expected, of profound unhappiness. Island intrigues and political jealousies exacerbated Lushington's moroseness, and on 28 February Lear wrote in his diary: 'Dined at L's – but wearied myself with talk, & when after dinner in that cold room, he took a good cigar himself from a box at the other end, but offered me none, – & when cafe came $\frac{3}{4}$ of an hour after, I grew black & silent, & went away at $9\frac{1}{2}$.'[11] Though they occasionally walked together they rarely communicated. '. . . now that he has got a dog,' Lear told Fortescue, 'one cannot help feeling how far more agreeable it is to him to walk with that domestic object, to whom he has not the compulsory bore of being obliged to speak.'[12]

Preparing for his visit to Palestine was the one thing that cheered Lear during that dreadful winter. As usual he read everything he could find about the countries he was visiting, then he had to buy medicines and a tent, leather saddle-bags and cooking things. It was all very expensive, but he did think of a way to get more money, as he told Ann: '. . . nothing is talked of by the Corfu world but the Marchioness of Headford's diamonds, which cover her up so much, that few people have seen their wearer. As for me, I sat next to her at dinner yesterday, but she hadn't got no diamonds; only about 200 big turquoises & emeralds & bangles & spangles & chains & griggly-miggly dazzling messes, a few of which I should have liked to have had for the fun of turning them into pounds & shillings for my Holy Land trip.'[13] Clowes still could not get away, so Lear planned the whole trip on his own. '. . . perhaps it is better,' he wrote. 'There are but few I could travel with & yet keep my own threads of thoughts unwispy & unentangled.'[14]

He needed to go armed because travellers were being attacked and robbed by Arab tribesmen. Lushington offered him his revolver and taught him how to use it. 'I have been practising shooting at a mark, (I can hardly write for laughing,) & have learned all the occult nature of pistols,' he told Fortescue. 'Don't grin. My progress is slow, – but always – (I trust) – somewhat. At 103 – I may marry possibly. Goodbye, Dear 40scue.'[15]

They reached Alexandria at sunrise on 17 March, but as there was not a boat to Jaffa until the 26th, they decided to fill in a few days by going to Cairo. Lear knew the city well, but to Giorgio, brought up in peaceful Corfu, it must have seemed astonishing.

The steamer, when it came, was crammed with pilgrims going to Jerusalem for Easter. Luckily it was a short voyage and in less than a day they were at Jaffa, a scrubby little place with no proper harbour. They dropped anchor offshore, and were at once surrounded by boatloads of shouting, waving Arabs: it was a milling, pressing, clambering scrabble of people and baggage.

They stayed at Ramleh that night, and found it both uncomfortable and expensive. 'During the night I did not sleep at all,' Lear told Ann, 'but passed the time in catching innumerable animals, which, – with the sagacity & desire of knowledge a zoological landscape painter should combine, – I placed upon a sheet of paper – wishing to know what manner of insects they were, & rejoicing to find on the first break of day, that 17 were fleas, 3 mosquitoes, 8 ants, only 2 bugs, & nothing at all of a less creditable nature.'[16]

The next morning they travelled on the busy road towards Jerusalem, and then began to ascend 'the last steep tiresome pull of all – before conquering which we could not see the Holy City

. . . It was 2.30 before I saw all the places I at once recognised as portions of the scene I so long have desired to paint, – & when we were opposite the west side of the city – I at once found it far more beautiful than I had expected.'[17]

But for Lear 'the universal hubbub throughout the place, prevents any *quiet plan or reasoning*'.[18] He decided to return when it was emptier and quieter, and to spend the time now in visiting places beyond the city which he wanted to see.

The next day, Palm Sunday, he crossed the rocky valley of Jehosophat to the Mount of Olives and climbed 'to the spot Christ must have been on when he "saw the city" – on coming from Bethany'.[19] From the top he could look across to the Dead Sea ⁻ 'clear pale milky far blue, with farther pale rosy mountain – fretted & carved in lovely shadow forms, – this long long simple line melting into air towards the desert'.[20] When the light had gone he went back to his room thrilled with the excitement of what was all around him: '. . . as I came up the stairs, how glorious was the full moon of blessed Israel – & how beautiful the dim pale film of Moab! – the round domes of the city & a thousand other glorious quietudes recalling older days.'[21]

He left Jerusalem on 2 April and travelled south to Bethlehem which he liked, and to Hebron which he did not. There he found a guide called Abdel who would take him on to Petra. He was offered an escort of altogether fifteen men, and this he was going to need, for travellers then were frequently attacked by Arab tribesmen. They asked £30 for the trip, a big extra on his budget. 'Yet,' Lear wrote to Ann, 'it appears to me that having come here for definite purposes, & for the sake of paintings which may convey pleasure & knowledge to others, I ought not to do the thing by halves.'[22]

The journey on camels took them through some of the lowest, hottest land on earth. Each night they pitched their tents on the sand, and after dinner he would sit outside in the quiet stillness watching the large round moon and the stars in the vast desert silence. Dawn had a different kind of beauty: 'What a strange calm world was the tawny hollow glen landscape, dusky-tufted and becamelled with ghostly wanderers, before the sunlight came gloriously bursting over the dark sapphire heights of Moab!'[23] he wrote in his journal.

They travelled for five days and on the morning of the sixth they came to Petra, the ancient centre of caravan trade between Arabia and the countries west and north. 'About 9 we reached

the highest part of the mountain ascent, and passing the ridge immediately below the rocks of Gebel Haroun (Aaron's mountain), now upon our left, entered the first or upper part of Wady Mousa on its western side. But it was nearly another hour before, still descending by winding tracks, we reached the first cavern tombs and the first coloured rocks. The slow advance chills with a feeling of strange solitude the intruder into the loneliness of this bygone world, where on every side are tokens of older greatness, and where between *then* and *now* is no link. As the path wandered among huge crags and over broad slabs of rock, ever becoming more striped and glowing in colour, I was more and more excited with curiosity and expectation. And after passing the solitary column which stands sentinel-like over the heaps of ruin around, and reaching the open space whence the whole area of the old city and the vast eastern cliff are fully seen, I own to having been more delighted and astonished than I had ever been by any spectacle ... The attraction arising from the singular mixture of architectural labour with the wildest extravagances of nature – the excessive and almost terrible feeling of loneliness in the very midst of scenes so plainly telling of a past glory and a race of days long gone – the vivid contrast of the countless fragments of ruin, basement, foundation, wall, and scattered stone, with the bright green of the vegetation, and the rainbow hues of rock and cliff – the dark openings of the hollow tombs on every side – the white river-bed and its clear stream, edged with superb scarlet-tufted blossoms of oleander alternating with groups of white-flowered broom – all these combine to form a magical condensation of beauty and wonder which the ablest pen or pencil has no chance of conveying to the eye or mind ...*

* '"Oh master," said Giorgio (who is prone to culinary similes), "we have come into a world where everything is made of chocolate, ham, curry-powder, & salmon."'

'What art could give the star-bright flitting of the wild dove and rock-partridge through the oleander-gloom, or the sound of the clear river rushing among the ruins of the fallen city . . . I felt, "I have found a new world – but my art is helpless to recall it to others, or to represent it to those who have never seen it." Yet, as the enthusiastic foreigner said to the angry huntsman who asked if he meant to catch the fox – "I will try."[24]

And try he did: until it was too dark to see any more he drew one scene after another, and only when the light had gone did he return to where the Arabs had pitched the tents. Then he saw, on one of the rock terraces above the camp, a line of ten black squatting figures silently watching them. A small goatherd boy who had seen their party had told the Bedouin that they were there, and now they had come to demand money as tax for travelling across their land. Lear had already paid a levy to the Sheikh of Haweitât, but these Arabs were from Dibdiba and wanted their own payment. They told Abdel, the leader of Lear's men, that if they were not paid they would return with fifty men, and Lear realised that his journey to Petra, which was already so expensive, might become both exorbitant and useless. He refused to pay them more, saying that the Sheikh of Haweitât would divide the money he had been given amongst them all. They left muttering belligerently, leaving one man perched above the camp, watching them until it was too dark for them to move on again that night: then he too disappeared.

Lear went uneasily to bed. At midnight he was wakened by shouting. The scene outside his tent was strange and almost comical. Fifty or so Arabs were dismounting noisily from their camels, and after cheerily greeting Lear's men, they lit fires and settled down to wait for the morning. All through the night more kept arriving, and it was impossible to sleep. Instead Lear packed his things so that he was ready to leave. At dawn, when he cautiously opened his tent flap, he saw more than a hundred Arabs squatting outside.

Now a group of Haweitât rode into the camp. Their Sheikh was coming and he had the money with him. It looked as though there would be no trouble after all, and as his only thought was to get drawings of Petra, Lear slipped quietly away. It was still very early, and he drew until ten o'clock. Then he went back to the camp to see what was happening. Now there were nearly two hundred Arabs, and the Sheikh, dressed in scarlet robes and riding a white Arab stallion, had arrived. They were quarrelling violently over the division of the money, and Lear could see that it would be impossible to stay on. He gave orders for the tents to come down, and then disappeared again to draw. In the chamber of Khasmé he melodramatically wrote his name on the wall so that a search party would know that he had reached Petra.

When he returned he found his men ready to leave, but the money had still not been divided. The Sheikh was in a cave with some of the other leaders, and they were arguing angrily. Now the Arabs grabbed Lear's camels and gathered menacingly around him. On and on went the argument in the cave as Lear was pushed and thrust from one Arab to the next, though he had time to think what splendid studies their expressions would make. Then a cry went up and he was seized by the arms and his pockets emptied – except surprisingly for his watch and Lushington's pistol. The same happened to Giorgio, and Abdel was pulled to the ground and his turban wrenched off. Lear managed to get away and into the cave, and he pulled the Sheikh outside so that he could see what was happening. 'You must pay twenty dollars at once to these men of Dibdiba or I can do nothing for you,' he told Lear; 'after that I will help you on if I can.'[25]

Lear no longer cared about the expense, and he told Abdel to fetch the money. When it had been paid the Sheikh helped them to their camels and led the way out of the camp. But it was not all over. First one group and then another and another, dissatisfied with their share, came after them and demanded more. He paid them all he had, and when at last they realised that he had nothing more they turned back and left him.

Their route back took them along the western shores of the Dead Sea to Masada then north to Jerusalem. The crowds had gone, and he could move easily round the city: '. . . there is enough in Jerusalem to set a man thinking for life, – & I am deeply glad I have been there,' he wrote to Lady Waldegrave. 'O my nose! O my eyes! O my feet! how you all suffered in that vile place! – For let me tell you, physically Jerusalem is the foulest & odiousest place on earth. A bitter doleful soul=ague comes over you in its streets – & your memories of its interior are but horrid dreams of squalor & filth – clamour & uneasiness, – hatred & malice & all uncharitableness. – But the outside is full of melancholy glory – : exquisite beauty & a world of past history of all ages: – every point forcing you to think on a vastly dim receding past – or a time of Roman War & splendour – (for Aelia Capitolium was a fine city –) or a smash of Moslem & Crusader years – &. the long long dull winter of deep decay through centuries of misrule. – The Arab & his sheep are alone the wanderers on the pleasant vallies & breezy hills round Sion – : the file of slow camels all that brings to mind the commerce of Tyre & other bygone merchandise.'[26]

But the tragedy of Christian dissent there saddened him – the bickering and the scandalous quarrels, the hypocrisy and the shows of power and wealth which denied everything that Christ had ever taught.

They went north towards the Sea of Galilee and Nazareth, but when they stopped in Jericho it was hot and insect-ridden and he could not sleep. He was beginning to feel exhausted and unwell, and when the next day a party of Arabs stopped them to demand money it seemed like a nightmare. He could not go on, and turned back to Jerusalem without seeing Nazareth or Galilee.

After he rested there for a few days, he decided to go on to the Lebanon, which he hoped would be more peaceful. To avoid travelling overland through Palestine they went by boat from Jaffa to Beirut, which they reached on 11 May 1858. The country was a disappointment and the scenery like any he had seen in Greece or Albania, though the Cedars – ancient and enormous – were a marvellous sight. Damascus too was beautiful, like '16 worlds full of gardens rolled out flat, with a river & a glittering city in the middle'.[27] But the hottest time of year had begun, and he was moving from the oppressive heat of the plain to the extreme cold of the mountains. Suddenly he had had enough.

12 Rome
1858–1860

It had been an extraordinary and exciting three months, and back in Corfu a deep post-travel depression settled on him. 'O! that this blank of life would break into some varied light or shade!'[1] he wrote in his diary. He was run down and developed a sty: '. . . my brain is confused between cause and effect,' he wrote to Fortescue, '& I don't know if my being a pig has produced the sty – or whether the sty makes me a pig. But I know I am a pig.'[2]

Whilst he had been away the island intrigues had come rushing to a head, and now Lushington had resigned his post and was going back to England. Lear wondered whether he should stay on there alone, or find somewhere else for the winter. Clowes had suggested that they should go together to Rome, but it was a long time since he had left there and it could be a mistake to go back now.

Early in August he travelled to England with Lushington, and they parted at Dover. He was alone again. Of course there were friends by the score for him to visit, and one of the first was Holman Hunt. He stayed at Hunt's rooms at Campden Hill, and even wondered if he could live with him permanently. 'One thing is a fact,' he wrote, 'living with Daddy Hunt is more a certain chance of happiness than any other life I know of.'[3] But it would not really work. He visited Helena Cortazzi, and indulged in a 'world of thought'[4] about her – but there was no solution there either.

He felt more and more desolate, and entries in his diary ache with unhappiness. 'Wake, to impatience blindness & misery. Incapable of deciding whether life can be cured or cursed – I totter giddily, refusing to take any road, yet agonised by staying irresolute.'[5] His painting went badly, and he felt desperate at the thought of the unending struggle which faced him on and on into the future. His Palestine drawings were seen and enjoyed though. Woolner told Emily Tennyson, 'they are the most beautiful things he has ever done: if you have not seen them I hope you will, for they would give much delight and interest you extremely, not only for the mystery and history attached to the places themselves but also for the excessive fineness, tenderness and beauty of the art displayed in them.'[6]

Some audiences viewed them with less commitment however, as he discovered when he took his work with him to the Lord Chancellor's house. 'Upstairs, after fuss – arranged drawings –: but the whole thing was a failure, but for the attention of R.P. and Ly L. I don't think I should have carried it through. Tittering & laughing & bore. – And Sir R. talking Cicero, & Dr Roberts – but no lifelike care for Palestine itself, tho' they asked to see views of it . . . At II. I came away – I confess – very angry.'[7]

In the autumn he decided to accept Clowes's invitation, though he did so without enthusiasm. 'You have no idea my dear boy, what a grief this going to & fro is,' he told Fortescue. 'I had rather, methinks, come & settle & die straight away, only the half life half death of physical bore & worrying is a trial one flees from as yet.'[8]

At the beginning of November he packed his things. Before he left he went to the Zoo, and he drew – vultures.

When Lear had left Rome in March 1848 the threat of nationalist revolution had been drawing in on the city. The new pope, Pius IX, had at first been welcomed by Italian patriots who believed that he would join in their fight for his country's unity, but he was absorbed in reforming papal administration and the government of his territories and he did not want to be involved in a war. His position was an impossible one – as an Italian he supported the idea of unity, but if he went to war with Austria he would compromise his position as leader of the universal church. All he could hope to do was to steer an uncommitted middle course. But in a time of crusading revolution lack of support means opposition, and the papacy was seen as the reactionary bulwark which would hold back the revolutionary tide. To try to placate the people he appointed popular ministers, but this was not a time for half-measures and in November 1848 he had to flee from Rome when Garibaldi's nationalist troops overran the city.

Louis Napoleon, anxious to woo Catholic support in France, decided to send soldiers to win back Rome for the Pope. In the summer of 1849 the French defeated Garibaldi's men, the Republic collapsed, and Pius IX was brought back with a French garrison to protect him and guarantee his territorial rights. For nine years now the city had been quiet, but the balance was un-real and would inevitably topple.

Lear and Clowes reached Rome on 1 December 1858 almost exactly twenty-one years after Lear had arrived there first, happy and excited. Then the world had been bursting with expectation and hope which needed only time to be fulfilled. Now he knew what he had almost forgotten then – that life was unhappy and that it would never change: '. . . so dismal has been the return here,' he told Fortescue 'that only the friendliness of ancient acquaintance, & the even temper & kindness of Clowes could have kept me above water.'[9]

Then, two weeks after their arrival, Clowes fell from his horse and broke his collar bone, and for the next few weeks he was in bed. Lear felt so lonely that when letters began to arrive from England he could not help 'the tears a busting out of my eyes incontinent'.[10] Even visiting friends was a sad task, for they had grown older and tireder. They were pleased enough to see him, but he had been away for a long time and after the first pleasantries they were not really very interested in his return.

When he began to search for rooms he saw that changes had been made in the city since he had left. The Tiber still over-flowed its banks in winter, and carts were still pulled through the city streets by buffaloes, but the streets were cleaner and there were new houses and shops. There were new prices too, and he had to pay £80 a year for the apartment he found in the Via Condotti, opposite the Spanish Steps. He moved in on 21 December. Three days later Giorgio arrived, and life began to run smoothly once more.

He had a three-year lease on the rooms, and he carpeted all the floors and bought a new wall-covering for the study, he ordered fenders for all the fireplaces, blinds for all the windows and green baize curtains for all the doors, he hired a piano and then went shopping for 'a portable water-closet, a bedstead, 6 chairs, a pair of bellows, & a pepperbox'.[11] It seems strange that he should have gone to so much trouble and expense when he did not yet know if he would like living in Rome again, but he needed to find a permanent winter home and Rome had one overriding advantage, for '. . . everyone comes here with an express purpose to buy something in the way of painting'.[12]

When he had set up a room where he could show his draw-ings, he began holding twice-weekly open-days. At about mid-day on Wednesday and Saturday the bell would start to ring, and Giorgio would open the door to twenty or thirty or sometimes even more than forty people. They would be shown into the gallery where a fire had been lit and seats arranged in front of a folio stand, and when everyone was settled Giorgio would go to Lear and say 'with a grave grin "the Arabs are come".'[13] For the next hour and a half Lear would show his drawings of Palestine and Egypt. He sold a few paintings, but not many, and generally he found that the process just wasted a lot of his time. '. . . as yet I eschew general society, being wholly cross & bigongulous,'[14] he told Fortescue, precisely.

The guest of honour in the English community that winter was the young Prince of Wales. He had been four when Lear had given his mother drawing lessons; now he was seventeen and on his first trip abroad.

On 29 March Lear received a note from the Prince's tutor, Colonel Bruce, saying that his Royal Highness would like to come and see his drawings. It was three in the afternoon – would it be convenient if they arrived at four? At once Lear and Giorgio set to work with brooms and dusters. Then Giorgio was sent to put on his Sunday suit so that he could open the door to the Prince, whilst Lear stood on the landing to greet him when he arrived. 'Nobody could have nicer & better manners than the young Prince, nor be more generally intelligent & pleasing,' he wrote that night. 'I was afraid of telling or shewing him too much, but I soon found he was interested in what he saw, both by his attention, & by his intelligent few remarx. Yet I shewed him the Greek pictures, & all the Palestine oils, – & the whole of the sketches, & when I said, – "please tell me to stop, Sir, if you are tired by so many" – he said – "*o dear no!*" in the naturalist way.'[15] The visit, he told Ann, 'lasted just one hour & 5 minutes'.[16]

It was a good thing for Giorgio to have this extra excitement, for he was unhappy in Rome. He had never lived in a city before and knew nobody there apart from Lear. He did not like the Italians, he thought Roman laundries quite ridiculously expensive and the workmen shamefully lazy, and he was very distressed that Roman bread rolls could only be broken in four pieces instead of three like bread rolls in Corfu – in fact Lear was worrying that he would ask to go back to the island.

During that winter, Cavour and Louis Napoleon were making secret plans to drive the Austrians finally from Italian soil, and by the late spring rumours of war had begun to spread. The English started to pour out of the city to Civita Vecchia where they waited in crowds for enough boats to take them all off. Lear scorned their rush, but was alarmed to see the disappearance of the people who should be buying and commissioning his work. Exactly the same had happened to him there in 1848, and he realised that if it went on for any time he was going to be left with two years' unexpired lease and no income. War was declared at the end of April 1859, and a month later he left safely for London.

He began the summer with a round of visits to friends, and for six weeks he rattled round the countryside from one country house to another, from Lewes to Wells, and from Winwick to the Isle of Wight, showing his drawings and collecting commissions. He spent a happy few days at Farringford, striding over the downs beside Alfred – with his tousled black beard and flowing cloak booming out his new 'Idylls of the King' in a deep measured voice, or playing with the two boys who were now seven and five and 'very darling chaps indeed'.[17]

Emily seemed tired and ill, and he thought Alfred should have realised that she was wearing herself out working for him. 'I should think, computing moderately,' he wrote to Fortescue, 'that 15 angels, several hundreds of ordinary women, many philosphers, a heap of truly wise & kind mothers, 3 or 4 minor prophets, & a lot of doctors & schoolmistresses, might all be boiled down, & yet their combined essence fall short of what Emily Tennyson really is.'[18] There was an atmosphere of sadness mingled with a 'kind of sensitive excitement'.[19] Yet he felt happier at Farringford than anywhere, and when he left a heavy post-happiness depression settled down on him. 'I am doing little, but dimly walking on along the dusty twilight lanes of incomprehensible life,' he wrote to Fortescue. 'I wish you were married. I wish I were an egg & was going to be hatched.'[20] And perhaps if he could begin life again he would have a mother like Emily Tennyson.

His visits accomplished, he began to look for rooms in London where he could settle to work. He was already in debt and now he had spent £20 travelling round England. Though it brought him work it was money he could ill afford. Fortescue offered to help him through the summer, but Lear told him: 'My dear boy: – I don't want any money & fresh borrowings would only distress me more . . . I am thought wrong by some for want of independence in ever borrowing at all: but I am sure that is not a right view of things, for my whole life from 14 years has been independentissimo: & on the other hand, the man who will not put himself under obligation of any kind to even the friends who entirely sympathise with his progress – nourishes, in my opinion, a selfish & icicle sort of pride.'[21]

He felt cross and disheartened by London life, and decided that he must go somewhere with fewer distractions so that he could get down to work. This always meant either Sussex or the north, the two places where he had been happiest, and in July he found rooms in St Leonards on Sea. From there he wrote to Fortescue, '. . . although the queer solitude in which I live & the displeasing mill=round of toil is not particularly joyful, yet apart from the thorough necessity of the daily life – (in order that I may be out of debt if possible before November,) I quite believe it is a better extreme for me than the lounging existence to which I can look back with no comfort . . .

'This is what I do here: – rise at 5/2., & after 6 or so, am at work till 8. Bkfᵗ – Then work till 5 – occasionally obliged to leave off on account of sight, or from utter weariness – when I do a line or two of Sophocles, or compose some new song music, – & at 5 dinner – to 5¾. at most. Thence to 7/2 paint again, & by the time the brushes are washed, it is nearly dark, & I potter out to the post with some notes I may have written, or puddle along the shingly beach till 9/2 – Then, half an hour Sophocles, – & bed. This is unvaried, barring the Sundays – when I go to Hastings to dine with somebody or other. No "followers" or visits allowed in the week, nohow.'[22]

Really he was rather enjoying himself. 'I do feel a kind of placid sort of progress here,' he told Fortescue, 'where no one hardly interrupts me, – a kind of feeling like a snail's belly= crawling existence.'[23] A state of steady progress towards a goal of self-improvement was something Lear always aimed for, both

professionally and personally, and an ordered, full life helped him along this path. There was a beautifully mellow late summer and autumn, and the gentle warmth sank into his soul. 'Of all the very loveliest days of the wonderfully loveliest summer =endless – perhaps this might be the softest & calmest & brightest,'[24] he wrote one day in the middle of October. It was a year now since he and Lushington had parted; emotionally he was disengaged, and for the time being his mind was freed from its obsession of unhappiness.

Throughout the summer the newspapers had been filled with reports from Italy. In July the nationalists were betrayed when Louis Napoleon made peace with Austria behind Cavour's back, but the news did mean that Lear would be able to go back to Rome for the winter.

When he had finished his work at St Leonards he returned to London with the paintings and clear his debts. November was settling in, London was odious and he wanted to get away south as soon as he had tied up his business and said goodbye to his friends. He wrote to Fortescue telling him his plans:

O! Mimber for the County Louth
    Residing at Ardee!
Whom I, before I wander South
    Partik'lar wish to see; –

I send you this. – That you may know
    I've left the Sussex shore,
And coming here two days ago
    Do cough for evermore.

Or grasping hard for breath do sit
    Upon a brutal chair,
For to lie down in Asthma fit
    Is what I cannot bear.

Or sometimes sneeze: and always blow
    My well-develloped nose.
And altogether never know
    No comfort nor repose.

All through next week I shall be here,
    To work as best I may,
On my last picture, which is near=
    er finished every day.

*

So then I hope to hear your ways
    are bent on English moves
For that I trust once more to gaze
    Upon the friend I loves.

(Alas! Blue Posts I shall not dare
    To visit e're I go –
Being compulsed to take such care
    Of all the winds as blow.)

But if you are not coming now
    Just write a line to say so –
And I shall still consider how
    Ajoskyboskybayso.

No more my pen: no more my ink:
    No more my rhyme is clear.
So I shall leave off here I think. –

               Your's ever,
               Edward Lear[25]

Someone – probably Lushington – had suggested that his painting of the Temple of Bassae should be presented to the Fitzwilliam Museum, and he had to spend some time in London writing to ask his friends if they would subscribe towards the purchase. '. . . the "Bassae Septuagint" – or as some call it "the Subscription of the 70 Elders" – or "the Bassaerelief", is riz up to 50,'[26] he told Holman Hunt on 9 December, and a few days later he went up to Cambridge to see where the picture would hang.

His final task before leaving was to arrange for the publication of his settings of the 'Idylls of the King'. This was his third published set of Tennyson songs. The second, which contained a reprint of those published in 1853 together with five new settings, had come out earlier in the year.[27] On 22 December 1859, Lushington saw him off to Rome.

In Rome there was an uneasy peace, and he returned to a half-deserted city. Usually there would be nearly 2000 English residents, but that year he thought there were probably no more than 250. The artists who relied on casual sales to visitors were going to have a hard winter, and Lear was glad that he had brought back commissions on which to work. But even though he was busy he found Rome oppressive.

'O dear Emily T! & various people! –
how I live a living death here!'[28] he wrote in his diary.

The weather was '*abomminnable*: *filthy*: *beeeeeeeeeestly*: so I shan't
talk about it. I am always in a rage – always.'[29]

'I grow so tired of new people, & silly people, & tiresome
people, & fanatical people, & robustious people, & vulgar
people, & ugly people, and intriguing people, & fussy people,
and omblomphious people – & people altogether,'[30] he told
Emily Tennyson. But there were some whose company he did
enjoy. The Stratford Cannings, with whom he had stayed in
Constantinople, were there, and so was the American actress
Charlotte Cushman, who gave excellent dinner parties. At one of
these he met Robert Browning, who 'was all fun – pun – foaming
with spirit . . . altogether the evening was splendidophoro-
pherostiphongious'.[31] He went to visit Elizabeth Barrett Browning, but found her so smothered with bores and snobs that he
asked Emily Tennyson, 'what good does one get of anyone's
society when it is merely like a beautiful small rose tree planted
in the midst of 43 sunflowers, 182 marigolds, 96 dahlias and 756
china-asters?'[32]

Giorgio was gloomy and cross. Then, early in March, he
suddenly told Lear that he had a wife and three children in
Corfu. Lear had employed him now for four years but had had no
idea of this, even though part of this time had been spent in
Corfu where Giorgio's family lived. He realised now that his
servant would not want to come back to Rome for another
winter. It had been a mistake coming at all, and he told
Fortescue: 'I hate & loathe this place so utterly – for its petiness,
its cliquerie, – its art before nature, – its faith pro works, – its wet
& dirty atmosphere, its compulsory boredom, – its imprisoning
life, – & a thousand more reasons, – that I know I do right to quit
it at all risks.'[33] Next winter he would look for somewhere new.

His wish still was to return to Palestine, for 'the great views of
Jerusalem, should I be able to execute them, will be of more
permanent service to me for Engraving & public Exhibition than
any other work I could fix on'.[34] 'I am convinced of this more &
more,' he had written, 'if you have a wife – or a woman, – or are
in love with one, – (all phases of the same state of self=division,
the only real & proper state of life in this world –) if I say such be
your condition, ὦ ἀνθρωπε [O man!] – then you may stay in
any place in any circumstances: – you are raised out of the
necessity of contemplating the cursed nuisances of poverty or

bores by sympathy: – but if you are absolomly alone in this world – & likely to be so – then move about continually, & never stand still. I therefore think I shall be compulsed . . . to go to Japan & New York – or Paraguay – or anywhere before long.'[35] Part of him longed to stop wandering, though another part wondered if he ever could. 'How I wish I had some settled aboad – at least until the last narrow box,' he told Fortescue. 'But if I settled myself I should go to Tobago the next day.'[36]

Meanwhile, until he could save enough for the trip to Jerusalem, he was going back to England. Leaving Rome early meant that he would lose a whole year's rent, but he had managed to save £350 from the previous summer's work.

On 13 April 1860 he began to pack 'furibundiously'. Then he spent a fortnight travelling with Giorgio round the Bay of Spezia. At the end of May he saw Giorgio on his way to Corfu, and then he turned back for England.

13 Landscape Painter
1860–1863

Creative artists are strangely placed. There is a lingering mystique of their apartness – the idea that they are men of vision and that with the great leaders, and now the great scientists, they will be the people most remembered by other generations. Because of this, and the dignity of their talent, they may find their way into the highest layers of society. Yet they are also tradesmen who must sell their goods, and in Lear's time – indeed sometimes even now – tradesmen were considered quite simply beyond the pale.

And so they find themselves in an ambivalent situation in which they may be both admired and despised, and where as a result they will often be regarded with magnanimous condescension. When an artist is in demand he can afford to ignore this, and this in its turn will inspire confidence in his value. On the other hand, a man who allows himself to be patronised, who is inordinately grateful to anyone buying his work, can leave the purchaser with an uneasy feeling that he has taken an inferior work off a second-rate artist's hands.

Viewed objectively now, Lear's water-colour drawings are enjoying a reputation they never had in his lifetime. One reason for this, one amongst several, is that Lear let himself be patronised. The trouble, of course, was that he simply could not afford to upset anyone who was thinking of buying his work, but the result was that though many of the people who had his paintings derived a great deal of pleasure from them, few felt that they had bought anything of value.

There were other reasons as well. His water-colour drawings varied in quality a good deal – particularly later in life when his sight was going and he had rheumatism in his right arm – yet he would exhibit the bad beside the good. Then he underestimated the value of even the best of them and tended to see them either as slight, inexpensive 'pot-boilers' or as sketches for the oil paintings which he regarded as his real achievement. He never fully understood what he was doing when he painted in oils, and in his anxiety he often overworked the pictures until all the sparkle had gone and the fluid, rhythmical movement which made his water-colours so delightful had been ground to a standstill.

But Lear was certain that it was with his oil painting that he would become known, and in a sense he was right, for his water-colour drawings were lost in the great exhibition halls and galleries. His mistake was in even trying to compete with the fashionable painters of his day who surpassed him in both sentimentality and mastery of their medium. If he had concentrated on water-colours he might have enjoyed in his own lifetime the respect that he now commands, and he would probably have made a steady if undramatic living. But he never realised this, and when he came back to England in 1860 he was planning to paint the large and conspicuous oil painting which would finally establish him as the respected and sought-after painter he felt he should be.

He did not settle to work at once. In the middle of June he was invited with Lushington to stay at Farringford. It was the first time they had been together for more than an hour or two since they had left Corfu, but Lear felt easier with him now: '. . . a fanatical=frantic caring overmuch for those who care little for us, is a miserable folly. And after all ordinary natural pride revolts at selfish coldness,'[1] he wrote in his diary.

It was a strange and rather unhappy visit. Emily was as perfect as ever but as Lear was sinking back into the rare contentment of family life, Julia Cameron, the photographer, swept into the house followed by eight men carrying a grand piano so that Lear could play and sing for them: '. . . odious incense palavar & fuss succeeded to quiet home moments,' he wrote sadly. 'After all, it is perhaps better now, never to feel happy & quiet: so one gradually cares less for life.'[2] Then he added the phrase which he quoted over and over again as he found earlier happiness slipping away: 'We come no more to the golden shore, where we danced in days of old.'

The next day was Sunday, and the three men – Tennyson, Lushington and Lear – set out to walk across the Downs. Tennyson had begun to loathe the strangers who wanted to pester him, and the walk was miserable: 'AT was most disagreeably querulous and irritating and would return, chiefly because he saw people approaching,' wrote Lear. 'But FL would not go back, and led zigzagwise towards the sea – AT snubby &

SLOPES OF MYRTLE

cross always. After a time he would not go on – but led me back
by muddy paths (over our shoes,) a short cut home – hardly, even
at last avoiding his horror, – the villagers coming from church
. . . I . . . believe that this is my last visit to Farringford: – nor can
I wish it otherwise all things considered.'[3]

Back in London he was alarmed at how old and tired Ann was
looking. It was a warm summer, and the close June weather
seemed to be crushing down on her. She had moved now to
Stonefield Street in Islington where she shared a house with two
of her oldest friends, but in her gentle old age she was lonely.

In August Lear was invited to stay at Nuneham, where Lady
Waldegrave had asked him to do two paintings of the grounds.
There was to be a house full of people, and he could combine
work with the chance of talking with Fortescue. He was not
always at ease with Lady Waldegrave, though she was beautiful
and kind and commissioned a great deal of work from him. She
had been delighted with the paintings he had done for her in
Palestine, and sent him a letter of doubtful praise: 'I fell in love at
first sight with your beautiful pictures,' she had written. 'They
far and far surpass my expectations and I am miserable at not
knowing where I can find a good place for them.'[4]

> 'Bother all painting! I wish I'd 200 per annum!
> Wouldn't I sell all my colours and brushes and damnable
>   messes!
> Over the world I would rove, North, South, East and *West*, I
>   would –
> Marrying a black girl at last, & slowly preparing to walk into
>   Paradise!'[5]

he wrote to Fortescue on 9 July. But, unlike Tennyson who had
an annual grant from the Exchequer, he did not have £200 a year
and he must get back to work.

He arrived at Nuneham at the beginning of August, and found
the house gurgling with people. Then he heard that the whole
party was moving on to Strawberry Hill and that he was to stay
on with the housekeepers, the governess and Lady Waldegrave's
seven-year-old niece, Constance. He was to eat with the
governess, for apparently this was considered his rightful
position. He had not been treated like this since his earliest days
at Knowsley, and as he wandered in the rain under the dripping
trees and across the sodden park he was reminded of lonely days
there. He became so despondent that he could not get on with
the paintings. Instead he made a few drawings to work from and

left as soon as he could.

Back in London he began to concentrate on his plans for the large painting. In fact, he had decided to work on two pictures – one nine feet long of the Cedars of Lebanon, and another seven feet long of Masada and the Dead Sea. 'One *must* plan & risk & think something,' he wrote to Emily Tennyson, 'or if not, turn into a stagnant snail.'[6]

He needed some cedar trees that were within easy reach of London, and he found them at Oatlands Park Hotel at Walton-on-Thames. 'It stands upon elevated Terrace land, within its own grounds of forty-four acres. The rooms are spacious, and replete in every comfort, and the Mansion being placed on a dry, gravelly subsoil, is particularly well adapted for a winter residence.'[7] So ran an advertisement in the *Saturday Review*, and since Lear would be working there through the winter, it sounded ideal. The oldest cedar, still there today, was reputed to have been one of the first imported into England from the Lebanon, and was planted to commemorate the birth of Prince Henry, the son of Charles I, in the royal palace which had stood on the site.

At the end of September 1860 his things were sent to the hotel, and he went down and settled in. He did not usually like hotel life, but he was well and busy and he found himself rather enjoying it. It was 'a large & sumptuously commodious place, in a part of the old Oatlands Park – with nice broad terrace walks, & a wonderfully lovely view over the River Temms & the surroundiant landskip'.[8] He was given 'a large light bedroom – delightful to behold, & wanting for nought'.[9] Each morning he was up at six o'clock. '. . . what deep strange delight in that morning air & sun, – & bird singing, & tree rustling freshness!!!'[10] he wrote in his diary. His first task was to feed the 'unfortunate birds', then he would spend an hour or so on small

143

commissioned works before breakfast at eight. He would 'breakfast audibly in the public coughy=room',[11] and immediately afterwards begin working outside. He painted until six in the evening on the Cedars or the Masada, or on two big commissioned works of Damascus and Beirut. Dinner was at a quarter to seven and afterwards he would be sociable downstairs until nine o'clock. Then he would spend one hour translating 'Thousididdles – & so by very slow degrees attain to Greek nollidge',[12] and one hour penning out his Mount Athos drawings, and at eleven o'clock he went to bed.

It was the kind of full, regular life which most satisfied him, and he was getting through the winter remarkably well: '. . . the soil is so dry that at present I have neither Asthma nor roomatizum when I am there. On the contrary I have been making some new nonsenses in my old age',[13] he told Lady Waldegrave. It was fourteen years since *A Book of Nonsense* had been published, and he had been writing new limericks all the time. Now he wanted to bring out an enlarged edition 'with 42 new & enchanting subjects',[14] only this time he would offer it outright to a publisher instead of publishing it himself.

Right through December and into January he painted out of doors, feeling remarkably fit. Christmas had been unusually cold, and when the thaw came it was disastrous. '. . . lo! as I began to write this afternoon,' he told Emily Tennyson, 'horrible borrible squashfibolious meligoposhquilous sounds were heard, & ever increasing, like 5000 whales in hysterics.

'Then – huming screams & shouts. – Then stamping; – roaring; – rushing; – bouncing; – booming; – by-go-bustling; – ——O—— the great cistern, along of the sudden thaw – had bust all the pipes – which spouted forth arm=broad torrents of water like fire from cannons.'[15]

His room was all right, but when workmen arrived to repair the mess and began hammering all around, he decided that it was time to get back to London.

His painting of Masada was in the British Institution, and Lord Stanley, visiting the exhibition, found it 'the only one that especially pleased me'.[16] But Lear wrote to Lady Waldegrave, 'I begin to have an idea that bye & bye I shall have a gallery of my own. Exhibitions in a mass of thousands of paintings – the greater part of which are painted so as to look well as regards the surrounding pictures, – seems to me more & more a false practice.'[17] During the winter he had taken a new lease on some rooms at 15, Stratford Place, two doors away from the house

1. Ann Lear, Edward's sister

2. The 13th Earl of Derby

3. Knowsley Hall, home of the Earl of Derby, where Lear was invited to draw the animals and birds in the menagerie

MACROCERCUS ARACANGA.

Red and Yellow Macaw

4. The Red and Yellow Macaw, from Illustrations of the Family of Psittacidae, or Parrots

5. Lear by Wilhelm Marstrand, drawn in Rome in 1840

6 & 7. Ann and Jeremiah Lear, Edward's mother and father

8. Bowman's Lodge, Upper Holloway – Lear's birthplace

9. Gussie Bethell

10. Vitoe Monkey, drawing for Gleanings from the Menagerie at
Knowsley Hall

11. Franklin Lushington

12. Lake Fucino, from Illustrated Excursions in Italy

13. Athens, 13 July 1848. Watercolour

14. Cairo, 10 March 1858. Watercolour

Rose ~5.30. Worked at the last of the longer ~ size A
Autotype trials. Left at 7.30. with General Walpole 212
& Admiral Robinson. Walked nearly to Upper Bella-

1882 31 Days. 31 MONDAY [212–153] July
Royal Academy closes

=vista, but returned, along of a kicking mule.
Meeting Nicola, he told me that his father was full of
complaints. I have made him ridiculous by the spidaments, &
he could not return to Sanremo — he would get torpid — &c &c. He has
never made these "sbaglios" in so many years service, &c &c.
Later, Nicola came up & said his French lessons well. How
to act it is difficult to know. No letters. Wrote also
to Gastaldi — begging him to let me know what
debts have been claimed for George's brothers.
Paid weeks accts — 21.4. 60. Came up & wrote
out accounts — beginning August with
Drummond's £184 — Acquiescence £, £40 in hand

184 ⎫ in all
30 ⎬
40 ⎪
£278 ⎭

Sate some time with the R.'s before
my dinner — a cutlet & potatoes, & a bottle
of Chiavenna: Came up & slept & drew till
30. Then shewed S & R & Miss L. the A subjects,
& then read, slept, & penned out No 1 of the A lot,
till 5. The day is lovely & glorious — all beautiful
without — within depression & vexation. Opposed to my
being so utterly at sea mentally & morally, my better
health contrasts most curiously. I suppose the
ever-presence of the Demon since I was 7 years old
would have prevented happiness under any sort of
circumstances. It is a most merciful blessing that I have
kept up as I have, & have not gone utterly to the bad
mad & sad. When I have done the last of these penned out
Autotype bosher, shall I go in for doing some in a
similar way, but large? — Or shall I go for 10 days or so
about Switzerland? — or to Sanremo? —
At 5 went down to Castelletto, &
read somewhat: Nicola came up, but nothing
more had been said by Giorgio.
Adml Sir L. Robinson

Lady Robinson Miss Lewis.

16. *Edward Lear and Chichester Fortesque at Ardee in September 1857*

17. *Emily Tennyson from the portrait by G F Watts R. A.*

18. Frances, Countess Waldegrave, 1850

19. Alfred Tennyson

20. *The Cedars of Lebanon, May 1858. Watercolour*

21. *The Temple of Apollo at Bassae, 1859. Oil*

22. *Hubert Congreve*

23. *Giorgio Kokali – detail from a portrait in oils by Lear*

24. *Thomas Baring, 1st Earl of Northbrook*

25. *William Holman Hunt*

26. 'And someone walking there alone . . .' one of the Tennyson drawings

27. Mount Parnassus, 1860. Oils

28. Villa Tennyson, San Remo

29. Last photo of Lear, 28 April 1887

where he had lived whilst he was at the RA. Now he set up one of them as a gallery. Then he sent out invitations, and settled back to wait for visitors. They came, 'sometimes 20 at a time – of all kinds of phases of life: sometimes – for 3 hours no one comes: – so then I partly sleep, & partly draw pages of a new Nonsense book. If I sleep, I wake up savagely at some new comer's entrance, & they go away abashed. If I write Nonsense, I am pervaded with smiles, & please the visitors.'[18] Two paintings sold almost immediately, 'so I shall pay off all my debts – & possibly – if there is any overplus, buy a pleasing tabby cat, or a guitar, or some currant jelly: – but I don't think there will be anything over.'[19]

Ann called frequently, just to sit quietly with him. Often he would walk back to Islington with her, and she would tell him about their brothers and sisters and the years in Pentonville before he was born. She revelled in his company and they spent some of the most contented days together that they had ever known. In January she had her seventieth birthday and she looked little and frail. On 2 March she came as usual to his studio and sat with him through the morning whilst he painted, then they lunched together and at 3.30 they parted.

Two days later she began to have terrible bouts of sickness, and a swelling appeared on the back of her neck. She became really ill, and each day Edward went up to Islington, sometimes taking flowers to brighten her room, and would sit quietly with her holding her hand. She seemed calm and contented, '& speaks of dying as a change about to bring such great delight that she only checks herself for thinking of it too much. She has always been indeed as near Heaven as it was possible to be.'[20]

On 9 March the constant sickness began to tell and her strength seemed to fall away. Edward sat with her, and she was happy just to have him there. 'Dear dear Ann! Always joyous at seeing me,' he wrote in his diary. '. . . Sometimes she spoke suddenly – "What a blessing you are here! – not among the Arabs!" . . . "bless you my dear Edward! what a comfort you have been to [me] all your life!"'[21]

The next day she grew weaker. 'The dearest Ann *never* murmurs: thanks us for all we do: – always thinks of us! – "Go to bed Ellen dear! you are tired!" – "Nurse have you had your supper?" – "Edward my precious – take care you do not hurt your head against the bed iron."'[22]

In the early hours of 11 March she sank into a coma, and Lear could not bear to watch what was happening to her. He went back to Stratford Place to wash and make an attempt at eating breakfast, then returned to her; he walked up to Highbury to see the Nevills, and then went back to her again. As the morning wore on she grew weaker, and he knew that he could not be with her when she died. Instead he went out into Stonefield Street and walked up and down the pavement outside the house. Just after noon he looked up and saw the blinds in her room being drawn across. '. . . she died as a little infant falls asleep! Painless – motionless! As her life has been one of good & blessing – so is her death.'[23]

He wrote at once to Fortescue: 'My dear Ann is gone – she died a little after noon today – in such quiet!

'I am going down to Lewes to try to get Husey Hunt, (who is her executor –) to come on Saturday to my darling sister's funeral – for I shall be so terribly alone.'[24]

He stayed two nights at Lewes, glad to be with someone who had known Ann, and then he went back to sort her meagre belongings. So many of them related to him: his drawings from the age of four, letters, all the hundred and one trinkets and mementos he had sent her from every place he had been to – necklaces and scarves and brooches and carved paper-knives – they had all been faithfully kept. How she must have longed for his company in the years that he was away, though she had never tried to persuade him to come home to live. 'Ever all she was to me was good: – & what I should have been unless she had been my mother I dare not think,'[25] he wrote.

The funeral at Highgate cemetery was quiet, and afterwards he went for a few days to Oatlands Park Hotel.

Lear did not feel like being alone. Emily Tennyson had written to him, 'You must come to us when you are equal to it',[26] and she was the person who would most understand his loneliness. He reached Farringford on 19 March – but it was the wrong moment. Alfred's brother, Horatio, was expected with all his family, and the house was in a bustle of preparation. Lear found himself a room at the Royal Albion Hotel at Freshwater, and on the first day he was able to have a talk with Emily. After that he was in the way. Then there was a misunderstanding about an invitation for dinner, and he was so distressed by the whole atmosphere that on the 24th he slipped away without going up to the house to say goodbye. 'Perhaps after all, the less one stays in places one likes the better – & so one escapes some pain,' he wrote in his diary. 'Therefore, wander.'[27] For the next two weeks he moved from one friend's house to another, and on 11 April he came back to London.

He found it difficult to settle. 'My dear child,' he wrote to Fortescue, 'not only H. of C. or Official life is a dream – but all sorts of life, – & to all people really – only some don't think so at all times. But, I should say, to all men & women not absolutely fools, there must be seasons in which the so called realities of this life appear as only ombra of something to come, – the strange links between this & a future existence.'[28] 'The past is the past – the present seems nonsense, & the future darkness.'[29] Gradually he began to work again, and by the middle of May the 'Cedars' were finished. This was the first large painting he had done without any help from Hunt, and it was going to be his crowning success. Since the sale of his first large oil painting – 'The Quarries of Syracuse' which had sold in the Academy in 1853 for £250 – both the size and the price of his paintings had been increasing. In 1857 he had been paid 500 guineas for the 'Corfu', and the following year he asked the same price for Lady Waldegrave's painting of Damascus. Now he was thinking of asking an even larger sum for the 'Cedars', but he had not finally decided, when one evening in May he was invited to dinner with Millais and his wife, Effie.

'The dinner was very good,' he wrote in his diary, 'but the 2 hours I passed there, a bore. Mrs. R's – I mean Mrs. M's – cold Scotch accent, her vulgar queries & half suppressed jealousy about Hunt – (who is as the Sun to a Candle compared with J. E. Millais) – her catching at any Aristocratic names, – her pity of Bachelors – "it's just so melancholy!" – (as if one half of her 2 matrimonial ventures in life had turned out so happily!) – & her drawling stoniness disgusted me – wrongly or rightly I don't yet quite know – so that I don't care ever to see her again. J.E.M. has far better qualities than she – such is my impression. He walked, at 9. with me to Oxford St.: but I must say I do not care ever to see him much more. As I consider Daddy H. far his superior, this cannot be envy – nor is the feeling, I believe, anything but one arising from the utter difference of his nature & my own: he, at 30 is like a crafty aged French dancing=master, – & has neither depth nor softness in his character.'[30] By comparison Hunt, whom Lear saw two days later, was 'a very solid good fellow, & wonderful in contrast to J. E. Millais – all outside & froth'.[31]

Millais's painting, 'Apple Blossoms', had just been sold for 450 guineas, and Lear decided that if that was worth 450 guineas then the 'Cedars' were worth 700. 'If the Cedars don't sell for

735£, now, I shall put a higher price on them if exhibited, – and shall be *wholly indifferent* to their not selling then,'[32] he told Fortescue. But there was one important difference – Millais was the most popular painter of his day and people were eager to spend their money on his work, whilst Lear was known to only a few.

With the big picture finished, he felt that he needed a change, and as Lady Waldegrave had asked him to paint two views of Florence he decided to spend a few months on the Continent.

The Folkestone train rocked and swayed and jumbled along, and two small children travelling with their nurse were frightened and unhappy. So Lear lifted them on to his knee, '& told them my long name & all kinds of nonsense till they forgot the shaking bother ... I NEVER saw 2 sweeter & more intelligent children than those 2: & and I LONGED to keep them both,'[33] wrote the lonely man.

Giorgio joined him in Florence, and he worked there for two weeks. 'Plumpudding – treacle, weddingcake, sugar, barley-sugar, sugar candy, raisins & peppermint drops would not make a more luscious mixture in the culinary world, than Florence & its Val d'Arno does as Landscape,'[34] he told Holman Hunt contentedly.

It seemed odd to be away from England and not be writing long and frequent letters to Ann, and he told Fortescue, 'the want of the constant journal I have sent to my dear sister for so many years, makes every hour seem very strange & sad & blank'.[35] From America, where the Civil War had broken out earlier in the year, came the news that four of his nephews had joined the Northern army and another the Southern. Then he heard that his sister, Mary, had died on her way home from New Zealand.

He was back in England at the beginning of August and went straight down to St Leonards to work on the Florence pictures. When he had been young he had enjoyed his work, but now it had become an odious and objectionable task. 'No life is more *shocking* to me than the sitting motionless like a petrified gorilla as to my body & limbs hour after hour – my hand meanwhile, peck peck pecking at billions of damnable little dots & lines, while my mind is fretting & fuming through every moment of the weary day's work,'[36] he told Fortescue, who wrote: 'You are a curious compound of love of Art – or at all counts power of absorbing yourself in it – with hatred of the actual work.'[37] 'Yes,' replied Lear, 'I certainly *do* hate the act of painting: & although day after day I go steadily on, it is like grinding my nose off.'[38] 'When you & I go to heaven,' he proposed to Hunt, 'we won't paint any more, but will sit in Chestnut trees & smoke and drink champagne continual.'[39] In the end, it came back to money, for painting, painting, painting to pay the bills took away every ounce of creative enjoyment. 'Really if I could realise enough money to give me 200 a year, I think I would begin a new kind of life altogether; but I suppose this cannot be.'[40] His dislike of painting was to some extent balanced by the pleasure he gave, for 'it is better to be the means of giving armless pleasure to a limited number of people, than to be the means of slaughtering indefinite thousands – though I grant the latter function requires the greater ability.'[41]

One thing did cheer him – it seemed that he had been right about the 'Cedars'. The painting was on exhibition in Liverpool and a critic there had written: '"Mr Lear has in this great picture not only achieved a professional success – but he has also conferred an obligation of the highest order on the whole Christian world." (! ! ! ! ! – After that, take care how you speak or write to me.)' he warned Fortescue. 'I shall not be surprised if the Cedars are purchased at Liverpool.'[42] But they were not, for they were too highly priced.

By the beginning of October the paintings of Florence were finished, and he was back in London. Now he had one more task before the winter began, and that was to find a publisher for the revised edition of *A Book of Nonsense.* He took it to Smith & Elder, and then to Routledge, Warne & Routledge, but neither of them wanted it. This was rather a shock, for whatever his success as a painter he had thought that as a Nonsense writer he was assured. He asked Dalziel to make wood-engravings of the drawings – this was cheaper than the lithography he had used in earlier editions – and to print and bind the book. Now that he was paying for the entire book production, Routledge said that they would take 1000 finished copies for distribution.

Winter was coming on again, and as there was nothing now until the Great International Exhibition in London in the spring he thought it was time to get away south. He had decided to try another winter in Corfu: the past was over, for at the beginning of October Lushington became engaged. Instead he would look to the future: the nonsense book would be out in time for Christmas, and with the 'Cedars' he was approaching the climax of his painting career.

He wished he had never come. He was weary and lonely and missed Lushington's sombre company, for though it had not made him happy it had given a purpose to his life. The weather certainly was marvellous – 'All without, – the sea, mountains, olive woods – are as lovely as color & calm atmosphere & cloudless sky can make them: – but within I confess to being blank & weary & sad to a shocking amount –: & perhaps a lesson may be learnt from this state of things that the outside is not what we should so much think of – but then how the devil is it to be otherwise with a dirty Landscape painter.'[43] 'I am mortissimo in body & soul,' he wrote in his diary. 'Yet looking back – even as far as 6 years old – (at the clown & circus at Highgate,) & then to all since – how can it be otherwise? The wonder is, things are as well as they are through constant fighting.'[44]

But he began to settle in, and after the dullness and heaviness of his Roman exile he actually enjoyed the bustle of the garrison town. Having military friends had its disadvantages though, as he told Fortescue: '. . . just now I looked out of window at the time the 2[d] were marching by – I having a full palate & brushes in my hand: whereat Col. Bruce saw me & saluted – & not liking to make a formillier nod in presence of the hole harmy, I put up my hand to salute, – & thereby transferred all my colours into my hair & whiskers – which I must now wash in turpentine or shave off.'[45]

The Nonsense book was out for Christmas, and within a few days five hundred copies had been sold. But a critic writing in the *Saturday Review* described the verse as 'anonymous, & a reprint of old nursery rhymes',[46] which made Lear cross and sad. 'I wish I could have all the credit due to me, small as that may be,' he wrote. 'I wish someone would review it properly & funnily.'[47]

It was a quiet winter. He had a few small commissions to work on, and as usual he opened his gallery twice a week to visitors, but he soon realised again the one advantage of Rome for he sold absolutely nothing. He went back to his Greek lessons and told Fortescue, '. . . if I had my way & wor an Axiom maker & Lawgiver, I would cause it to be understood that Greek is (or a knowledge of it,) the first of virtues: cleanliness the second: & Godliness – as held up by Parsons generally – the 3[d].[48]

Lear had forceful opinions about parsons generally, and what he saw as the distortions that they preached. 'I begin to be vastly weary of hearing people talk nonsense, – unanswered – not because they are unanswerable, but because they talk in pulpits,' he once wrote. '. . . Are not the priests of the age blind indeed not to discern that though from the unassailable vantage ground of custom they may oppress the human intellect for a long long while, yet that some day the hour will come for them to go the way of all other priesthoods? ... A broader creed, – a better form of worship – the cessation of nonsense & curses, – and the recognition of a new state of matters brought about by centuries, science, destiny or what not, – will assuredly be demanded, & come to pass whether Bishops & priests welcome the changes or resist them.'[49] He deplored righteousness without charity, piety without love, and he sought in the interpretation of Christ's teaching, as in so much else, the natural generosity of wide horizons. 'When will it please God to knock Religion on the head, & substitute charity, love & common sense?'[50] he asked. Above all, he feared the Athanasian Creed with its 'exclusion clauses', for he would not believe that 'the Almighty d——s the greater part of His creatures'.[51] Gradually he ceased to go to church regularly. 'Perhaps it is better that I should altogether stay away,' he told Fortescue, 'since one day if I am so over-constrained to folly, I may get up & snort & dance & fling my hat at this abomination of sermon preaching where sermons are simply rot.'[52]

When the spring came round he crossed the island to do some drawing at Paleokastrizza, a village on the western coast which was perfect and utterly peaceful 'excepting only a dim hum of myriad ripples 500 feet below me ... It half seems to me that such life as this must be wholly another from the drumbeating bothery frivolity of the town of Corfû, and I seem to grow a year younger every hour. – Not that it will last. Accursed picnic parties with miserable scores of asses male & female are coming tomorrow, & peace flies – as I shall too ...

'One thing, under all circumstances I have quite decided on – ἀποφάσισα ἀκριθως* – When I go to heaven "if indeed I go" – & am surrounded by thousands of polite angels, – I shall say courteously – "please leave me alone! – you are doubtless all delightful, – but I do not wish to become acquainted with you: – let me have a park, & a beautiful view of sea & hill, mountain & river, valley & plain, – with no end of tropical foliage: – a few wellbehaved small cherubs to cook & keep the place clean: – & – after I am quite established – say for a million or two of years, – an angel of a wife".'[53] 'The Elements,' he wrote in his diary, 'trees, clouds, &c – silence ... seem to have far more part with me or I with them, than mankind.'[54]

* 'I unconditionally refuse.'

In April he began to be anxious about his paintings in the Exhibition. Their success now depended very much on how well they were hung and lit, for exhibition walls then were crowded with pictures and a badly hung painting could scarcely be seen. Anxiously he wrote to Fortescue: '. . . please let me know, un-varnishedly, how my Cedars & Corfu look: – for the sale of the Cedars depends much on its place, & *my* plans on *its* sale for 735£.'[55] The reply came back – the pictures are hung high.

In the middle of May 1862 he left for England, ground down with disappointment. His great painting, lionised in Liverpool the year before, was not only hung high – it was slated by Tom Taylor reviewing the exhibition for *The Times*. When Lear saw this he was desperate. He had believed that this painting would establish his reputation. He also had to live and he had spent most of one winter working on it, expecting to see an ample return for his time and the expense of staying at Oatlands Park. He had hardly sold a thing since he left Rome in the spring of 1860: the large paintings of Beirut and Damascus on which he had worked in 1860 and 1861 had been paid for in advance to get him to the Holy Land. Ann's property had been sold and this brought him in an annual income of £50, and from the sales of his books he had saved money for the day when his sight was too bad for him to paint any more, but he did not want to break into this as he knew that he would never be able to replace it. 'How debts of frames and colours are to be paid, I do not know,' he told Emily Tennyson, 'but I think I shall become a cheerful bankrupt, & begin a new life in a tramper's caravan.'[56]

He thought of cutting all his picture prices by half. In the next breath he considered buying one of the houses in Stratford Place from his savings and setting himself up there with two servants and a permanent exhibition of his work. His quandary was dread-ful. However much he might dream of it, he could not seriously think of buying a house in England because of the climate. To get enough money to live – and though his tastes were not extravagant they were at least generous – he needed to be where people bought pictures, and that meant either London or Rome.

One thing he did know: he could not again spend months working on a large, important, but uncommissioned work. Instead he must paint the small water-colour drawings which he knew would sell. There is a popular fallacy that artists are stimulated by poverty, and that enough money saps their creativity. As Lear saw and experienced it, lack of money meant that he must bury his real creativity and produce instead pot-boilers just so that he could pay his bills.[57] 'I agree with you Daddy,' he wrote to Holman Hunt, 'Art is the Devil. I believe that originally in the Hebrew version of Job, the Devil was made to set Job about a painting, & that that excellent & unfortunate individual took it in hand until he was worn out, & bust into cusses no end. But the later transcribers of the Bible could not see the wit of this, so they cut it out. More fools they.'[58]

In fact, from this time can be observed quite clearly a change in Lear, a growing disillusionment and isolation, and an impatience and increasing irascibility, particularly with the arbiters of taste. The hanging of the Manchester Exhibition had been in the charge of two Academicians – Creswick and Red-grave – and in a letter to Fortescue he vented the anger that many artists of his day felt against this all-powerful, closed society. 'Two R.A.s having had to decide their destiny it is a gt. thing they were hung at all,' he wrote. '. . . A society like the W. Color has the right to place who it pleases as 1st rate members & to exclude whom it pleases: – but on what grounds do R.A.'s of any small or of no power monopolise the eclat & substance accruing to them from Royal Patronage & recognised position? If 25 painters were the elite of the nation in 1780 – why is the list in 1862 to exclude good & include bad & yet ever remain 25? (I do not speak of Architects or Sculptors – 40 being the whole number.) Talented as many of the body are – I fear that dis-honesty is a thriving deity of their pantheon: for those very talented men who can fully appreciate the merits of such as are shut out – are the most to blame for not moving the extension of the number of members, or, if they cannot do that, for not leaving the Academy . . . if the R. Academy is a National Institu-tion, then it ought to be forced to reform: – or it might cease to be a Royal & National affair, – & then nobody can complain that it is rotten & narrow if it pleases itself so to be.'[59] 'Now if one were but an Academician – if ever such a fool or dauber – how joyful it would be!' he wrote to Emily Tennyson, 'only then one would suffer as an honest man by representing this 30th part of the best English art. – After all such men as Watts, Holman Hunt, Linnell, Antony, Maddox Brown, Rosetti and many more have no "position" in art, & must *therefore* be quacks.'[60]

It was not only the RA that angered him. He raged too against those people who could afford to buy paintings, but did so only according to fashion, the sheep who 'leap where others leap'.[61] Their influence, rightly used, could have achieved so much by wise patronage. Beyond that, he deplored their way of life. He noted, as he had done at Knowsley, how they filled their idle hours with 'utter frivolity'[62] and studied emptiness. If only he had had the time and the freedom from money worry that they had, what opportunities he would have grasped! '. . . oh! ! how sick I am of the upper 10000! – I mean – as acquaintances – for friends I have in their station as in others'[63] He was always careful to distinguish between his friends and all others, though his irritation at this time extended most noticeably to Fortescue who, through his wife, represented to Lear the type of society and social gatherings he most disliked. '. . . the small dinners of highly intelligent or scientific middle class friends are about the really best society going,'[64] he thought, and he told Emily Tennyson, '. . . of all things most to be remarked, this is a fact: – the middle classes – professional & otherwise, are by far the best fun for pleasure & knowledge as to converse. The big folk are in most cases a norful bore.'[65]

But it was the big folk who bought pictures, and since Lear did not belong to the RA, nor even to the Water Colour Society, he needed their patronage. Instead, as the years went by he came to rely more and more upon his friends, who continued to buy his pictures. Writing in 1877, he said: '. . . as I was saying 2 days ago to Carlingford one of the most curious points in my Artistic Career, is the steadiness with which my friends have relied on my doing them good work, contrasted with the steadiness with which all besides my friends have utterly ignored my power of doing so. Said a foolish Artist to me – "you can hardly be ranked as a Painter – because all you have done, or nearly all, – is merely the result of personal consideration, & you are comparatively if not wholly unknown to the public." – Says I to he, – "that don't at all alter the qualities of my pictures – whether they are done to the commissions of Ld N. or Ld. A – or Lord C – or Lady W – or Sir F. G. – or F. Lushington, or R. Bright, or F. W. Gibbs – or any other friend, – or whether they are bought in a gallery by Mr. Timothy Timkins or the Duke of Popmuffin: – For the Public, says I, I have no sort of respect not none whatever – for provided pictures are cried up & well hung up – they are safe to be bought – be they by Whistler or anybody else. But the voice of Fashion whether it hissues hout of a Hart Cricket in a Paper, or hout of the mouth of a Duke or a Duchess – ain't by no means the voice of Truth. So you see o beloved growler – your ozbervations don't affect me a bit, who haven't got no ambition, nor any sort of Hiss Spree de Kor at all at all."'[66]

It was another stage in the progressive isolation which was to find its final expression in the great nonsense poems, and it is interesting to speculate whether, if Lear had become a successful and sought-after painter, these would ever have been written.

At the end of September the exhibition came down. 'What I do with the Cedars I do not know,' he wrote to Fortescue, 'probably make a great coat of them. To a philosopher, the fate of a picture so well thought of & containing such high qualities is funny enough.'[67]

Even the Nonsense was becoming a millstone, for Dalziel was pressing him for money and though the whole edition had sold Routledge had so far paid him nothing. Then they decided, after all, to buy the copyright, but Lear refused now to let them have it for the £100 he had originally asked. Instead, he sold the entire rights of a book which went into nineteen editions in his own lifetime, for £125. Seven hundred guineas for the 'Cedars', £125 for the copyright of *A Book of Nonsense* – he did not realise where his unique value lay. But he was pleased. 'I went into the city today, to put the 125£ I got for the Book of Nonsense into the funds,' he told Lady Waldegrave. 'It is doubtless a very unusual thing for an Artist to put by money, for the whole way from Temple Bar to the Bank was *crowded* with carriages & people, – so immense a sensation did this occurance make. And all the way back it was the same, which was very gratifying.'[68] That evening, he went to dine with some friends. 'Bye & Bye, on showing the receipt for the Bk of Nonsense, they seemed to think it was worth nil, – wh. distressed & disgusted me, & made me cross,'[69] he wrote in his diary.

Lady Waldegrave was now a widow, for Mr Harcourt had died the previous winter. Since it was considered improper for a widow to become engaged until at least a year after her husband's death, Fortescue was having an anxious time. He knew that he had rivals, including the Duke of Newcastle under whom he worked in the Colonial Office, and as the summer wore on he began cautiously to push his suit. Lady Waldegrave encouraged him, and in September she accepted his proposal. It was to be kept a secret which Lear, who had been a confidante all along, was entrusted to keep. And so another dear friend was marrying. 'Every marriage of people I care about rather seems to leave me on the bleak shore alone,'[70] he wrote, and the shore was becoming a very lonely place.

'"but never more, o! never we –
Shall meet to eggs & toast & T!"

'Never mind. I don't grumble at the less I see of friends – so they gain by it.'[71]

But there was a germ of an idea coming into his own mind. Early in November he went to see Richard Bethell, who was now Lord Westbury, the Lord Chancellor. He had a twenty-four-year-old daughter called Augusta whom Lear had known from a child, '. . . dear little Gussie, who is absolutely good & sweet & delightful,' he wrote in his diary, 'BOTHER'.[72]

In the middle of November he left for Corfu, and as soon as he had settled in he began a completely new system of work. First he sorted through the sketches he had made on his travels, and chose sixty from which to work. Then he prepared and mounted thirty pieces of paper of one size, and thirty more rather larger. Next he drew in thirty outlines and a few days later thirty more. Then, moving from one picture to the next he painted in all the blues, and all the greens and all the browns. '. . . his method seemed to be to dip a brush into a large wide-necked bottle of water-colour, and when he had made one or two touches on the drawing, to carry it to the end of the room and put it on the floor, the performance being repeated till quite a row was arranged across the room.'[73]

The process was not entirely unenjoyable: '. . . worked all day – to 4.: getting the whole of the larger 30 tyrants – another step forward. This sense of progress – however dark the terminus – is inspirating.'[74] His plan was to make a large number of pleasing paintings which would sell. 'For the present I have done with oil painting,' he wrote to Lady Waldegrave, '& have collapsed into degredation & small 10 & 12 Guinea drawings calculated to attract the attention of small Capitalists.'[75] 'They are an odd sort of drawings – in as much as they recall vividly other places & times – yet have no "upward aspirations" as vorx of hart.'[76] Instead, he was giving the public what he felt it deserved.

As usual when he worked hard, Lear was much happier. Whenever he could, he committed himself to things completely, refusing to do things 'by *halves* and *squitters*'.[77] When he travelled he pushed himself on and on until he was exhausted, when he was painting he might work from 6 in the morning until the evening light had gone, when he wrote letters they would be several carefully composed pages and he might write more than twenty at a time until he 'became like unto a spawned salmon, & was exhausted, & could work no more.'[78] 'The Beaver, the Ant, the Bee, & suchlike brutes are my model communities,'[79] he

once wrote, and for him work was a 'universal panacea for the ills of life'[80] – it left no time for brooding or recrimination. 'I do not think he ever wittingly or willingly wasted an hour,'[81] Lushington said of Lear. 'January is nearly gone,' he wrote in his diary, '& I must say I have never passed one so serenely for many many years.'[82] 'I lead as quiet life as I can, being strongly convinced that a regular application to some kind of self=improvement by way of work is more necessary to ensure comfort than any great variety of social fuss.'[83]

It took him sixty days to complete the sixty Tyrants, as he called them, and by the end of February they were all framed and hung in his studio. Throughout March they were on exhibition, and within a few days £120 worth had been bought. Some of the visitors were most provoking, especially one 'who saw all 60 drawings in 19 minutes – calling over the names of each & saying – "700£! ! why you must give a ball!" – Blasted fool: – as yet I have sold 120£ worth – but have not received one farthing – for great people generally suppose that artists gnaw their colors & brushes for food.'[84]

He found new friends that winter. The High Commissioner, Sir Henry Storks, had as one of his aides a zealous young Royal Artillery subaltern. This was Evelyn Baring, a cousin of Lear's close friend Lord Northbrook, who was later created Earl of Cromer for his work in Egypt. He was young, intelligent and enthusiastic, and despite the thirty years' difference in their age he and Lear formed a spontaneous and happy friendship which lasted until Lear's death. A few of Lear's letters to him have survived, like this one:

> Thrippsy pillivinx,
> Inky tinky pobblebookle abblesquabs? – Flosky! beebul trimble flosky! – Okul scratchabibblebongibo, viddle squibble tog-a-tog, ferrymoyassity amsky flamsky ramsky damsky crocklefether squiggs.
>
> Flinkywisty pomm,
Slushypipp.[85]

Sir Percy Shelley, son of the poet, was there 'in a yott' and he set down the music Lear had composed to Shelley's words, 'O world, O life, O time!' Other friends were a family called De Vere who had a small daughter, Mary. Lear was always happy when he was with her, making up Nonsenses and drawing pictures, and delighting in her childlike appreciation. 'Would *one* have been as happy as *one* fancies if *one* had been married & had had children?'[86] he pondered sadly.

Really it had been a marvellous season. 'The same perfect weather. Hardly a cloud in all the sky: every crag & winkle of Salvador – every gull & goose – every sail & boat, reflected clear & calm in the bright sea from 7.30 to 6 P.M. It is not possible to imagine greater beauty of nature.'[87] 'So happy a "winter" as this – one thing with another – passed I – never,'[88] he summed up on 6 March.

He seemed at last to have found a way of combining a happy winter home with making enough money to live, for nowhere suited him as perfectly as Corfu: '. . . the more I see of this place, so the more I feel that no other spot on earth can be fuller of beauty & of variety of beauty. For you may pass your days by gigantic cliffs with breaking foam-waves below them . . . – or on hills which overlook long seas of foliage backed by snow-covered mountain ridges . . . or beneath vast olives over-branching dells full of fern & myrtle & soft green fields of bright grass: or in gardens dark with oranges & lemon groves, those fruits sparkling golden & yellow against the purple sea & amethyst hills: – or by a calm sandy shore below aloe=grown heights – rippling= sparkling curves of sea sounding gently around all day long.'[89]

He was thinking now that he would settle permanently abroad and not come back to England each summer. The expensive double journey brought him nothing, and '. . . the few friends I care much for, I see only for a few hours, and really don't communicate with as much as when abroad: – the sitting for six weeks or 2 months in a room on the chance of purchasers coming is far from pleasant: – & the Country house life is rattling & expensive . . . & moreover cannot be carried on by those who have ever to work for life.'[90]

But his Corfu days were coming to an end, for the Cabinet had decided that the islands must be returned to Greece. The Greek monarchy was to be restored, and the throne was offered to a number of people, including Lord Derby. Lear himself pondered on the opportunity. 'You may not have heard,' he wrote to Drummond, '(it is not generally known,) that I refused the throne of Greece – King Lear the first – on account of the conduct of Goneril & Regan my daughters, wh. has disturbed me too much to allow of my attention to governing.'[91]

At the end of March he took the exhibition down and decided to make a tour of the islands before they ceased to be under British rule. He was away for two months, walking and drawing on each island; if the following summer in England brought him no new commissions, he would at least have material for another book.

He returned to Corfu for a few days early in June, and then left for England. The journey took him nearly a month, for he was taken ill in Italy. He had landed at Ancona which was a free port, but he could not leave by the road out of town until all his baggage had been examined. It was noon, and the sun pulsed down on him as he struggled to undo the straps and bindings on his cases. He managed to get to Turin, but there he collapsed with sunstroke. For a few days he was really ill, and he was still feeling horribly weak when he reached England at the end of June.

The large paintings had been on exhibition throughout the winter at Stratford Place, but there was no sign of their being sold. 'Will nobody be wise enough to buy those great vorx?' he wrote to Henry Bruce. 'Not such as you, but childless, gold-possessing, house=purchasing, room=devising individuals.

'Never mind. They will be useful when I am dead – those pictures – as the reflective & expiring bear thought when he considered that his skin would become muffs.'[92]

As he had no other work planned, he settled down to the Ionian Islands book. Instead of using lithography, a task he dreaded, he decided to experiment with photography. This meant doing the drawings in black and white so that they would photograph, and he tried using charcoal, lamp-black, pencil, chalk – but they were all hopeless. Instead he made a delightful water-colour drawing of Paxo which could not be reproduced by any method, then sat back and wondered what to do. 'All other years I have had some large work to do & have had to go through with it & look forward to its completion by gradual progress & labour: – but this year I have nothing of the kind –: & the only work I wish to pursue seems to elude my search by the difficulty of its execution . . . Squiggs. Beetles. Bother. Bullfrogs. Buttercups. Let us change the subject.'[93]

Really he had no choice. Nobody wanted his work, and at least he should make some money from the book. Besides, if he did it well, it 'would keep up my prestige as a draftsman of Mediterranean scenery: – & would moreover hold up or pave a way to my more general smaller-sized Topography of Greece – to be one day printed with my journals.'[94] This work covering the whole of Greece had been in his mind since his very first visit there in 1848.

He knew that he must simply start on the book and stay in England until it was finished, and as his photographic experiments had been failures he would have to use lithography again. 'The 60 drawings I began in December last were a longer toil, – but then I could often get out & walk, & see the mountains. Now & here, that is not possible, – & I am in a prison.'[95] 'I go grinding on most sadly & painfully, for it is not altogether the physical annoyances of banishment from fresh air & nature combined with many hours' daily work of a constrained kind, that bothers & depresses me, – but beyond these – the impossibility of getting any compensation=spiritual from the views I am drawing, since their being all executed reversed causes them to seem unreal, & without any interest.

'You may ask – then why undertake a task so odious? – The reply to which would be, what else could I do? – The remains of my Watercolor gains could not carry me through the winter, & therefore, as ever the ·case with Artists who have no settled income, – something else was necessary. And as it would be folly to commence more oil works – those I have done being still unsold, – or to begin more Watercolors when there are none to see them, – Ionian Book was my only apparent open=door of progress.'[96]

He made up his mind to see nobody until he had finished. He did go to Highgate to see Ann's grave, and as he walked back through Holloway he passed Bowman's Lodge. The gardens and paddocks had already gone to make room for new roads and buildings, and now the house was advertised for sale as building materials. He decided to take one last look over it. 'Some of the steps were gone –: a woman showed me in to the hall. The parlour at once annihilated 50 years. Empty – but – there were the 2 bookcases, & the old "Secretary" my father used to write at. – I saw every possible evening for years. Would I could see the pictures as they were! ! – then I went up stairs – the Drawing room is really a fine good room – but spoiled now by the back buildings. *My* room – ehi! – ehi! – Henry's – Mary's – Mother's, and the spare room. Down stairs again – the nursery, a large low room – just as it was – only with no view. Dear Ann's – & the painting room – the happiest of all my life perhaps – the "dark room" – and the "play ground". The little parlour was shut – & the study & greenhouse room extinct. Gave the woman 2 shillings – a cheap & wonderful lesson.'[97] Unless several other rooms were also extinct, it seems to have been a very small house for such a large family. The Bowman's Lodge days are certainly a mystery.

The last of the lithographs was finished on 20 October, and he wrote to a friend, '. . . if you hear of my being seen a walking on my head or in any other remarkable mode about town, set my eccentricities down to extreme delight at my work having come to a conclusion.'[98]

Now he had to write six hundred letters asking people to sub-scribe. This too was an endless task, and he confessed to Fortescue, 'if I were an angel I would immediately moult all my quills for fear of their being used in calligraphy.'[99] He was still in England in December, and on the 17th he went to Strawberry Hill for dinner. 'The people I sate next to bored me to death . . . the large drawing room was *horribly* cold: & all things horribly dull. Society at Strawberry Hill – unless a great fête, – is a misery.'[100] Compared with this a quiet visit to Holman Hunt was perfect, 'A really delightful evening – very rare now a days . . . Daddy always seem semi-fabulous to me – : either quâ good-ness – or for depth of thought: conscientiousness: – talent &c. &c.'[101]

On 1 December 1863, *Views of the Seven Ionian Islands* was published. It was similar to the second volume of *Illustrated Excursions in Italy*, and had twenty plates each with a short descriptive text. It had been a test of his endurance, and it was not all over yet for he had to chase up fifty subscribers who had not bothered to pay, and 'who naturally think 3 guineas can be nothing, forgetting that 150 guineas are much'.[102] But from the book he was able to put £300 into the 3 per cents for his old age. Ten days after Christmas he left once more for Corfu.

14 Wanderer
1864–1866

During the summer of 1863 the seventeen-year-old Prince William of Denmark had accepted the Greek throne, and when Lear reached Corfu early in January 1864 he found the British preparing to leave. Hopeful that he might stay on, he had written to Fortescue: 'I want you to write to Lord Palmerston to ask him to ask the Queen to ask the King of Greece to give me a "place". – As I never asked anything of you before – I think I may rely on your doing this for me. I wish the place to be created a=purpos for me, & the title to be δ 'Αρχανοηδιφλναρίαποιος [First nonsense chatter maker], with permission to wear a fool's cap (or mitre) – 3 pounds of butter yearly & a little pig, – and a small donkey to ride on. Please don't forget all this, as I have set my heart on it.'[1]

But he had to leave with the rest of them. The members of the garrison would receive new postings, and some of the civilians were moving on to Athens to live. Lear wondered if he should go there to look for a home for himself. He had still not quite abandoned the possibility of settling in England, and wrote in his diary, 'It seems to me that I have to choose between 2 extremes of affection for nature – towards outward nature – i.e. – English, or Southern. – The former, oak, ash & beech, – downs & cliffs, – old associations, – friends near at hand, & many comforts not to be got elsewhere. The latter – olive – vine – flowers – the ancient life of Greece, warmth & light, better health – greater novelty – & less expense in life.'[2] Sadly he packed his things. 'Goodbye, my last furniture is going: – I shall sit upon an eggcup & eat my breakfast with a pen . . .'[3]

He left the island on 4 April, and watched 'the loveliest place in the world'[4] diminishing into the horizon. After dinner, he and Evelyn Baring sat out on deck under the stars, and before he went to bed he composed a sad little ditty, perhaps the purest piece of nonsense he ever wrote:

She sits upon her Bulbul
Through the long long hours of night –
And o'er the dark horizon gleams
The Yashmack's fitful light.
The lone Yaourt sails slowly down
The deep & craggy dell –
And from his lofty nest, loud screams
The white plumed Asphodel.[5]

Athens was not as he remembered it. It seemed pervaded with a 'queer analytic dryness of soul & mind & atmosphere',[6] and he knew he could not make a home there. But winter was still a long way off so there was no hurry to find somewhere else, and as it was too early for England he decided to visit Crete. Within a week Giorgio had joined him, and they left together for Khania.

'Out in the dark blue sea there lies a land called Crete, a rich and lovely land, washed by the waves on every side, densely peopled and boasting ninety cities . . . One of the ninety towns is a great city called Cnossus, and there, for nine years, King Minos ruled and enjoyed the friendship of almighty Zeus.'[7] So wrote Homer in the *Odyssey*, but King Minos was no more than legend to people travelling in Crete in Lear's time. 'Its antiquities are *so* old as to be all but invisible,'[8] he wrote sadly, and with more truth than he realised, for it was not until the end of the century that Arthur Evans began to excavate and re-construct the palace at Knossos.

Today we know that the Minoan civilisation was the fore-runner of the Mycenean and Athenian cultures and that they were a colourful, uninhibited people apparently free from the fears of wrathful gods and the worries of convention. If Lear had known this too he would have respected them for the very characteristics he most admired. But he did not, and he was dis-appointed with the island. Indeed, even the description 'rich and lovely' seemed legendary, for when they arrived it was windy and wet and altogether horrible. Ten days later it was no better. 'Alas! for Crete, it seems a sell,' he wrote, '& when I think of Sicily & its every step & every moment of interest, while here is so little, except that of floral nature & the delight of the sweet morning air & thorough calm.'[9] The only good thing was that the peasants did not bother them as they had done in Albania and Palestine – though one did call out to Giorgio, 'Why don't you draw?' to which the Suliot replied inconsequently, 'Don't you see, I am too short.'[10]

One place Lear could see and draw was Mount Ida, the birth-place of Zeus, and as they crossed from the northern coast the island seemed to brighten. 'Lovely leafy thickets & glens! Birds! birds! birds! ... The vast multitude of blackbirds, nightingales, & many other sorts of birds is wonderful & most delightful, as is this mountain scene: sitting below oaks————, – a cornfield sloping down to the stream & to the thick groves of walnut & cherry: – above these, opposite to where I lie, rises a steep hill, slanting off into a summit of rox, but the sides are covered with plane, walnut, olive & oak, – cornfields, – & here & there rocks, & a few cypresses. Far off, the cawing of rooks – which brings back days – "days that are no more" – so long gone as those in 1823 – when I first heard the voice of rooks in Sussex. – o life! – o earth! – o time! – on whose last steps –'[11]

He made the drawings of Mount Ida and watched the antics of the mountain goats, and at the end of May he left for England.

One of the first people he went to see was Gussie Bethell. 'There is but one Gussie so one need not comment,'[12] he wrote in his diary, and thoughts of her wandered unhurried through his mind. More pressing was the decision about a house. Now that his things were on their way back from Corfu he had to decide between taking bigger rooms at Stratford Place or putting everything, including the large oil paintings, into store whilst he concentrated on finding a permanent winter home. The paint-ings were still unsold, though Lear was certain of their value, and he decided to take the larger rooms on a three-year lease. He would exhibit the 'Cedars' and the 'Masada' in them during the winter whilst he was abroad, and use them as a gallery in the summer to show his winter's work.

He thought of trying the Pyrenees or Gibraltar for the winter, or possibly southern France and the Corniche. In the end he

chose the Riviera, and at the beginning of November he left
England.

Prices in France were very high, and the rooms he found in Nice
were horribly expensive. Accommodation was always a problem
for Lear, for if he was in the wrong place the right people did not
come to look at his paintings.

He settled to work at once. The previous winter he had
produced sixty water-colour drawings – this time he was going to
do 240. He laid out paper in batches of eighty at a time. It was a
strange way to work: '. . . the constant change of subject, & the
inability – according to this system, – to work out any improvement or feeling, worries & drives me wild,'[13] he wrote in his
diary. For a month he drummed through this soulless task, then
he and Giorgio set out to walk along the coast to Genoa.

It was bitterly cold, and on the whole he was disappointed with
what he saw – 'Obscure torrents, & unpleasant villages: roaring
sea: – but no peacock hue bays nor any other pleasure.'[14] They
walked between sixteen and twenty miles a day, and were back in
Nice again on New Year's Eve. Despite the wintry weather and
the disappointing scenery he had 144 drawings.

Before returning to the Tyrants for his summer exhibition he
made a collection of 'slight small 5 pound pot-boilers'[15] of local
views to sell in Nice, and soon the local 'swells' began to crowd
into his room. 'At 12 or 1 – came Ld. & Ly. Fitzwilliam, in the
simplest kindest way, wanting 6 more drawings, & to give me a
cheque for £100,' he wrote in his diary of 11 February, 'Dear old
Mrs Wentworth of Woolley would have rejoiced.'[16] It was
strange that he should have mentioned Mrs Wentworth at this
point. She had helped him at the very beginning of his career,
and now he was beginning again but on something quite different, for in February 1865 he wrote the first of his Nonsense
stories, 'The History of Seven Families of the Lake Pipple-
popple,' and presented it to Lady Fitzwilliam's little son.

He found old friends wintering in Nice. Helena Cortazzi was
there, but that particular flame, which had never burnt very high,
had quite gone out. More exciting was Gussie Bethell, who
travelled through with her sister on their way to Rome, 'to my
delight, who with them walked & drove about thro' all the live-
long day'.[17]

But though there were many English, theirs was not the kind
of society he liked. '. . . the sun blazes away all day blue sky &
blue sea, red roses, green pease & all sorts of southern luxuries,'

he told Mrs Bruce. 'But as a set off, the atmosphere of swelldom & total idleness of this place is odious ... Society here, is gregarious not social.'[18] 'Lord! how I hate the bustle & lights & fuss of "society" – social in reality as is my nature – not gregarious. Geese, swine, gnats, &c are gregarious.'[19]

On the whole he had few interruptions in the task he had set himself, but he sometimes grew despondent. '... my pictures never can be perfect,' he wrote to Holman Hunt, 'it is not their nature: they are born with one leg shorter than t'other, or one side of their nose crooked – & so they must die. I sometimes wish I were able to study more & so produce more nature=like work: but the whole groove & tenor of my life is against that, & it is perhaps better to aim at exclusive Topographical representation, of a better order than has hitherto been called such, than at producing fewer paintings of a more perfect class.'[20]

In April he returned to London, where he spent the first few weeks completing the Tyrants. 'Unpacking & arranging has been a long & hardish work, & now there is the fitting – framing – finishing of the Drawings I have brought over, which are wonderful in number even for your humble servant.'[21] '... if I am not repaid for the great outlay of rooms – fittings up – frames – wintering abroad with double rent – &c. &c. – I think I shall collapse in the Autumn, & go & live at Pâra on the Amazon. There ... are abundance of fat caterpillars highly edible & refreshing – & thus life for its few remaining years, would be cheaply sustained.'[22]

When the exhibition opened the drawings sold quickly. At one point Lady Ashburton considered buying the 'Cedars', but then she decided that after all they were too expensive, 'wh. she might methinx have known earlier',[23] grunted Lear. He was given a commission for a painting of Jerusalem, and the Prince of Wales came again, this time buying ten drawings. But London gallery life depressed him, and he told Emily Tennyson, '... even if I get enough tin to cover all expenses, the method of doing so is so harrassing & odious – seeing the vapid nature of swells, & the great amount of writing, & the close confinement to the house, – that I loathe London by the time I have been here a month. The walking – sketching – exploring – noveltyperceiving & beauty-appreciating part of the Landscape painter's life is undoubtedly to be envied: – but then the contrast of the moneytryingtoget, smoky dark London life – fuss – trouble & bustle is wholly odious, & every year more so.'[24]

In July he went to stay with the Westburys. Gussie was home from Italy, and he seriously began to wonder if he should ask her to marry him. 'Poor Gussie! – but how to decide? if her life is sad, – united to mine would it be less so? or rather – would it not be more so? . . . The risk of trying the marriage – the marriage itself so gt a risk of making 2 people more unhappy than before?'[25] He left the next day, still wondering. 'Poor dear little Gussie. I know not what to do?'[26]

Holman Hunt, the last of his close friends still unmarried, became engaged in August, and in September Lear was again at the Bethells. 'Gussie – poor dear – played the "Cloches du Monastéri" & for a moment one's heart returned. But no. It would not do. Better suffer alone, than cause sufferings in others.'[27] And so it seemed that his brief thoughts of marriage were over, and when Lady Waldegrave commissioned him to do a painting in Venice, he decided to begin the winter in Italy.

Venice was foggy, but as it cleared he was excited by the magnificent architecture and the splendid sunsets. Lady Waldegrave had left the choice of subject to him, and he gondoled slowly up and down the canals trying to decide what to draw, but 'thickphoggs' kept coming down making it impossible to see. In the end he chose a canal scene, though he found in it none of 'the poetry of plains or mountains – or woods – or rocks, Man=work – not God work.'[28]

Whilst he was there he picked up *The Times* at breakfast one morning, and saw that Fortescue had been appointed Irish Secretary, a post which gave him a seat on the Cabinet: '. . . being of an undiplomatic & demonstrative nature in matters that give me pleasure, I threw the paper up into the air & jumped aloft myself – ending by taking a small fried whiting out of the plate before me & waving it round my foolish head triumphantly till the tail came off & the body and head flew bounce over to the other side of the table d'hôte room. Then only did I perceive that I was not alone, but that a party was at Bkft in a recess. Happily for me they were not English, & when I made an apology saying I had suddenly seen some good news of a friend of mine – these amiable Italians said – "*Bravissimo Signore! ci rallegriamo anche noi! se avessimo anche noi piccoli pesce li butteremmo di quâ e lâ per la camera in simpatia con voi!*"* – So we ended by all screaming with laughter.'[29]

* Hurrah, Signore, we also are delighted. If we had only got some little fish, too, we would throw them all about the room in sympathy with you.

When he had finished the drawings he decided to go on to Malta. Sir Henry Storks, who had been High Commissioner of the Ionian Islands, was now Commander in Chief in Malta, and Evelyn Baring had gone with him as one of his aides, so there were friends already there. If he liked it he might make it his permanent winter home.

But when he arrived he discovered that Sir Henry Storks had just left, with Baring, to preside over a commission of enquiry in Jamaica. The only suitable house he could find was across the bay from Valetta and three miles by road from the town and, as he remembered, there was practically no scenery on the island. He drew whatever he could find, 'more because I happened to be there, & some work had to be done – than for any good it is likely to do me'.[30] The only good part of the winter was a trip with Giorgio to the island of Gozo, where the 'Coast scenery may truly be called pomskizillious & gromphibberous, being as no words can describe its magnificence.'[31]

In the three months he was there he sold only £25 worth of work, but this may have been because he was thoroughly cross and grumpy with the visitors who came to see his studio. 'The Anglo Maltese intelligence does not seem ever to have heard that Artists require particular light aspect, quiet, &c.: & because I cannot have some 3 or 4 hundred visitors lounging in my rooms – I am dubbed a mystery & a savage: – tho' the very same people can understand that they could not go to a Lawyer's or Physician's rooms to take up his hours gratis. Were I to ask a Military Cove, if this climate on account of its dryness required him always to pour water down his gun before firing it, – or a Naval one if he weighed anchor before he sailed or a week afterwards, – I should be laughed at as a fool: yet many not much less silly questions are asked me. No creature has as yet asked for even a 5£ drawing, though 28 amateurs have volunteered to shew me their sketches – nor have I sold even one of my few remaining Corfu books. My rooms though spacious are painted, one blue – one orange – one green – so that my sight is getting really injured as to color, just as if a musical composer should have to work in the midst of hundreds of out of tune instruments.'[32]

It had been a lonely winter, 'for though by nature hating crowds & hustle=gaiety, yet some social sympathy is necessary & one don't get any'.[33] He left Malta in April. The boat taking him to Trieste via Dalmatia and Montenegro, where he spent a few days exploring, stopped on the way in Corfu. The island made an overwhelming impact on him. 'The beauty of this place would strike a savage: how much more *me*, & me fresh from Malta! !' he wrote in his diary. 'As I lie now, green & flowers everywhere, – this is Lotuseating with a vengeance! – 2 P.M. Lovelier ever! a regular intoxication of beauty! Walked up towards the hill church, & down, down, where terraces of close green sward with large patches of bright yell: gr: fern, & sheets of blooming rosy & white asters spread away. Myrtle also. Over head ever the loved olive: far below "bowery hollows" of green – ever & ever retreating: spotless blue above: glimpses of darker blue sea, & pearly radiant mountain through the transparent foliage. No wonder the Olive is undrawn – unknown: so inaccessible=poetical=difficult are its belongings. So bright & glorious is all I now see & feel, it seems to overpay any outlay of pain – time – money! Can I give *no* idea of this Paradise island to others? Would Gussie like to live here?'[34]

15 A Proposal of Marriage?
1866–1867

His first thought when he reached England was of Gussie. On the day after his arrival he called on the Westburys, but she was out. A few days later he dined there '& passed a pleasant evening. Pleasant did I say? – This – the last dream – to burst in a bubble or flourish into a reality – is indeed a strange matter.'[1] Three days later he was there again:

> 'Like a sudden spark
> Struck vainly in the night –
> & *Back returns the dark*
> With no more hope of light.

Alas. The building seems to fade away & the dream to flit.'[2]

But the next day he wrote, 'the "marriage" phantasy "will not let me be" – yet seems an intangible myth. To think of it no more, is to resolve on all the rest of life being passed thus – alone – & year by year getting more weary: – to encourage it, is to pursue a thread leading to doubt & perhaps more positive misery . . .'[3]

He simply could not make up his mind. He longed for companionship, and she was so unlike most women he knew, for she was kind and gentle – 'poor little Gussie' he called her – and was far happier sitting and talking than rushing into society. But for Lear it was not easy. She might refuse him which would be distressing, or accept him which could be worse, for he would have to tell her about his epilepsy – and then she might change her mind.

> 'Lady Jingly! Lady Jingly!
>   'Sitting where the pumpkins blow,
>   'Will you come and be my wife?' –
>   Said the Yonghy-Bonghy-Bò.
> 'I am tired of living singly, –
> 'On this coast so wild and shingly, –

   'I'm a-weary of my life;
   'If you'll come and be my wife,
   'Quite serene would be my life!' –
Said the Yonghy-Bonghy-Bò,
Said the Yonghy-Bonghy-Bò.[4]

He went to see Lady Waldegrave to ask what he should do, and she warned him that as Gussie had no money it would be too much of an extra burden for him. He became anxious and depressed, and developed nervous symptoms of neuralgia and an itching skin. Her sister, Emma Parkyns, made it quite plain that she favoured the match. 'Emma's wishes & thoughts are not difficult to divine,' Lear wrote in his diary in August, 'but again I say, it would not do.'[5] She called sometimes at Lear's studio, but he was not always 'at home', 'for, much as I like her – I dread the reopening of the Gussie question'.[6] If he could not propose to Gussie then he did not want to come back to England again. There was still a year to go on his Stratford Place lease, but he had had an offer from Maclean's Gallery to exhibit his work there. He could accept this, close Stratford Place, and wander away.

   He did not let himself sit and think. As usual he had more dinner invitations than he could possibly accept. 'I believe if I were the last man – someone would be created to ask me to dinner,'[7] he wrote, somewhat ingenuously, to Gussie.

'Depressed & weary, so talked much & foolishly to hide the fax,'[8] he wrote after one such dinner. During the day he worked through 250 new Tyrants for Maclean's to exhibit during the winter, then he went on to finish more limericks which he offered again to Routledge. At first they did not want them, but then they changed their minds, though in fact they were never used. Really Lear had satisfied the public with his old favourites, and the book of limericks, which he published as *More Nonsense* in 1871, was never as popular as *A Book of Nonsense* had been. Routledge were constantly reprinting this earlier book and one afternoon in October, when Lear went by train to see Husey Hunt in Lewes, he shared a compartment with a globular gentleman and two ladies with some children who were reading *A Book of Nonsense*. The gentleman explained '"that thousands of families were grateful to the author – (which in silence I agreed to) who was not generally known – but was really Lord Derby. – And now came a showing forth, which cleared up at once to my mind why that statement had already appeared in several papers. Edward Earl of Derby (said the Gent[n]) did not choose to publish the book openly – but dedicated it as you see to his relations, – & now if you will transpose the letters LEAR – you will read simply EDWARD EARL." – Says I, joining spontanious in the conversation – "that is quite a mistake: I have reason to know that Edward Lear the painter & Author wrote & illustrated the whole book." –"And I" – says the Gent[n] says he – "have good reason to know Sir that you are wholly mistaken. *There is no such a person* as Edward Lear," "But – " says I – "there IS – & I am the man – & I wrote the book!" Whereon all the party burst out laughing – & evidently thought me mad or telling fibs. So I took off my hat & showed it all round – with Edward Lear & the address in large letters – also one of my cards – & a marked handkerchief: on which amazement devoured those benighted individuals & I left them to gnash their teeth in trouble & tumult.'[9]

He had already accepted Maclean's offer to exhibit his work that winter and had finished the 250 Tyrants for them to show, but now Husey Hunt persuaded him that he should come back and try one more summer in England in case he could still sell the large paintings. He had decided, however, to reduce their prices, bringing the Cedars from 700 guineas to 500, the Masada from 500 to 300, and the Beirut from 300 to 200. He wrote to Drummond, who had expressed some pleasure in the Beirut, telling him of his decision, reminding him of his interest, and suggesting that he might like to buy it in instalments.

Drummond bought the painting, but such an overture was a mistake and the beginning of the somewhat shameless approach that Lear developed towards his patrons in his later years.

Now, with the money from the sale of his water-colours, he had enough to make his long-delayed return trip to Egypt and Palestine. 'I have never been so utterly weary of 6 months as of these last,' he wrote to Fortescue, 'never seeing anything but the dreadful brick houses – & latterly suffering from cold, smoke – darkness – ach! horror! – verily England may be a blessed place for the wealthy – but an accursed dwelling for those who have known liberty & have seen God's daylight daily in other countries. – By degrees however, (if I dont leave it by the sudden collapse of mortality –) I hope to quit it altogether, even if I turn Musselman & settle at Timbuctoo.'[10]

He left England at the beginning of December 1866, just too soon to be cheered by a notice reviewing the seventeenth edition of *A Book of Nonsense* which was out in time for Christmas: 'Never was a book published that so exactly hit the child's mind as this one,' it read, 'the fine artist that produced it, is without doubt prouder of the joy these sketches and nonsense rhymes have given to a million children, than of the powerful pictures with which he has delighted the artistic world.'[11]

It had been nearly thirteen years since Lear had left Egypt. 'It seems a dream that I am about to see the blinding brightness of the south once more!'[12] he wrote as the boat neared Alexandria.

As soon as he reached Cairo he began to enquire about the cost of boats to take him up the Nile. This time he wanted to go through the Nubian desert to the second cataract, but it was a long way and the cheapest price he was quoted was nearly £400. He did not have so much money at the moment, but he knew that if he did not go now each year would just add to the price. There were two hundred and fifty of his water colours on exhibition at Maclean's, so he should be earning money in London whilst he was away: he would risk borrowing now, and hope to repay it when he got back to England. So he sat down and wrote to eight of his friends asking each of them for a loan of £100. 'Verily I am an odd bird,'[13] he thought. On his return to England the money was repaid promptly, but – as with the approach to Drummond – it was a mistake, summed up by Lord Derby. 'He works hard, sells well, yet seems always in difficulties,'[14] he wrote. '... in the world, where nothing succeeds like success, he has done himself much harm by his perpetual neediness. An artist who is always asking his friends to buy a picture, & often to pay for it in advance, makes outsiders believe that he cannot know his business: which in Lear's case is certainly far from the truth. But he has been out at elbows all his life, & so will remain to the last.'[15]

Certainly Lear was unwise, and he cannot have been unaware of this himself. Yet he saw that the influence of fashion in painting was such that, whilst one painter might be swept to the top, others of no less talent could scarcely begin. He was exploiting friendship, but only partially, for he knew that his work was worth considerably more than anyone paid for it.

His problem was two-fold. Part of it was that, by choosing to be a painter of faraway places, he involved himself in substantial expenses which did not always see a proper return. Secondly, he lacked initial capital. Almost all his paintings were paid for after completion – sometimes distressingly long after completion. If he had spent less on travel, both on journeying abroad and on his coming to and from England, he might have got ahead of his expenses. Instead, he chose to use the money he earned in seeing more places and gathering more material from which to work – in some ways a happy decision, but with its inevitable outcome.

Giorgio joined him in Cairo, and they spent a few days looking round the city. 'O! dear! what wonderful street scenes – & scenes of all sorts!' he wrote in his diary. 'And to me what wonders of broad beautiful green & lilac vegetation & far hills & mosques – seen thro' & beyond gt palms & acacias! O sugar canes! O camels! O Egypt!'[16]

This time they did not drop anchor at night, for they had much further to go and Lear had already seen the lower Nile. He had arranged to stop at Luxor to pick up a cousin from Canada called Archie Jones, who was touring Europe and the Mediterranean. Lear had not yet met him, but he was glad to have some companionship on such a long, tedious journey.

Again he was amazed by the Nile scenery. Each morning he rose early and watched the dawn come up. As the sun broke over the horizon the shadows of the palms stretched across the sand in exaggerated leanness, and the moving leaves touched by the morning sun glittered against the darkness of the shadows like slivers of beaten silver. The colours of the day were superb, and when he saw the places that he had drawn so often in the last thirteen years he realised that his work was too red, or not richly grey enough, or just simply dull. The whole scene was vast in its atmosphere of disappeared greatness. 'The intense deadness of old Egypt is felt as a weight of knowledge in all that world of utter silence – looking down on the great green valley with its modern life beyond,' he wrote. 'The Myriad bees are the only living world here, & where one peeps into those dark death-silent giant halls of columns – a terror pervades the heart & head.'[17]

But there were hundreds of birds, and they were very alive. 'O queer community of birds! On a long sand spit are 4 black storks – one legged: apart. – 8 pelicans – careless foolish. 17 Small ducks, cohesive. 23 Herons – watchful variously posed: & 2 or 3 flocks of lovely ivory ibis – (or Paddybirds –) flying all about.'[18] Sometimes they were busily absorbed: 'Here & there are bits of desert sand with a few palms, & some of the poisonous euphorbia. A few geese & ducks now & then in the still water – with ever a long necked Heron peering to keep watch, & informing the more busy ducks, who perhaps pay him in fishes for his assistance in saving their lives.'[19]

> We live on the Nile. The Nile we love.
> By night we sleep on the cliffs above;
> By day we fish, and at eve we stand
> On long bare islands of yellow sand.
> And when the sun sinks slowly down
> And the great rock walls grow dark and brown,
> Where the purple river rolls fast and dim
> And the ivory Ibis starlike skim,
> Wing to wing we dance around, –
> Stamping our feet with a flumpy sound, –
> Opening our mouths as Pelicans ought,
> And this is the song we nightly snort: –
> >Ploffskin, Pluffskin, Pelican jee, –
> >We think no Birds so happy as we!
> >Plumpskin, Ploshkin, Pelican jill, –
> >We think so then, and we thought so still.[20]

Cousin Archie came aboard at Luxor, and they went on to Esneh and Edfu and then to Philae, 'more beautiful than ever'[21]. Archie finished Philae in three hours, which Lear found sorrowfully unbelievable. In fact he was finding his company rather a strain. 'Cousin Archie, who prefers going to "Bazari" to walking, or looking at the scenery, & who I begin to find is "vague" – buys continually new objects.'[22] This, however, gave Archie something to do, for 'Archie takes (happily) to putting labels on all his

purchases, wh. keeps him employed'.[23] He rushed in and out of temples declaring that they had 'an affle bad smell',[24] and in the evening he sat on deck and whistled, beating out the rhythm with his finger-tips. 'I often feel – any amount of loneliness is necessary at times,'[25] Lear wrote sadly in his diary.

They went on south to Wadi Halfa, a place of desolate loneliness with long lines of hills and great expanses of sand. The Nubian desert was a complete contrast to the green-fringed Nile of Egypt. Here there was 'Sad, stern, uncompromising landscape – dark ashypurple lines of hills – piles of granite rocks – fringes of palm – & ever and anon astonishing ruins of oldest Temples'.[26] Life seemed 'a casual gift, not a necessity of the district'.[27]

From Wadi Halfa they turned north again, and on 8 February they came upon the magnificence of Abou Simbel. 'I was absolutely too astonished & affected to draw – so I lost my sketch & must go back for it. Happy I am to feel that I nearly cried with a burst of amazement & delight – even after all I had seen & heard & read of these statues';[28] '. . . all other visible things in this world seem to me to be as chips, or potatoparings, or any nonsense in comparison.'[29]

Cousin Archie left them near Luxor, and on 8 March 1867 Lear and Giorgio were in Cairo. They made a short trip to Sakkara and Memphis, and with this Lear's Egyptian work was done.

Now he turned his thoughts again to Palestine. His plan was to cross the desert to Gaza and go inland to Jerusalem, then travel north to Galilee. In Cairo he took on a dragoman called Abdul, and on 22 March they set off on camels across the desert. 'Some things in this world *are* NOT pleasant,' he wrote philosophically in his diary, three days later: 'to wit beetles in your hair, – the odoriferous nature of respected domestics, fleas: and the gulpyroarygroanery of camels.'[30] These were not the only things, for he soon discovered that Abdul had brought only one tent, no curry powder, and not nearly enough warm blankets.

He was glad to reach the sudden greenness of Gaza, and at Askalon they turned east to Jerusalem. It was now mid-April and Lear had been travelling since the beginning of December. 'I don't feel up to much of it – mentally & physically,'[31] he wrote in his diary. He thought Jerusalem more exquisitely beautiful than ever, though two days later he felt exhausted and low again. But he had missed Nazareth and Galilee before, and he must get there this time. On 15 April they left Jerusalem for the north and as they came to Bethany they saw that the road ahead was crammed with pilgrims coming up to Jerusalem for Easter. Suddenly he knew that he could go no further. Once again Nazareth and Galilee would have to wait. By nightfall he was back in Jerusalem and by noon on the 20th they were in Alexandria.

It was too early in the year to go to England so they went by boat to Brindisi, and for a month wandered quietly along the coast. They saw the Forest of Ravenna where Byron had lived, then travelled to Rimini before turning back to the Lombardy Lakes. At the beginning of June Giorgio left for Corfu, and Lear returned to England.

Of course the large painting had not sold, and he told Fortescue: '. . . sometimes I consider as to the wit of taking my Cedars out of its frame & putting round it a border of rose colored velvet, – embellished with a fringe of yellow worsted with black spots, to protypify the possible proximate propinquity of predatorial panthers, – & then selling the whole for floorcloth by auction.'[32]

He was able to repay most of his debts within a few weeks, and with each £100 he sent a small picture by way of thanks. It was a sad summer, as they all were now, for each year he had less and less contact with his old friends, and he must sometimes have been depressing company. At Strawberry Hill Fortescue asked him to sing, but he refused, '& was disgusted at their tiresome upper 10000 ways'.[33] He found no more happiness in his visit to the Tennysons; the Laureate's poetry seemed to be a repetition of the old, and he loathed the brutal and snubbing way in which he treated Lionel and Hallam. He went to Lord Northbrook's home at Stratton, but he wrote in his diary: 'Vainly, vainly I strive to keep merry & lively: it is *not* always possible.'[34]

'. . . the recollection of past days – & the worry about the few to come – all conspire to depress me horridly. Happily I can bear up against this better than of old – yet it is hard work.

'Yet when I look back on life – even from my 5th year, I know step by step how all has occurred – & knowing (what I alone know,) it seems to me wonderful that I have gone on thus far as well as I have!'[35]

The only spark in his gloomy blackness was Gussie. He had seen very little of her that summer, but in October he received a letter from her which gave him a sudden new hope. Within a week his mind was made up. He would go to the Westburys and he would propose to her – at least he would go to the Westburys and then he could decide.

He packed two trunkloads of clothes for he did not know how long he might stay. 'It is absurd to think that at 54 years old I am within a point of doing what will fix the rest of my life – be it short or long – in one groove – good or bad,' he wrote in his diary before he left. 'I do not say I am decided to take this leap in the dark, but I say that I am nearer to doing so than I ever was before.'[36]

It was Saturday evening when he arrived at the Lord Chancellor's house. Lear tells us that he had decided to talk to Gussie's sister, Emma, before he spoke to Gussie herself. On Sunday morning he saw her alone. We do not know what was said, but by the end of the interview all his hopes were crushed. 'Yet after what she said a year ago – her "certainty that now A & I could not live together happily" – seems strange. Anyhow – *it broke up a dream* rudely & sadly.'[37]

One wonders whether Lear did in fact raise the question directly with Emma, or whether he was able to discern her wishes and realise that he was safe. Certainly, he committed himself to his diary most dramatically, but later statements about his wish to marry Gussie were more imagined than real. If he had been a free man, able to marry, then Gussie would have been an ideal wife. But he was not. As he saw it, the barrier of his epilepsy was total. Had he proposed and been accepted, it would have been a secret he would have to have shared with her, and possibly even with her family. This was unthinkable.

Certainly, Lear would have liked to have married, to have had children of his own instead of the world's children. 'I went as far as their door,' he wrote of some visitors in 1879, 'wishing, as I left them that I had sons or daughters. But it was decreed I was not to be human . . .'[38] But there would have been too much possibility of new suffering, of his children going through the terrors that he himself had gone through. In fact, the whole human situation was so sad that perhaps it was cruel to have children at all. 'I have come to the conclusion,' he wrote once to Emily Tennyson, 'that nobody ought to marry at all, & that no more people ought ever to be born, & so we should be gradually extinguified, & the world would be left to triumphant chimpanzees, gorillas, cockroaches & crocodiles . . .'[39]

Then there was the terrible possibility that another woman might leave him one day as his mother had once done. As far back as 1851 he had told Fortescue: '. . . there is nothing of which I have so distinct a recollection as the fearful gnawing sensation which chills & destroys one, on leaving scenes & persons for which & whom there are no substitutes till their memory is a bit worn down. I say – "there is nothing I so distinctly remember" – because those feelings are with me already taking the form of past matters – never again to recur like cutting ones teeth – measles &c. – Not that one has actually *outlived* the possibility of their repetition – but rather, I *prevent* them by keeping them at arm's length: – I *won't* like anybody else, if I can help it – I mean, any new persons – or scenes – or places – all the rest of my short foolish life.'[40] He had not lived up to his resolution, and because of this he had to suffer all the unhappiness of his love for Lushington. 'Accept a lonely destiny – ordained perhaps – or the clear result of causes – & make the best of it,'[41] he wrote resignedly in his diary.

He did not leave at once, in fact he stayed until the following Thursday. The day before he left he sat down and wrote a story for Gussie's niece and nephews. 'Once upon a time; a long while ago, there were four little people whose names were Violet, Slingsby, Guy and Lionel; and they all thought they should like to see the world . . .'[42]

On 26 November 1867 he left England for the South of France.

Down the slippery slopes of Myrtle,
Where the early pumpkins blow,
  To the calm and silent sea
Fled the Yonghy-Bonghy-Bò.
There, beyond the Bay of Gurtle,
Lay a large and lively Turtle; –
  'You're the Cove,' he said, 'for me;
  'On your back beyond the sea,
  'Turtle, you shall carry me!'
Said the Yonghy-Bonghy-Bò,
Said the Yonghy-Bonghy-Bò.[43]

16 The Greatest Nonsense
1867

He went to Cannes this time, and found a suite of rooms over-looking the bay with 'sun=aspect for health – light to work, & position &c. for swells to come to'.[1] The air there was un-pleasantly cold, 'simply cayenne pepper frozen',[2] and for a month nobody bought anything.

But he found a kindred spirit with whom he could talk. John Addington Symonds, later the author of a seven-volume history of the Italian Renaissance, was there with his wife Catherine, daughter of Lear's old friend Frederick North of Hastings, and they sat together discussing Byron and Shelley and the modern writers, Swinburne and Walt Whitman. Although in many ways quite unalike, Lear and Symonds had much in common. Both had been separated from their mothers at the age of four and had been brought up in predominantly female households; they were often ill as children and carried psychosomatic illnesses into adult life; each was inclined to self-dramatisation and craved affection; both sank into periods of abysmal depression; and they were both homosexual, though as Lear never seems to have discussed this aspect of himself with anyone, and Symonds at this time was desperately trying to suppress his longings, it is unlikely that they ever touched on the subject when they were together. They certainly grumbled together though, and this Lear found most satisfying.

EDWARDUS: What makes you look so black, so glum, so cross?
      Is it neuralgia, headache, or remorse?

JOHANNES:: What makes you look as cross, or even more so?
      Less like a man than is a broken Torso?
           *

EDWARDUS: Why did I leave my native land, to find
      Sharp hailstones, snow, and most disgusting wind?

JOHANNES: What boots it that we orange trees or lemons see,
      If we must suffer from *such* vile inclemency?

EDWARDUS: Why did I take the lodgings I have got,
Where all I don't want is: – all I want not?[3]

The Symondses' small daughter, Janet, was ill in bed, and just before Christmas Lear went up to see her, taking with him a picture poem to make her feel happier. It was 'The Owl and the Pussy-cat' – the first of his nonsense songs.

In his limericks, Lear had travelled to the off-shore islands of the Nonsense world. With his songs, he reached the mainland where the horizons were wide and clear. In his early work he was concerned with the restraints imposed by society: later, he added those laid down by life itself. 'There's something in the world amiss will be unravelled bye and bye,' he would quote in his diary. In his case, epilepsy set him apart as an isolated oddity. 'Alas! Alas!' he wrote in the last year of his life, 'how fearful a birthright was mine! I wonder if others suffer similarly? Yet I dare not ask or endeavour to know.'[4] He sought, through his writing, an escape from its burdens.

In his songs, such anomalies might cause embarrassment: they could also be the source of real suffering. In 'The Pelican Chorus', the apparent deformity suffered by the King of the Cranes is politely ignored. With 'The Daddy Long-legs and the Fly', however, it is all more serious and distressing. Each to the other seems so fine and composed, and yet . . . 'Why,' asks Mr Daddy Long-legs, 'do you never come to court?'

'O Mr Daddy Long-legs,'
    Said Mr Floppy Fly,
'It's true I never go to court,
    And I will tell you why.

> If I had six long legs like yours,
>   At once I'd go to court!
> But oh! I can't, because *my* legs
>   Are so extremely short.
> And I'm afraid the King and Queen
> (One in red, and one in green)
> Would say aloud, "You are not fit,
> You Fly, to come to court a bit!"'

But Mr Daddy Long-legs also has his secret sadness. He, who once sang so beautifully, can no longer do so:

> 'For years I cannot hum a bit,
>   Or sing the smallest song;
> And this the dreadful reason is,
>   My legs are grown too long!
> My six long legs, all here and there,
> Oppress my bosom with despair;
> And if I stand, or lie, or sit,
> I cannot sing one single bit!'

Yet there is a remedy. They can escape to a land where none of this will matter any more.

> Then Mr Daddy Long-legs
>   And Mr Floppy Fly
> Rushed downward to the foaming sea
>   With one sponge-taneous cry;
> And there they found a little boat,
>   Whole sails were pink and gray;
> And off they sailed among the waves,
>   Far, and far away.
> They sailed across the silent main,
> And reached the great Gromboolian plain;
> And there they play for evermore
> At battlecock and shuttledoor.

This is where Lear takes his children. Together they had hopped on one leg down the great gallery: now they set out on a long and possibly difficult journey. You must have courage to go to sea in a sieve, or indeed to sail away for a year and a day, but such courage will be rewarded. Narrowness of outlook – whether imposed by false conventions, by the distortions of a dogmatic rather than a loving Christianity, or by the pursuit of other people's spiritual and physical perfection – robs man of his humanity, with all its oddities and faults. But you can leave such narrowness behind, for the faint-hearted will not follow here. When the Jumblies returned home

> . . . everyone said, 'If we only live,
> We too will go to sea in a Sieve, –
> To the hills of the Chankly Bore!'

but we know perfectly well that they will not.

Lear's quest – paradoxically perhaps for a Nonsense writer – was for reality: people and things must be seen and accepted as they are, and not as they ought to be. The essentials of life were to be found in tolerance, affection and liveliness. He saw these attributes most frequently in children, although he found them also in his real friends. Indeed, though Lear spoke of his child songs, he was not only writing for children: anyone who has known loneliness and isolation might understand what he is saying.

Of course, you may discover when you reach the sunset isles of Boshen that you have moved from loneliness into loneliness. Neither the Yonghy-Bonghy-Bò nor the Dong redeem their isolation: there are sadnesses which can never be overcome, and which may indeed grow more acute. But, in the end, it is all a game, perhaps of battlecock and shuttledoor, certainly of words and of the imagination, and this is what gives it its safety. 'There only remains a general, but very strong, pervading sense of wellbeing and innate rectitude from the standpoint of eight years old,' a child friend said of Lear. 'I knew he was "safe" and that I was safe and that we were all safe together, and that suspicion might at once be put aside.'[5] In a potentially alien world, Lear made children feel secure. You may sense that you are strange and different, there may be things which set you apart, but in an imaginary world where people have unlikely noses and legs and the strangest modes of expression, where they seek out oddities with whom they can identify, and where they yet find kindness and spontaneity, you are never likely to feel alone.

Nonsense is a universe of words. Lear was unusually aware of the sounds words make and he would analyse them phonetically. He was regarded by his friends as a dreadful punster and he enjoyed making up riddles. 'What's the difference between the Czar & the *Times* paper? – One is the type of Despotism & the other the Despotism of Type.'[6] With his strong musical sense he would mull over words and phrases that he heard, so that Díghi Dóghi Dà reappears twenty years later as the Yonghy-Bonghy-Bò, and Mr & Mrs Discobbolos are named after the Grecian sculpture – a cast of which still stands in the Royal Academy Schools. He would use words incongruously as in 'The Cummerbund', and he liked rounded words like promiscuous and pusillanimous which he used out of their place as meaningless, musical adjectives. And of course he invented words, like runcible, because he liked the sound they made: he had a runcible goose and a runcible wall, a runcible spoon and a runcible hat, a runcible raven and even a runcible state of mind.

When Lear was first writing there was no such thing as an established literary genre of Nonsense.[7] To him the word meant something happy and inconsequential, but he and Carroll both altered that meaning. Even now it is difficult to define succinctly, and any definition needs qualifying clauses: perhaps it could be said that incongruity of characters, situations, or words, plus a predictable, stable element such as numbers, choruses, alliteration, or, paradoxically, an insistence on the correct use of words, equals Nonsense. Without this unifying element it tends towards dream: with it, it is more logical, for Nonsense is a game played by a rational, methodical mind. Carroll was a professional mathematician, and though Lear was not trained in logic his mind was 'concrete and fastidious'.[8]

One of the characteristics of pure Nonsense is detachment – neither the writer nor the reader is to be involved with the characters. To establish this Lear showed quite clearly by his drawings that the hero, even when human, is not for a moment to be treated seriously, and he created imaginary characters like the Quangle Wangle and the Pobble. Once this detachment has been established it is quite acceptable and not at all distressing to find a man being baked in an oven or coiled up like a length of elastic. In the same way Nonsense characters can have alarming physical defects, and Lear returns often to the feature of himself that most bothered him – the size of his nose. There are people with noses which reach to the ground, noses which finish in tassels, noses like trumpets and noses which simply disappear out of sight, and the Dong gathered the bark of the Twangum tree and 'he wove him a wondrous nose'. But though in the limericks, which are pure Nonsense, violence and distortion leave us unmoved, in the Nonsense songs they begin to disturb, for the detachment is no longer complete.

Lear's Nonsense falls into three overlapping groups. The first comes under the original classification of the happy and inconsequential. Here are the parody, the limericks, the botany, the cookery, the alphabets and the Nonsense he put into letters to amuse his friends. Humour is found in this group, but in the other two it gradually diminishes.

In the second group are stories, in both prose and verse, nearly always of wandering and travel, and either with happy endings – 'The Owl and the Pussy-cat', 'The Duck and the Kangaroo' – or with sad endings which do not worry us for they are pure Nonsense – 'The History of the Seven Families of the Lake Pipple-popple'. Between this and the third group the un-happiness becomes disturbing, for the detachment is beginning to break down. 'The Daddy Long-legs and the Fly'

> Sat down in silence by the sea,
>   And gazed upon the sky.
> They said, 'This is a dreadful thing!
>   The world has all gone wrong,
> Since one has legs too short by half,
>   The other much too long!'

By the time we have reached the third group the detachment has gone and we are moving from Nonsense into sad and moving poetry. Here are verses which express Lear's deep personal feelings, written no longer for children but for himself, songs like 'The Pelican Chorus':

> And far away in the twilight sky,
> We heard them singing a lessening cry, –
> Farther and farther till out of sight,
> And we stood alone in the silent night!
> Often since, in the nights of June,
> We sit on the sand and watch the moon; –
> She has gone to the great Gromboolian plain,
> And we probably never shall meet again!
> Oft, in the long still night of June,
> We sit on the rocks and watch the moon; –
> – She dwells by the streams of the Chankly Bore,
> And we probably never shall see her more.

The emphasis now is on looking back to a time of happiness that has gone for ever, as the creature wanders grief-stricken like Demeter in search of Persephone, seeking someone who in Lear's songs will never return. Lear scarcely mentions his parents in his diary, but it is impossible to believe that he did not think of them. His memory of that childhood evening with the clowns was poignantly vivid, as was the overwhelming nostalgia and sadness that settled on him afterwards. He dreamt of the happiness he could dimly remember, which had ended so suddenly when they went away, and he put this into his songs.

> Happily, happily passed those days!
>   While the cheerful Jumblies staid;
>   They danced in circlets all night long,
>   To the plaintive pipe of the lively Dong,
>   In moonlight, shine, or shade.
> For day and night he was always there
> By the side of the Jumbly Girl so fair,
> With her sky-blue hands, and her sea-green hair.
> Till the morning came of that hateful day
> When the Jumblies sailed in their sieve away,
> And the Dong was left on the cruel shore
> Gazing – gazing for evermore . . .

Only once did Lear see anything but sadness in a seashore, and that was at the end of 'The Owl and the Pussy-cat', when they danced by the light of the moon. 'We come no more to the golden shore where we danced in days of old,' he quoted to himself over and over again, but for Lear the days of dancing had been so short that they were nothing but the dimmest of memories, and the golden shore was a place where happiness ended and loneliness began.

In Cannes, nobody was buying his work. By Christmas he had used practically all his ready money. 'It is really absurd at 55 to be so utterly without prospects for the future,'[9] he wrote. But on Boxing Day he heard that Lady Ashburton had decided to buy the 'Cedars'. She wrote offering him £200, which was not even a third of its original price, but he was glad that at last the painting was sold, and he told Fortescue: '. . . they will be well placed, & thoroughly appreciated.'[10] This was important for Lear, partly because it might bring him work, but also because he cared about where his pictures were hung. 'I hate, when I have done any pictures, which, it is to be hoped, may confer more or less fun on their possessors, – to seem indifferent to them, like unto the ostrich which evacuateth her eggs, & leaveth them thenceforth.'[11] He spoke of them as his 'children', and they were something of himself.

With the sale of the 'Cedars' his luck seemed to turn. Within a few days he had begun to sell some water-colour drawings. The new year was beginning well.

17 Last Travel Book
1868–1869

'By degrees I want to topographise & typographise all the
journeyings of my life – so that I shall have been of some use
after all to my fellow critters – besides leaving them drawings &
pictures which they may sell when I'm dead,'[1] Lear told
Fortescue, and he spent the rest of the winter writing up his
journals of Crete and his two journeys down the Nile. By the end
of March these were finished, but although he now had eight
unpublished journals he decided to spend the spring in Corsica
gathering material for another book.

He left on 8 April 1868 and travelled with John Symonds and
his family who were going to Ajaccio. They arrived in the rain,
and all the people seemed to be wearing black. In fact the only
sign of colour was the French sailors' scarlet trousers, and their
brisk walk and busy chatter was a complete contrast to the dour
drabness of the Corsicans: '. . . this is truly the land of the *Helix
tristis*, the melancholy snail,'[2] he pondered sadly.

Instead of going on horseback or on foot, as he had always
done, Lear hired a two-horse carriage to take them swiftly round
the places he wanted to see. This was a way of travel he usually
deplored, for 'the quick passage of ordinary tourists is very different from my stopping, prying, lingering mode of travel.'[3] But
his excitement in exploring new scenery had been replaced by a
calculated decision to see and draw as much as he could as
quickly as possible – not a good beginning for a book.

Before he left Ajaccio the weather cleared, and as they
travelled south things improved even more. Birds and flowers
and mountains began appearing one after another, and though
the people were still dour they were 'thoroughly kindly &
obliging'.[4] This may have been partly because the coachman, a
bad-tempered man called Peter, was telling the villagers that
Lear was the Finance Minister of England. 'But why?' asked
Lear. 'Oh, partly because you wear spectacles, and have an air of
extreme wisdom, and partly because one must say something or
other,'[5] he replied.

On 28 April they reached the pine forests of Bavella, which grew 'as it were in the pit of an immense theatre confined between towering rock-wall, and filling up with its thousands of pines all the great hollow'.[6] Whilst they were there there was a sudden thunderstorm, and they sheltered from the downpour in a forester's cottage: '. . . when the storm ceases for a time, and the sun gleams out through cloud, the whole scene is lighted up in a thousand splendid ways, and becomes more than ever astonishing, a changeful golden haze illumes the tops of the mighty peaks, a vast gloom below, resulting from the masses of black solemn pines standing out in deepest shadow from pale granite cliffs dazzling in the sunlight, torrents of water streaming down between walls and gates of granite . . . profound silence, broken only by the cuckoo's notes echoing from the crags, and from the fulness of melody chanted by thousands of blackbirds.'[7]

But Peter's temper did not improve. A few days after they left Bavella he took the carriage on up a narrow mountain road ahead of Lear and Giorgio, and when they caught up with him again he was beating the horses wildly over the head. At each stroke the animals backed in terror, and suddenly there were screams and a splintering crash as they fell shattering over the edge, cascading down the rocks until they came to rest in a clump of chestnut trees. Pieces of coach and cases were scattered about, one horse was injured and the other lay dead, and on the road Peter knelt appealing to the Madonna and saints whom only moments before he had been blaspheming.

Lear spent two months in Corsica, and on 7 June was in Cannes once more with 350 drawings and a journal of his travels. A few days later he left for London.

Only one of his paintings had sold during the winter, and as there were no new commissions awaiting him it seemed sensible to spend the summer working on a new book. His choice was between Crete and Corsica, perhaps the least interesting of all his unpublished tours. It seems strange that he did not decide to publish his tour of Mount Athos which so few people had visited, or Egypt which had really interested him, or that he did not begin on the book about Greece which he could have done so well. Instead he chose Corsica.

Symonds had given him an introduction to the publisher Smith & Elder who had turned down his Nonsense in 1861, and at the end of July he went to see Mr Smith to talk over the idea of the book with him. He was interested, but would only consider it if the costs were kept very low. Lear had published all his other travel books himself and had never economised on their production. He was not happy at the thought of doing so now, but never again could he write hundreds of letters asking people to subscribe to his work – so he asked Smith how he would like the book done. He was told that instead of the two volumes he had in mind he could have one small volume, and he must use wood engravings and not the more expensive lithography. Ever since his book of *Parrots* Lear had used lithography, for he knew that his work lost almost all its sweeping grace and subtlety when it was engraved. It was bound to be inferior to anything he had done before, and it is sad that he should have agreed to these conditions, especially as Smith & Elder had not even accepted the book. But he went ahead as they suggested, and sent some of his drawings to be engraved.

At the end of July he decided not to keep on even the small rooms at Stratford Place: the lease on the large rooms had expired the previous year. Maclean's had now taken over the sale of his drawings and he did not need a London home any more. 'Verily – this coming to England is Hell,'[8] he wrote, and each visit made him realise his loneliness a little more. He was beginning to find that he preferred receiving letters from his friends to actually being with them – there was a kind of harsh reality in being with people from whom he had grown away which could be disguised in letters. Yet, in spite of this he thought of buying a plot of land near to the Tennysons' new home at Aldworth, and he even went down to look at a site – but he knew that he could never live in England. 'I am very dimbemisted=cloudybesquashed as to plans,' he told Fortescue. 'Neverthless, they go on slowly forming like the walls of Troy or some place as riz to slow music.'[9]

Meanwhile, he had seen samples of the engravings, and they were terribly disappointing. They were also very expensive, for the small vignettes alone were going to cost nearly £7 each. But as the alternative was for him to draw his own lithographs he decided to go ahead, and by December they were done and ready to take to Smith & Elder.

On the spot they decided that they were not interested. They were too expensive, and the book would not pay. If the blocks were any less good it could not be called an illustrated book, and it would not pay as a literary work. Poor Lear! he had done as they had suggested, incurred a bill of £130 – and now they did not want them.

He could not afford to waste all this time and money, and he became dreadfully worried. 'I have one of my cruellest fits of depression,' he wrote in his diary on 11 December, '& can only say – God's will be done. Yet, looking back to, & carefully analysing all the curious physical phenomena of myself from 4 years old, & the consequent effects on the mind, I ought to see I am little to blame & therefore must hold on & abide.'[10]

Now there was only one thing he could do – he must publish the book himself. A few days before Christmas he went to see a printer called Bush who agreed to do it 'if cheaply got up'.[11] This would mean beginning again and cutting smaller, cheaper blocks.

At this point Lear should have left it. If 'cheaply got up', the book would do him no good, and he would be adding the cost of new blocks to the £130 he had already spent. Besides, he would have to go through the dreadful process of finding subscribers. But he decided to persevere.

By now it was late into December, and his rooms in Cannes were paid for and waiting. He would finish writing the book in France and arrange to have cheaper wood-engraving done over there.

In Cannes he felt happier at once. The sun was shining and the sea was blue. 'Evening & sunset beautiful, & certainly the view from these rooms IS something in life. I am not sure though that it is good to have such violent weight in the one scale, because, when the weight is taken out, – how low goes the other side!'[12]

His epilepsy was better, at least he was having fewer attacks though when they came they were more violent than they had ever been, and when they were over he would fall into a deep sleep. Giorgio was there to look after him, and Lear began to ask him in each Sunday evening for half a glass of wine and a cigar.

The Symondses were not in Cannes that year, and Giorgio was, after all, the only companion Lear had.

He worked on the book until the end of February, then he began on a group of sixty Tyrants. It was the first painting he had done for nearly two years. 'My life, or rather what I do with the rest of it must be essentially topographical, & I do not look to painting much more at all,'[13] he told Holman Hunt in July. Certainly, though he continued to paint, the topographical side of his work increased in importance for him, for this was the area in which he could make his own particular contribution. 'The peculiarity of my work lies, I believe, in its accuracy, & in its representing, – owing to my extensive travelling – so many renowned places.'[14]

But he felt that his work went beyond merely representing the places he had seen. 'Painting is silent poetry; poetry is painting that speaks,' wrote Simonides of Ceos, and this thought of ancient Greece was built increasingly into Lear's whole approach to painting. However defective his work was technically, he felt that he did achieve 'good Topographical likenesses, & I trust poetical also',[15] and nothing made him happier than being described as 'The Painter of Topographical Poetry'.[16]

Meanwhile he sent for some wood-blocks so that he could start on the vignettes himself, and a friend – Prosper Merimée, the distinguished French writer – recommended some wood-engravers in Paris for the big engravings.

He was in Paris at the end of June 1869, spreading the work around and hoping that some at least would be passable. 'Of course the cuts will be coarse & queer, & the book will not have the shadow of a pretention to merit quâ art, but it will give a good notion of the scenery of an island little known,'[17] he told Holman Hunt, and to Wyatt he wrote, 'I firmly believe there is some quality in my drawings untransferable to wood engraving. If they keep the accuracy of form (wh. they do here,) they make the whole hard & hideous: in England they sacrifice that – & with that goes half the value of my stupid style. O that I had been born a pig, or a spider, or a broomstick!'[18] In fact, the quality did vary considerably, but even the best brought out nothing of the delicacy of Lear's drawings.

In London he accepted Bush's estimate for the work, but before giving him the manuscript he went to stay with Lushington.

Since Lushington's marriage, this friendship had changed in character; it had come, perhaps, more as Lushington had always wanted it. The intensity of Lear's love had declined after their parting at Dover in 1858, and later, when he could think more dispassionately, he was grateful to Lushington for not having allowed the friendship to develop as he might have dreamt: '. . . when I, who know all, remember how much more a friend he has been to me than even he himself knows; – I have reason to be grateful,'[19] he wrote. They had continued to see one another occasionally, but it was not until after Lushington's marriage that they established a more satisfying relationship. It began gradually with Lear, as now, going to stay for a few days to talk about business or to ask for Lushington's advice in negotiating with publishers. Later, Lushington took upon himself the responsibility of helping Lear with the problems that beset his old age. In the sad Corfu days, Lear had thought him 'though a diamond as to value – yet hidden in a tortoise's shell',[20] and as they grew older the shell was drawn slowly back.

First impressions of Lushington's wife, Kate, had not been favourable. A friend found Franklin 'even more silent since his marriage', adding, 'she is so very commonplace'.[21] Over the years, Lear came to like her more, until he could tell Emily Tennyson that she was 'as good and loveable as any woman can possibly be'.

He stayed with them now for two weeks, and it was a visit of contrasts. '. . . their everlasting silence is horrible – & makes me foam & burst,'[22] Lear had written the year before. He had to face their English Sundays, a day he always disliked for its 'deadly AngloSunday Godhating idolatrous puritan Pharisee silence & sermonreading'.[23] '. . . the melancholy of the L atmosphere culminates on Sundays – & is absolutely dreadful,'[24] he wrote. At other times during the stay, however, he walked with them along the beautiful Southwold foreshore, was chased across a field by a bull, and listened as his god-daughter Gertrude, 'the sweetest & funniest creature',[25] sent him 'into fits of laughter by saying the Owl & Pussy & Calico pie, wh. she has got by heart'.[26] Whilst he was there, he wrote another song to share with them, 'The Daddy Long-legs and the Fly.'

At the end of August he received a letter from Fortescue. 'Have you read "Alice in Wonderland"?' it asked. 'It is very pretty nonsense.'[27]

That autumn the first of his Nonsense songs were published, in an American magazine called *Young Folks*. 'You will I know kindly print my name in full "Edward Lear",' he wrote to the publisher, Fields, 'wh. will, when I get the Magazine, delight my

feeble mind, & console me for remaining in this cold foggy place. After all, small as it may be, one does some good by contributing to the laughter of little children, if it is a harmless laughter.'[28] Now he began to take his Nonsense, as well as his paintings, when he went to visit friends, and he warmed with delight as staid Admirals and Knights of the Realm read aloud his songs and stories.

The Corsican book finished, Lear began writing letters to possible subscribers, doing over a hundred a day. '... rest is none,' he told Fortescue. 'When shall we fold our wings, & list to what the inner spirit says – there is no joy but calm? – Never in this world I fear – for I shall never get a large northlight studio to paint in. Perhaps in the next eggzistens you & I & Mylady may be able to sit for placid hours under a lotus tree a eating of ice creams & pelicanpie with our feet in a hazure colored stream & with the birds & beasts of Paradise a sporting around us ...

'I can't help laughing at my "position" at 57! – And considering how the Corfu, Florence, Petra, &c &c &c &c are seen by thousands, & not one commission ever coming from that fact, how plainly is it visible that the wise public only give commissions for pictures through the press that tell the sheep to leap where others leap!'[29]

He was able to fold his wings a little when he visited an old Knowsley friend, a Mrs Greville Howard, at Ashstead. Before dinner he went to his room: 'The evening is all gray – no sun: & when I put my head out of window, the sweet air, the rooks' voices, & the quiet, bring back memories of "days that are no more": – but as those were wont to bring with them regret, & as I have for a good time past felt that regrets are absurd, – I do not encourage sights sounds or sentiments which in reviving regrets of the past, do more harm than good to the present. What is past is past – gone – gone: – I, being alone ever, & having never now any with whom to talk on these subjects – (not E.T. nor A.B.* – the two last with whom one *could* talk) – cease as much as I can from thought during the last few years of remaining life . . . And on the whole as calm brings with it inevitable recollections & their pain, – it is perhaps better that calm should be as rarely found as it nowadays is . . .'[30] 'By degrees one is coming to look on the whole of life past as a dream, & one of no very great importance either.'[31]

Calm certainly seemed to have vanished on his visit to the Tennysons. Alfred had chosen two drawings of Corsica, but whilst Lear was in his room putting away his work the poet changed his mind – he wanted water-colours. Lear did not mind, but then Tennyson began to wonder if he should have any at all; after all the money might be better used on the outside of the house. Anyway, it was Emily who wanted them, and not he – Lear lost his temper – Tennyson said he was irritable (undoubtedly true) – Lear told him 'he was given to worry and everyone knew it' – they both exploded in rage and Lear went upstairs to pack. When he came down Emily had written out a cheque for £10 for one picture, and she persuaded him to stay.

Before he went to bed Lear apologised for speaking so angrily – Tennyson said 'how characteristic' – it wasn't that that worried him, but that '*Everybody*' said he was a worrier.[32]

* Augusta Bethell – 'Gussie'.

In fact, the relationship between Tennyson and Lear had been deteriorating over the years. They had never been close friends, but they had got on well and admired one another's work. Perhaps things began to go wrong when Lear turned to Emily for consolation over his frustrated love for Lushington. Certainly Tennyson found Lear trying. He had written a poem called 'Northern Farmer, Old Style', and when he followed this with 'Northern Farmer, New Style', Lear remarked that if he wrote any more 'he might publish them all in a Farmercopia – wh. disgusted him'.[33]

Despite this Lear never ceased to admire his poetry, though he thought his later work less good than his earlier writings. 'The way to enjoy Tennyson is to look to him for what he is – a superb landscape-painter, a consummate musician,'[34] wrote F. L. Lucas, and on these grounds especially Lear could appreciate his work.

But he did become disillusioned by Tennyson as a man, and he found his harshness and egocentricity hard to bear. 'I would he were as his poems,'[35] he remarked sadly on one occasion, and on another when he had just left Farringford, he wrote, 'I suppose it is the anomaly of high souled & philosophical writings combined with slovenliness, selfishness & morbid folly that prevents my being happy there.'[36] Yet, he was probably happier when he was with the Tennysons than in any other home. Emily remained his perfect ideal of womanhood, and he worshipped her.

During November he was busy correcting the proofs of his book, and on 8 December he paid a last visit to Bush to give him the remaining third of his money. *Journal of a Landscape Painter in Corsica*, Lear's last travel book and far and away his least successful, was nearly finished at last and would be out in time for Christmas 1869, modestly priced at £1.[37]

The next day he left London, and on the 10th he crossed to France.

PART THREE

SAN REMO
1869–1888

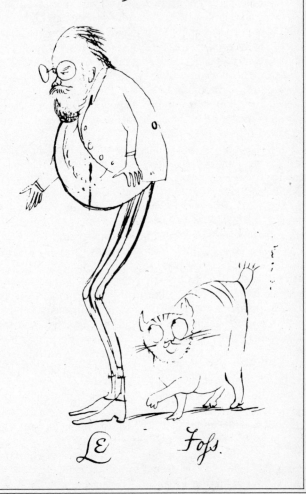

18 Villa Emily
1869–1871

In Cannes he settled down to do two oil paintings of Corsica, the first he had done for years. Then he sat back and looked carefully at his situation. 'I cannot decide "in my mind" – if it be wiser to await death in one spot,' he had written two years earlier, 'making that spot as pleasant as may be, & varying its monotony by such pleasant gleams of older life as can be obtained – or – to hurry on through constantly new & burningly bright scenes, & then dying al'improviso as may happen.'[1] But what he wanted now was a home where he could just work 'quietly at progressive art'.[2]

He had £3000 saved and this was bringing in £90 a year, but he was spending £30 on storage and insurance in London and another £70 on lodgings in Cannes. £90 in, £100 out – it would be cheaper to buy himself a house. Then where should he build? 'The extreme beauty of the Bay of Cannes is a gt temptation to fix here – but if a house be built opposite your windows, no good would come of such fixing'[3] – these were prophetic words. Besides, since Symonds had left he had found 'nobody of the faintest taste at Cannes,' but rather 'Belgravian idlers – who make calls & go to Church daily'.[4] They came to his studio but they bought nothing, and he grumbled against the 'beastly aristocratic idiots who come here, & think they are doing me a service by taking up my time! one day one of them condescendingly said "you may sit down – we do not wish you to stand".'[5] '"What books did you copy all these drawings from?"' asked another, whilst a third cried gaily, '"Oh don't look at the drawings – only come & see the view from the window!"'[6] 'Verily,' he wrote grumpily in January, 'the aristocracy are working out their own declivities; & sharply.'[7]

He was still undecided when rumblings of the Franco-Prussian war were heard, and he realised that it would be unwise for him to settle in France. So on the last day of February 1870, he travelled over to San Remo to look at land there. When he had walked along the Corniche five years earlier he had been disappointed with the San Remo scenery, and again he thought it looked bald, with 'skimpy meagre' olive trees – but land was much cheaper there. He stayed for two nights and was introduced to an Englishman called Walter Congreve who lived in San Remo – at least there would be one sympathetic soul, he thought. He saw a good piece of land next to Congreve's garden with a clear view across to the sea – but he was not sure.

Back in Cannes he was told of a house for sale in Corfu. English yachts had begun to call there again and perhaps that would be the place to settle. What should he do? Should he settle at all, or should he give up painting altogether and wander away? 'The more I work, the more I feel aware that the defects of hand & eye wh. always made painting so irksome & difficult, but which I used to think time would lessen, – are never to be conquered, but on the contrary increase with age. Whereon, I now speculate, – better perhaps to pass the rest of the years in seeing new places & in living how one can, – & not in endeavouring to make good pictures'[8] ... 'it is perhaps the best plan to run about continually like an Ant, & die simultaneous some day or other.'[9]

He finished the two paintings of Corsica, and for the first time for fourteen years he sent in for the Academy. With these out of the way he must make up his mind one way or the other. On Friday, 25 March, he went back again to look at San Remo – and the next day he decided to buy. Over the weekend he had discussions with the architect and went into the details of the purchase. By the time he left on Monday morning the contracts had been exchanged – there was no going back.

His first thought was that he had made a terrible mistake, and he reached Cannes feeling thoroughly gloomy. 'Disheartened & undecided about San Remo, & dreadfully oppressed & depressed.'[10] But the whole thing – land and house – was costing less than £2000, which meant that he could keep £1000 invested. Gradually he felt happier, and he wrote to tell Woolner the news:

'What do you think as I have been & gone & done? I grow so tired of noisy lodgings, & yet am so more & more unable to think of ever wintering in England – & so unable to bear the expense of two houses & two journies annually, that I have bought a bit of ground at San Remo & am actually building a house there ... As I have sold no drawings this winter & have no commissions ahead, I shall endeavour to live upon little Figs in summertime, & on Worms in the winter. I shall have 28 olive trees & a small bed of onions: & a stone terrace, with a gray Parrot & 2 hedge-hogs to walk up & down on it by day & by night . . .'[11]

At the end of June 1870 he moved across to lodgings in San Remo, but it was too hot on the coast and he went on up into the mountains near Turin. There, in a hotel which had been a Carthusian monastery, La Certosa del Pesio, he settled down busily to copy out the words and drawings for a hundred limericks and all the songs and stories he had written in the last few years, so that he could send them to England to be published in time for Christmas.

During the summer he had warnings of heart trouble, and the doctor told him that he must take things more easily and not run up hills or climb stairs quickly. Lear was not very good at taking things easily. 'I HATE LIFE unless I WORK ALWAYS,'[12] he wrote to Fortescue in July. But his father had died of a heart attack and he realised that he must be a little careful.

He did not like hotel life, and in particular he found the convention of *table d'hôte* trying. But it did give him a chance to see the children who were staying in the hotel, and a little American girl who met him that summer described their meeting. 'One day there appeared at luncheon sitting opposite to us a rosy, gray-bearded, bald-headed, gold-spectacled little old gentleman who captivated my attention. My mother must have met him before, for they greeted each other as friendly acquaintances. Something seemed to bubble and sparkle in his talk and his eyes twinkled benignly behind the shining glasses. I had heard of uncles; mine were in America and I had never seen them. I whispered to my mother that I should like to have that gentleman opposite for an uncle. She smiled and did not keep my secret. The delighted old gentleman, who was no other than Edward Lear, glowed, bubbled and twinkled more than ever; he seemed bathed in kindly effulgence. The adoption took place there and then; he became my sworn relative and devoted friend. He took me for walks in the chestnut forests; we kicked the chestnut burrs before us, "yonghy bonghy bos", as we called them; he sang to me "The Owl and the Pussycat" to a funny little crooning tune of his own composition; he drew pictures for me.

'I still have a complete nonsense alphabet, beautifully drawn in pen and ink and delicately tinted in water colours, done on odd scraps of paper, backs of letters, and discarded manuscript. Every day Arthur and I found a letter of it on our plate at luncheon, and finally a title-page for the collection, with a dedication and a portrait of himself, with his smile and his spectacles, as the "Adopty Duncle".[18]

The building progressed slowly whilst he was away, and from his mountain resort he wrote to tell Holman Hunt about the new house:

'My dear Daddy,

'I was very glad to get your letter in April last, & to know you were well & at work; – after all to be hard at work is pretty much the same as being well, at least with me (or at least, vice versa). – But I could not answer you at that time, & indeed can only do so meagrely even now, – for as you will hear presently, I have had enough to do in a new turn of this ludicrously whirligig life which one suffers from first & laughs at afterwards.

'You remember how I have always been wanting a real settled painting place – I having always been more or less convinced that I have talent enough to do some good Topographical painting yet, what though I am 58 – if only I could attain "North light" & "quiet". The idea of getting permanently rooted in England I gave up totally last year – reluctantly however, – for I could well have liked to live near the Tennysons. But how to pass from October to May shivering & coughing? – & how, if I lived that time abroad, – to pay for 2 dwellings continuously, an attempt I have already broken down in? – So therefore, I decided that a permanent Winter place – not a summer place, must be found. – Next, for beauty of scenery, Cannes seemed the properest spot – but I, who have tried it for 3 years, judged otherwise. The first year I was there, there also happened to be many of my friends – & so I sold a good many drawings: – but afterwards, the true character of the place became evident, – a haunt of rich or Aristocratic people – all perhaps good – but all *absolutely* idle. All smiles & goodness if they could take up the whole of an artist's time – "we shall be so delighted if you will let us come & sit in your studio while you work!" – said one of many gt. ladies to me – "we will stay all the day! we should never be tired!" – but on the Artist showing a little notion of independence & self assertion – he was quite thrown by, & other painters – awful daubers! – taken up – or art altogether ignored. So it has come to pass that I have never had *one single commission* to draw or paint the beautiful scenery of Cannes, & only 30£ did I gain from visitors all last season! . . . Thereupon I came to San Remo, a place which while I live must be comparatively quiet (Cannes grows at the rate of 10 new hotels & 200 houses yearly,) – & there I got a bit of land – ¾ of an acre – for 400£ – & am building – or rather have half built a house, which is to cost me 1200£ – rather large – but its being so was requisite for various causes – to give a good chance of reselling &c &c. Neither too much *in*, nor altogether *out* of the world, – my plan may ultimately succeed, if I can only work hard enough to send to every kind of exhibition in England, for that tack I am now (perforce) going to try . . .'[14]

From necessity, he was returning to the large mixed exhibitions on which he had earlier turned his back. As well as this, he decided to try for election to the Old Water Colour Society so that he would have at least one guaranteed shop window in London. 'I'm sure 8 or 10 of my various subjects would attract more than everlasting Hampstead Heaths,'[15] he told Holman Hunt. This might secure him a basic income, leaving him free at last to settle to uninterrupted painting. Moreover, he could now realistically think of carrying out his long-held ambition of illustrating Tennyson's poems.

Before he settled down to his new system he had a sudden wish to do one final work for an old patron. In 1869 the 15th Earl of Derby had succeeded to the title. Lear remembered him as a small boy dressed in black velvet whom he had amused with his nonsense, and now he wrote asking if he could paint a picture for him. Back came 'a wonderfully kind & nice letter, wishing for a Corfù – for 100£.'[16] 'So I begin my San Remo life with the same Knowsley Patronage I began life with at 18 years of age,'[17] he told Fortescue. However, in his diary, Lord Derby wrote: 'Though successful as an artist, Lear is always in want of money, and his request is quite as much an appeal for help as an offer to supply what he thinks may be wanted: I am therefore unwilling to refuse him altogether.'[18] Happily, when the painting arrived at Knowsley a year later, he could write: 'It pleases me much, and the cost (£100) does not seem expensive.'[19]

In fact, 1870 was a difficult one for Lear, for in December he noted that: '. . . it is now nearly a year since I got a penny. All my last year's work is unsold . . . & my 2 large Corsica pictures I have just written to Foord's, to sell for 50£ each – (without frames,) instead of the 200 I ought to have had for each of them.'[20] 'I have more hope in a couple of mice I have seen in the garden of my "property" – who or which I trust the Lord may bless with infinitely multiplied offspring, for I don't believe I shall have anything else to feed on.'[21]

Giorgio went back to Corfu for the summer to see his family, so Lear was alone until October. As the months went on he found it trying having to wait so long for the house to be finished. Through the autumn his depression increased, and so did his fear of tying himself to a permanent home. He would sell the house and go and live in America. He would sell the house and just wander. He would never be happy living there. The excitement of his new plans flopped into a long, lonely depression. His introspection increased, and in November he wrote in his diary: 'Worried & miserable. – I review my whole life in such hours, & full of evil as it undoubtedly is, I am obliged to conclude as I always do, that the great physical misery & "particular skelton" of all these long years, which was not of my making – commenced when I was 5 or 6 years old, – & has influenced all the course of my existence. Blame there has been on my part no doubt – but the foundation of wretchedness was too solidly there, ever to have allowed of a greatly different chain of events & condition of living than has been my lot to bear.'[22]

There were two spots of light. One was an order of 500 copies of his new Nonsense book from Fields of Boston, and the other was the Congreve family. Walter Congreve had been Undermaster at Rugby under Tait, and had just been appointed second master at Marlborough when first his wife and then his eldest son became ill. Their only chance of recovery was to leave England at once, but soon after they arrived both the boy and his mother died, and Congreve was left with two small sons, Hubert and Arnold, to bring up.

Hubert later recalled his first meeting with Lear: 'I ran down the steep path which led up to our house at San Remo to meet my father; I found him accompanied by a tall,[23] heavily-built gentleman, with a large curly beard and wearing well-made but unusually loosely fitting clothes, and what at the time struck me most of all, very large, round spectacles. He at once asked me if I knew who he was, and without waiting for a reply proceeded to tell me a long, nonsense name, compounded of all the languages he knew, and with which he was always quite pat. This completed my discomfiture, and made me feel very awkward and self-conscious. My new acquaintance seemed to perceive this at once, and, laying his hand on my shoulder, said, "I am also the Old Derry Down Derry, who loves to see little folks merry, and I hope we shall be good friends." This was said with a wonderful charm of manner and voice, and accompanied with such a genial, yet quizzical smile, as to put me at my ease at once.'[24]

Apart from the Congreves Lear knew nobody, and for the moment he was happy it should be so. 'There are no peers or peeresses here, – no footmen or swell carriages, – all is quiet & stupid,'[25] he wrote to Morier, and to Lady Wyatt he made an offer: '. . . my white tails are useless – & Digby may buy them cheap: also the tails of my coat. I don't go out at all.'[26] '. . . nevertheless we have an Archbishop of Canterbury, & therein are unique among southern coastsettlements. 18 Clergymen also are portions of the Colony, and ecclesiastically speaking, Fortune cannot thus be accused of acting parsonimoniously towards us.'[27]

At the beginning of December copies of *Nonsense Songs, Stories, Botany and Alphabets* arrived – Bush had advised Lear to hold over the limericks for another book the following year. It contained the first of his songs including 'The Owl and the Pussy-cat' and 'The Jumblies'. It was a delightful collection, a real child's book, and Charles Kingsley wrote to Tom Taylor that it 'has more wisdom & genius in it than all that Bain & Herbert Spencer ever wrote.'[28]

'I am so pleased you like my "Nonsense songs & stories",' Lear wrote to Morier, '& that all the world is thereby delighted. – And I like to think that if a man ain't able to do any great service to his fellow critters, it is better wie nicht to make half a million of children laugh innocently.'[29] 'My only copy here,' he wrote on Christmas Eve, '. . . I have lent to the Archbishop as a pious & instructive work fitted for the season.'[30]

His painting plans were not going as he had hoped. Two of the three oil paintings which had been in the Academy were unsold, and he arranged for them to go to Foord & Dickenson, who were picture handlers, for sale at £50 each instead of £200. And he had not been elected to the Old Water Colour Society. Money was getting short again, and he wrote to Fortescue: 'Ain't it funny, at nearly 60, & with talents like mine, to be in such a mess.'[31] But he wanted 'to skriggle on without borrowing for the present',[32] and as the house was nearly finished he would not have to pay for rooms for much longer.

On 20 March 1871, almost exactly a year after he had bought the land, the house was ready. It was to be called Villa Emily, after – as he said – his niece in New Zealand. He moved in on the 25th, and wandered delightedly from one room to another. 'I never before had such a painting room,' he told Fortescue, '32 feet by 20 – & with a light I can work by at all hours, & a clear view S. over the sea. Below it is a room of the same size, which I

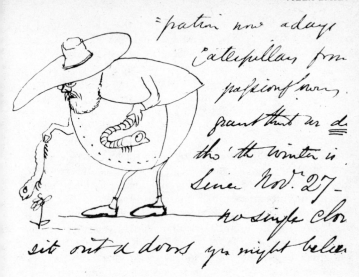

... patin now adays
Caterpillars from
passionflowers.
grant that we d
this 'th winter is
Since Nov. 27 —
no single clou
sit out d doors you might belive

now use as a Gallery, & am "at home" in once a week.'[33]

But he had nobody, except Giorgio, with whom he could share his excitement, '. . . no letters: no friends: no newspapers . . . & I can't think how I shall get through years of it.'[34] Soon the letters began to arrive, and one of the first was from Fortescue and Lady Waldegrave. 'I have just got your letter, left in my new post box in my new front door, over the old plate that used to be in 15 Stratford Place,' Lear told them. '. . . I took the letter out into "*my garden*" & read it under one of my own olive trees.'[35]

He was proud of this garden and found it 'a gt amusement, & the picking off of caterpillars & the tying up of creepers no end of distraction'.[36] He spent a long time arranging the lay-out of trees and shrubs and flowers, and planted exotic seeds which his sister had sent from New Zealand and others that Professor Bell's family had sent from Selbourne. He planted local species too, and the flowers that he had admired for so long on his travels were soon flowering on his own land. 'Very calm & quiet is life here – albeit away from friends,' he noted in his diary. 'If one had enough to live on, life would even be fun.'[37]

Now his thoughts were turning back more and more to his childhood. In June his cousin, his mother's sister's child, died in England. His name was Frederick Harding, and when Lear heard of his death he wrote in his diary: 'It is just 50 years since he did me the greatest Evil done to me in life, excepting that done by C: – & which must last now to the end – spite of all reason & effort.'[38] It was Easter Monday, 8 April 1822, and Frederick Harding, who was nineteen, had just been bought out of his regiment and was staying at Bowman's Lodge. Lear was not quite ten. He never elaborated on this, nor did he say who C was, but he thought of it often, and for many years afterwards when 8 April came round he would note the day in his diary.

He was not completely alone. He would wander over to the Congreves, 'dropping in often at our midday meal, when he would sit, generally without taking anything beyond a glass of his favourite Marsala, and talk in the most delightful and interesting way of his garden, his travels, people he had met, birds, botany, music, and on general topics interspersed with humour, which was never long absent', Hubert later recalled. Sometimes he would arrive in the evening, when he 'delighted us all by singing his "Tennyson Songs", set to music by himself, which he sang with great feeling and expression, and with what must have been at one time a fine tenor voice. He accompanied himself on the piano with spread chords, of which he was very fond. He generally finished up with some humorous songs, sung with great spirit, our favourite being "The Cork Leg".'[39]

Wednesday, from 1 till 5, was his weekly open day, 'for in these places of idle resort there is (as I found at Cannes,) no medium between total interruption, or regulated publicity'.[40] He filled his 'maggrifficent gallery, with 99 water color drawings – not to speak of 5 larger oils . . . (In one is a big beech tree, at which all intelligent huming beans say – "Beech!" – when they see it. For all that one forlorn ijiot said – "Is that a *Palm*=tree Sir" – "No", replied I quietly, "it is a Peruvian Brocoli".)'[41]

He had found at last a 'certain tranquility of life',[42] and in the settled isolation of his new home he began on the last phase of his Nonsense. In December he wrote the 'Yonghy-Bonghy-Bò' and the first part of 'Mr & Mrs Discobbolos'.

He longed for visits from his old friends, and tried bribing Fortescue to comè and see him: '. . . if you come here directly I can give you 3 figs, & 2 bunches of grapes: but if later, I can only offer you 4 small potatoes, some olives, 5 Tomatas, & a lot of castor oil berries. These, if mashed up with some crickets who have spongetaneously come to life in my cellar, may make a novel, if not nice or nutricious Jam or Jelley. Talking of bosh, I have done another whole book of it: it is to be called "*more nonsense*" and Bush brings it out at Xmas: *it will have a Portrait of me outside*. I should have liked to dedicate it to you, but I thought

it was not dignified enough for a Cabinet M(inister).'[43] These
were the limericks and other Nonsense left over from the previous book.

'My elth is tolerable, but I am 60 next May, & feel growing
old,' he wrote. 'Going up & down stairs worries me, & I think of
marrying some domestic henbird & then of building a nest in
one of my own olive trees, whence I should only descend at
remote intervals during the rest of my life.'[44]

Then, in September 1871, his quiet withdrawal from life was
disturbed by an invitation. Lord Northbrook had been appointed
Viceroy of India, and he wrote asking Lear if he would like to go
out there to live for six months at his expense.

19 Coast of Coromandel
1872–1875

Lear was not sure that he wanted to go to India. He had settled down for the first time in his life, and it seemed the wrong moment to be on the move again – though he had once predicted that if he ever did settle he would leave the next day for Tobago.

He went across to Cannes at the end of March 1872 to see Northbrook who was on his way out to India, and the invitation was put to him again. It was a difficult decision for Lear to make. '. . . with all my attachment to the whole lot, there is something antagonistic in my nature to travelling as part of a suite; – and indeed – though I am not in the strongest sense of the word Bohemian – I have just so much of that nature as it is perhaps impossible the artistic & poetic beast can be born without. Always accustomed from a boy to go my own ways uncontrolled – I cannot help fearing that I should run rusty & sulky by reason of retinues & routines. This impression it is which keeps me turning over & over in what I please to call my mind what I had best do. Sometimes I think I will cut away to Bombay – with my old servant, & writing thence to Northbrook – do parts of India as I can, & ask him to let me take out some money in drawings. On the other hand, I hate the thought of being ungracious or wanting in friendliness. The Himalayas, Darjeeling – Delhi, Ceylon, &c &c &c – are what I have always wished to see: – but, all' opposto, – here I have a new house, & to flee away from it as soon as it is well finished seems a kind of giddiness which it rather humiliates me to think of practising.'[1]

He thought he would spend the summer of 1872 in England. As well as more mundane arrangements – the ordering of new clothes and a new set of teeth, the checking of his spectacles – he needed to see if he could get commissions for work in India if he should go. During the winter he had bought himself a cat called Potiphar, 'who has no end of a tail – because it has been cut off'.[2] but Potiphar could go with Giorgio to Corfu. In England he could see his friends, for not many of them were likely to come and visit him:

But the longer I live on this Crumpetty Tree
The plainer than ever it seems to me
That very few people come this way,
And that life on the whole is far from gay![3]

he wrote just before he left San Remo. For the Quangle Wangle, of course, things turned out all right, and quantities of the kindest, most sympathetic creatures arrived to join him.

When he reached England at the end of June he had decided that he would see only a few friends – 'I will never again commence the ineffable worry of distant hurried journeys to country houses, at a serious expense, & to almost no purpose at seeing the friends whom nominally I go to see. The conditions & positions of life of most of these I knew in earlier years are so altered – that although they, (happily,) the friends themselves, are quite unaltered – no personal communication can now be had with them worth such sacrifices as must be made to obtain it ... I do not much suppose we shall ever talk as of old, until we come to sit as cherubs on rails – if any rails there be, – in Paradise.'[4]

Despite his resolution he spent a busy time in England, for in his mind was the thought that he might not return again. He saw Holman Hunt who had just come back from Jerusalem. 'He is little changed, – as he was indeed unlikely to be. We talked – naturally – incessantly.'[5] This was what Lear needed more than anything.

Strawberry Hill was dreadful. Last time he had stayed there he had been given a room facing the stables; this time he had a tiny room looking on to a wall. He left the next morning at seven o'clock, promising himself never to go there again.

He moved from one country house to another leaving his 'farewell testimonials' – and collecting commissions. '. . . will you not tell me if you have any especial wish for one view more than another?' he asked Henry Bruce. 'Shall I paint Jingerry Wangerry Bang, or Wizzibizzigollyworryboo?'[6] 'I will be sure not to forget the snakes, if I go to Hingy,' he reassured Lady Wyatt, '& I will also bring you 8 snipes, 24 bluefaced monkies, & a porcupine. This last you can use as a footstool.'[7] All the travelling had an alarming effect on him: '. . . rattling about so much as I have lately done, is fast destroying the small amount of intellect yet left me, and I am constantly on the point of believing in my proximate metamorphosis into a Railway Whistle or a Boiler about to Bust.'[8]

At the beginning of September he heard again from Northbrook, who this time enclosed a cheque for £50 for a drawing of Cairo which he wanted Lear to do on his way out to India. During the summer he had been given nearly £1000 worth of commissions, and he realised that he must go, though he hoped that his Vice-regal friends would realise that he was 'not a swell full of tin but a hard working painter'.[9]

Just before leaving England he fell and knocked his right temple. His right eye was 'like a rainbow in fits',[10] and the fall made him feel rather unsteady, increasing his anxiety about the hazards of the trip. But he had made up his mind, and he left London for San Remo to collect his luggage and close the house for the winter.

Lear picked up Giorgio in Corfu, and together they went on to Suez. In Egypt they heard that the boats were very full, and it was difficult to get berths. He was still feeling the effects of his fall and was in no mood to dally around, so when a French boat came in a few days later he decided to take a cabin on this rather than risk being left behind altogether. Some of his baggage was delivered to the quayside and the rest put on to a barge ready to go out to the boat, then they waited for Customs clearance. When the official arrived he told Lear that the bags already on the barge must be transferred to another before he would examine them. Lear was already afraid that he was going to miss the boat, and saw no point in moving his things from one barge to another. He started to argue with the official who then refused to examine anything, but mounted his horse and left.

The noise and the delay and the uncertainty of the voyage had already upset Lear. Now he was thoroughly angry, and he ordered that all his luggage was to be taken straight to the station. By seven that evening he and Giorgio were on the train to Alexandria, '& *the Indian bubble is burst*'.[11]

Within hours he was worrying. He had lost nearly £1000 worth of commissions which were rare enough these days, and his paints and canvases were already on their way out to India. What madness had made him give up his carefully planned journey in a sudden fit of pique? In fact, it is not difficult to see what was wrong. When he became very tired, Lear's handwriting changed, and this happened now. The long and exhausting journey back to England, followed by weeks of travelling once there, had thoroughly tired him. 'As at Jerusalem in 1867, & Larissa in 1849 – the abrupt change is very afflicting, as savouring of insanity . . .' he wrote in his diary. 'In vain, in vain I look back in search of a reason for the deterioration of health & mind in those days at Suez!'[12] He blamed the fall, coupled with the 'sense of "compulsion" – a want of total independence'.[13] More distressingly, he wondered if such sudden, irrational changes of mind betokened insanity growing from his epilepsy.

Back in San Remo he immediately began to make new plans for the trip. It was too late in the season for him to go now. He must wait until the following autumn.

Potiphar had disappeared during the summer in Corfu, but Lear found his twin brother available, and he called him Foss. One morning Foss was discovered tearing the letters to shreds, and was banished to the kitchen. 'Pity,' wrote Lear, 'for he was a sort of companion; – yet being literally & really alone, – it is perhaps as well to have no sham substitutes for society.'[14] But Foss soon crept back on to the hearthrug and became a much-loved cat, 'a good addition to one's lonely lonely life'.[15]

To pass the winter he settled down to read nine volumes of Horace Walpole's letters, then went on to eight more of Thomas Moore's diaries: he had built up a large library of books to which he was constantly adding and which he lent out to other English residents and visitors. As well as reading he began a batch of 120 new Tyrants, but as he was painting he felt that his right eye was not working properly and he was finding difficulty in seeing what he was doing.

As the months went by, the tension of waiting began to sap his energy. One moment he would be planning the trip, the next it was all off – he was not going. News of the death of friends saddened him. 'I must say that life becomes werry werry pongdomphious,'[16] he wrote. He was cheered by a mention of his work in a Commons debate, when William Vernon-Harcourt said that a 'friend of his – an admirable artist, had published a "Book of Nonsense". But Parliament published every year a much more celebrated "Book of Nonsense", called the Statute Book. (Laughter.) . . .' 'Sich is phame,'[17] Lear wrote in his diary.

In April he was taken ill, and spent several days in bed, a thing he rarely allowed himself to do. 'One thing . . . is certain,' he wrote to Fortescue, 'a sedentary life – after moving about as I have done ever since I was 24 years old, will infallibly finish me off SUDDINGLY. And although I may be finished off equally suddingly if I move about, yet I incline to think a thorough change will affect me for better rather than for wuss. *Whereby I shall go either to Sardinia, or India, or Jumsibojigglequack this next winter as ever is . . .*'[18]

In May his face swelled up painfully, and he wondered again about the Indian trip: '. . . sometimes it seems to me utterly ridiculous & impossible – at others, the real & only thing I have to look forward to.'[19] That month he wrote a new Nonsense song – 'The Pobble who has no Toes', and in July he composed an Indian absurdity about the Akhond of Swat.

Then in September came news which a few years earlier would have been a bitter shock, and even now distressed him. During the summer Lord Westbury had died and, free now from any obligations to her parents, Gussie had decided to marry. She was marrying a man called Adamson Parker who was much older than she, and an invalid. Lear had so often wondered if she could have been happy sharing his strange kind of life. Instead she had chosen for herself a life which would be much more demanding.

Though he often thought of her, it had been years since Lear had decided that he could never marry Gussie – yet he greeted the news dramatically: 'There is now no hope of any but a dark & lonely life. I must leave this place,'[20] he thought. A few days later he wrote a fanciful letter to Fortescue: 'I wrote you a long letter from Sanremo on Sept. 18, but at that time I do not think I had finally decided on India. Presently afterwards a circumstance happened that threw another weight into the "yes" scale – to wit, Gussie Bethell's engaging herself – on her father's death – to one who is disapproved of as her husband by all the family – but not as I could have wished to myself. You know how I have always had this dream – i.e. – for a good many years now – & just as the time came when I meant to let the decision of my proposal yes or no determine my plan as to India – the question suddenly resolved itself without my having pain of a refusal, which is so far a good feature in the case. *Please say nothing of this except to My Lady* – who with you knew of the matter. So altogether I considered that to go to India for 18 months would be really my best course – as a change of scene may do me good, & besides, – living as I do from hand to mouth by my art, I dare not throw away the many commissions for paintings & drawings I already have for Indian subjects.'[21] The last sentence was more to the point.

He spent some weeks sorting his possessions and papers in case he should not return. He had three 'chestfuls or chestsfull' of letters, and as he looked through them he thought firstly that 'every created human being capable of writing ever since the invention of letters must have written to me, with a few exceptions perhaps, such as the prophet Ezekiel, Mary Queen of Scots, & the Venerable Bede. 2dly. That either all my friends must be fools or mad; – or, on the contrary – if they are not so, there must be more good qualities about this child than he ever gives or has given himself credit for possessing – else so vast and long continued a mass of kindness in all sorts of shapes could never have happened to him. Seriously, it is one of the greatest puzzles to me, who am sure I am one of the most selfish & cantankerous brutes ever born, that heaps & heaps of letters – & these letters only the visible signs of endless acts of kindness, – from such varieties of persons could have never been written to me! – Out of all I kept some specimens of each writer more or less interesting – 444 individuals in all.'[22] 'I often say that if I get to heaven, the first question I shall ask will be, "How the deuce did I make & keep so many friends?" – (only of course, I shouldn't say "how the deuce").'[23]

Why was Lear so extraordinarily popular? He described himself as 'a most irregular & uncomfortable fool – partly swell – partly painter, who will never do any good – to himself or anybody else'.[24] He was often depressed and irritable, and when pressed upon by 'heaps of small botherations'[25] might fly off at his friends, a thing he always deeply regretted afterwards. Yet, after his death Lushington could say of him that the love of his friends was 'the best and sweetest of garlands that can in spirit be laid on his tomb'.[26] 'He has always been the most charming & delightful of friends to me,' Lushington wrote to Lear's niece, '& apart from all his various qualities of genius, I have never known a man who deserved more love for his goodness of heart & his determination to do right . . . There never was a more generous or a more unselfish soul.'[27]

Perhaps it was because he was a man who had known, and who never ceased to know, the meaning of grief. Sadness – especially sadness in childhood – which can destroy a personality, can also evolve into the richness of compassion. In Lear, friends observed 'a gentle sadness through which his humour shone'.[28] He cared about his fellow men, and was uninhibited enough to show it – indifference he thought the worst of all human characteristics. He was never afraid of placing himself in their debt, nor of acknowledging their help at every turn. Vulnerability did not frighten him. 'Feebleness & care is a better mixture than boldness & contempt,'[29] he once wrote. And as he was alone in the world he valued his friends enough to work at friendship. 'I will not withdraw my word "practical", my dear old friend, as applied to your friendship,' Fortescue had said, 'wh. is ready to show itself in acts & in taking trouble'.[30] '. . . a man of versatile and original genius, with great gifts, one of the most interesting, affectionate, and lovable characters it has been my good fortune to know and to love,'[31] summed up Hubert Congreve.

When he had tied the letters into bundles he wrote to Fortescue: 'I cannot help thinking that my life, letters, & diaries would be as interesting . . . as many that are now published: & I half think I will leave all those papers to you, with a short record of the principal data of my ridiculous life, which however has been a hardworking one, & also one that has given much of various sorts of stuff to others, though the liver has often had a sad time of it.'[32]

It is unfortunate that he did not go through with this half-thought, for all the letters he wrote to Fortescue have been carefully preserved. To each of his kindest friends he left one of his drawings, and as a final act in clearing his affairs he wrote a new will leaving any money realised from the sale of his house and pictures to his great-niece, Emily Gillies.

Now he was ready to leave for India. He sent Giorgio to Corfu to see his family whilst he 'shut & sealed & screwed up all the Villa Emily: & doddled about the Portofino coast some time'.[33] Then he boarded the boat going via Corfu to Suez. It was delayed for a day before it left Genoa and, almost unbelievably, Lear became so angry that he ordered his bags off the boat – the journey was off. The small cases were actually delivered back to his hotel, but the porters waited for confirmation before heaving the big ones off as well. This gave him time to cool his anger, and he asked for the small bags to be delivered back on board again. The boat sailed from Genoa on 25 October, and Lear was at last on his way to India.

It was a long, slow voyage. They docked at Bombay on 22 November, and Lear at once felt 'nearly mad from sheer beauty and wonder of foliage! O new palms!!! O flowers!! O creatures!! O beasts!! ... anything more overpoweringly amazing cannot be Conceived!!! Colours, & costumes, & myriadism of impossible picturesqueness!!! These hours are worth what you will.'[34]

From Bombay they went north-east by train through Jabalpur to Lucknow, where he joined the Vice-regal party and delighted in seeing Lord Northbrook and Evelyn Baring, who as Northbrook's secretary had made all the arrangements for his trip. But his luggage had not arrived and Lear found himself without the proper clothes. This was unfortunate, for Anglo-Indians took the formalities of life seriously. He found that he had to attend their glittering dinners, and he went in a procession through the streets of Lucknow riding in a carriage with Northbrook's daughter. '... they are so blessed viceregal!'[35] he grunted, wanting to get away to see India.

During the next thirteen months he travelled from Bombay to Calcutta, from Simla to Ceylon, spending days in trains and bumpy gharries in oppressive, overwhelming tropical heat and bitterly cold Himalayan winds. Giorgio was with him to push him up muddy banks made slippery by torrential rains, to sew on buttons and carry his sketch books. He lived in Vice-regal houses and slept in railway waiting-rooms, he ate enormously and drank more than was good for him, and when he was not working or travelling he was fretting about the time that he had to waste.

Travelling was exhausting, for they had to cover such large distances. They were on the move for days at a time, which was tiring for a man of nearly sixty-two with a troublesome heart. He disliked the 'Frightful fuss – tickets – baggage, bother – tumult'[36] so much that he wrote, 'I am half wild when I think of my folly in coming to India at all. The only thing now is to make the best of a miserable mistake.'[37]

But when they stopped at Benares, the holy city of the Hindus which climbs in tiers from the sacred Ganges sliced by ghats down which the pilgrims climb into the water, Lear thought it 'one of the most abundantly bruyant, and startlingly radiant of places of infinite bustle & movement! ! !'[38]

Calcutta, which they reached on 21 December, was a complete contrast. He stayed for three weeks in the Governor's house, and the whole place seemed permeated with the British. There was 'no rest in Hustlefussabàd',[39] and he was glad to leave and travel north towards the Himalayan mountains and Tibet. His changes of mood were rapid and complete. One moment he was bewitched with the colour and the beauty of the country, and the next he was horrified that he had ever agreed to come. It was all hurry, hurry, move, move. They stayed in hotels and private houses, but Lear was happier when he could sleep in one of the Dak bungalows. There they could look after themselves, get up early and go to bed when they liked, and not waste endless hours in chatting to hosts or waiting for meals. Giorgio looked after him splendidly, though it was soon pointed out to him that it was most unusual for an Englishman to travel with a European servant. There were even mutterings about the possible nature of their relationship. In fact, Lushington had encouraged Lear to take Giorgio with him, and Lear had readily agreed, for 'as much of my time in India will needs be full of out of the way tours . . . I do not care to be, in case of illness, without someone I know, & can trust.'[40]

They travelled up to Darjeeling by gharry, stopping frequently to change horses. The roads were bumpy, and as Lear's sketching stool had broken beneath him a few days earlier, he found the journey very uncomfortable. He had four commissions to paint the mountain of Kinchinjunga from Darjeeling, and as they came near the view became 'continually more and more lovely'.[41] But it was very high and so bitterly cold that he found it difficult to hold a pencil, and Giorgio piled coats and blankets on to him to try to keep him warm. 'Kinchinjunga is not – so it seems to me, – a sympathetic mountain,' wrote Lear, 'it is so far off – so very God=like & stupendous, – and all that great world of dark opal vallies full of misty, hardly to be imagined forms, – besides the all but impossibility of expressing the whole as a scene, – make up a rather distracting and repelling whole.'[42]

But the mountain at sunrise was 'a glory not to be forgotten'.[43] He was up whilst it was still dark and bitterly, bitterly cold, so that he could be out in time to draw at dawn. It was difficult, for he was not used to this kind of massive scenery and he thought that he had seen lovelier mountain views in Greece. The vegetation was beautiful, but there was a strange lack of animal life. There were birds, but they did not sing and it was strangely quiet.

When he had finished the drawings he went south again, and travelled along the Ganges to Alahabad where he found a letter waiting, telling him that his sister Sarah had died in New Zealand. 'We live & live & live, & live on & perhaps so living from day to day through long years, feel these losses less,'[44] he wrote, but he felt them no little bit less. In fact, as he travelled over India he had constantly to remind himself that looking back and thinking of the people and the places that he would never see again could only bring unhappiness. What was cheerful was that his poetry had come to India: 'While drawing Birds for Laurie's little girl before dinner another little girl – just as I was drawing an Owl, – called out, "O please draw a Pussy Cat too! – because you know they went to sea in a boat, with plenty of honey & money wrapped up in a 5£ note!" – On Enquiry, I found that she and all the school she went to had been taught that remarkable poem! !'[45]

In mid-February 1874, travelling on west, he came to Agra and the Taj Mahal: '. . . descriptions of this wonderfully lovely place are simply silly, as no words can describe it at all. What a garden! What flowers! . . . effects of colour absolutely astonishing, – the Great Centre of the Picture being ever the vast glittering Ivory-white Taj, & the accompaniment and contrast of the dark green of Cypresses, with the rich yellow green trees of all sorts! And then the effect of the innumerable flights of bright green Parrots flitting across, – like live Emeralds; and of the scarlet leaved Poinsettias, and countless other flowers – "beaming" bright off the dark green! ! The "Tinker" or "tinpot" bird, ever at work. Pigeons, Hoopoes, & (I think,) a new sort of Mayhna – pale dove colour and gray; also Squirrels – & all tame, and endless numerous.

'. . . Below the Taj is a scene of Pilgrim=washing & shrines &c &c. altogether Indian & lovely. – *What* can I do here? Certainly not the Architecture, which I naturally shall not attempt, except perhaps in a slight sketch of one or two direct garden views. Henceforth let the inhabitants of this world be divided into 2 classes, – them as has seen the Taj, – & them as hasn't.'[46]

He stayed for ten days in Delhi, 'making Delhineations of the Dehlicate architecture as is all impressed on my mind as inDehlibly as the Dehliterious quality of the water of that city'.[47] But it was ruined by British military barracks and iron railings, 'and other hideous British utilities'.

When he reached Simla he heard that Villa Emily had been broken into, and he wrote philosophically, 'Perhaps it is a good thing to be reminded that nothing on earth is permanent – which one might fancy was the case were nothing to go wrong, – to one's harm . . .'[48]

But there was good news as well, for Fortescue, who had lost his seat in the 1874 election, had been given a peerage as Lord Carlingford. Lear wrote happily to congratulate him:

O! Chichester, my Carlingford!
O! Parkinson, my Sam!
O! SP*Q*, my Fortes*cue*!
    How awful glad I am!
For now you'll do no more hard work
Because by sudden=pleasing-jerk
    You're all at once a peer, –
Whereby I cry, God bless the Queen!
As was, & is, & still has been,
    Your's ever, Edward Lear.[49]

Leaving the Himalayas behind him he hurried down to Poona to get there before the monsoons began. '. . . like AT's Rivulet once goes on "for ever and for ever",'[50] he wrote as he packed his things to dash south, 'I am a very energetic & frisky old cove,'[51] he thought.

Giorgio, on the whole, was coping well with the extraordinary conditions of travel: '. . . how very many of his best qualities only come out now in this hard Indian Journey!' Lear wrote, 'his quiet, content, & unmurmuring patience, – and his constant attention to me, – his often wrong=going Master!'[52] But at times he became silent and sullen and would refuse to talk to Lear.

They had to stay in Poona for two months, longing to get on but unable to do so until the rains eased. Whilst waiting, Lear had some tin cases made for his drawings – 500 sketches of Bengal, the North-West Provinces and the Punjab, the product of six months' hard work.

Waiting in Poona he wrote 'The Cummerbund', and for this he went back to the ditty – 'She sits upon her Bulbul' – that he had written as he sailed from Corfu with Evelyn Baring in 1864.

> She sat upon her Dobie,
>   To watch the Evening Star,
> And all the Punkahs as they passed
>   Cried, 'My! how fair you are!'
> Around her bower, with quivering leaves,
>   The tall Kamsamahs grew,
> And Kitmutgars in wild festoons
>   Hung down from Tchokis blue . . .
> Beware, ye Fair! Ye Fair, beware!
>   Nor sit out late at night, –
> Lest horrid Cummerbunds should come,
>   And swollow you outright.[53]

which is rather like a poem that had appeared two years earlier:

> Beware the Jabberwock, my son!
>   The jaws that bite, the claws that catch!
> Beware the Jubjub bird, and shun
>   The frumious Bandersnatch![54]

At last, in mid-July, the weather was good enough for them to get away south on the journey to Madras and Ceylon. At Hyderabad the Residency was in a fuss and bother for they were expecting the Nizan, the local ruler. Lear kept getting in the way, so he went out and sat with a sympathetic lizard. To help him pass the time he read Plato's *Phaedo*, and this set him on a stream of thought: 'The [   ] [and] misery of some 55 or 56 years of past life before me – & ever I have to turn away from too much thought of it, by a decision that it was no fault of my making, but inevitable and [growing] always from my 6th or 7th year – year by year,'[55] he wrote in his journal, an entry which was heavily inked out later.

From Hyderabad he went on south to Madras on the Coromandel coast. They were coming into tropical jungle and it was oppressively hot and humid. At Mamallapuram he saw the ancient temples and the 'Seven Pagodas' with their fine Pallavan sculpture, and he visited the temples of Conjeeveram. But the heat was beginning to get him down. Giorgio too was exhausted, and a little disagreement between them suddenly burst into an unhappy row. 'If I have been, as he says, a bad master to him, we ought to part,' wrote Lear afterwards, 'if not, – still we ought to part, because such accusations are unjust, & the relations of master & serv^t should not so go on. Therefore, I think it best he should go back, and so it must be.'[56] But within a few days the angry words had been forgotten.

By mid-October they had reached the Malabar coast and Calicut, but it was so hot and heavy that he decided in a rush to go on to Ceylon. Here Giorgio developed dysentery and for several days he was really ill. Lear tended him as he had done on Mount Athos, and when he was a little better they went on to Colombo and crossed back to the mainland. Then a few days later Lear strained his back, and soon it was so stiff he could not move. He knew that he could go no further.

From Calicut they went straight up the west coast to Bombay, where a letter was waiting with the news that Giorgio's wife had died in Corfu – it was a sad ending to the trip. Yet as they sailed from India on 12 January 1875, Lear was already planning to come back to see the places that he had missed.

20 The Cruel Shore
1875–1880

'I am come back safely to my native 'ome,'[1] Lear wrote to Lady Aberdare, but the return was depressing. Giorgio of course went straight back to Corfu and Lear reached San Remo alone. The house had been turned upside down by the burglary though little apart from winter clothes seemed to be missing.

After the bustle and colour and the movement of India, quietness and loneliness closed round him in a 'solitary weariness'.[2] He could not settle to anything: the change of climate had given him '42 thousand 857 colds in my head',[3] and his right eye was worrying him. In the end he decided to go to England for the summer. He needed new glasses, and might even come back with more commissions for Indian paintings. He was worried too about his one remaining sister, Ellen, who at 75 was almost completely blind and deaf.

He arranged that whilst he was away a new carriageway would be built and extra servants' rooms added to Villa Emily, making it more attractive in case he should ever decide to sell. The garden looked wonderful now. It had filled out and matured, and in the early summer flowers began to spill over it in giddy abundance. In the evening their heavy scent would fill the warm air, and after dinner he would sit out on the terrace and look over to the darkening sea: it was 'very much like Paradise – only Adam hath no Eve'.[4] Slowly, though, San Remo was changing, and Lear was fearful that 'quiet will for ever depart from my peaceful corner here, as new Hotels & Villas rise.'[5]

He left for London in the middle of June 1875, but arrived to find that most of his friends had gone into the country – though scarcely to escape the heat of the city for it was chilly and damp. There were not the usual rounds of dinner parties, and he told a friend, 'I intend to purchase a leg of mutton and eat it on one of the smaller trees in the Park by degrees daily.'[6] But he did sell a number of paintings, and Louisa, Lady Ashburton, who had bought the 'Cedars', commissioned a large painting of Kinchinjunga.

Giorgio was in San Remo to greet him when he arrived and they settled back into the quiet routine that had been interrupted by the trip to India. 'I strenuously resist all "acquaintance",' he told Fortescue. 'My idea of happiness in life, such as we can get, – growing more distinct as I grow older . . . & more remote from noise & fuss. At the very door of St Peter of the Keys, I shall stipulate that I will only go into Heaven at all on condition that I am never in a room with more than 10 people.'[7] His voluntary isolation from neighbours was short-sighted, as subsequent events were to prove. 'I wrote to Miss Kay Shuttleworth declining to dine,' he wrote in his diary in December, 'to my regret – for this lonely life is by no means good for me: & at times the depression from wh. I suffer, is almost intolerable. Yet to embark on general outdining would be far worse.'[8]

In the spring old friends began to visit him and dispel the quiet loneliness of his life. Frank Lushington stayed for a fortnight, and Lord Northbrook, who had resigned as Viceroy in January 1876, stopped in San Remo on his way back from India. Lord Aberdare came with his children, and in July Charles Church stayed for a week, so there was 'a plethora of friendship all in a lump',[9] visits which were a source of real happiness to Lear.

During the summer of 1875, he wrote the last of the Nonsense that was published in his lifetime, culminating in August with 'The Dong with a Luminous Nose'. Then he bundled up the manuscripts – amongst them, as well as the Dong, the Pobble, the Pelican Chorus and the Yonghy-Bonghy-Bò – and he sent them to Bush for publication for Christmas. This was *Laughable Lyrics* – Lear had wanted to call it 'Learical Lyrics & Puffles of Prose'.

The critics on the whole gave the book a good reception, though some preferred the earlier songs. The *Standard* critic, on the other hand, had this to say: 'We should not like to be condemned to read much of this kind of literature. Fortunately, in the present volume there is not much of it. The author must have supposed what he calls his lyrics to be laughable, since he gives them that title. If there is any man or woman whose features would curl, as novelists might express it, on reading them, we are certain it would not be with a smile.'[10]

1877 began badly for Lear. Though Giorgio seemed much better, he had not really recovered from his illness and from the shock of his wife's death. In February he told Lear that he wanted to return to Corfu to be with his three remaining children. Lear decided to go with him, and asked Hubert Congreve to come and take charge of the money and tickets, 'all money trans-actions being, as he said, "An nabbomination to this child".' In bitterly cold winter weather the three men set out for Brindisi. When they arrived a gale was blowing and it was snowing hard. It was a responsibility for Hubert to have two elderly, unfit men to look after, and he became thoroughly alarmed about Lear. 'I shall never forget the night we spent there,' he wrote many years later. 'It was cold and wretched in the extreme, and Lear was thoroughly dejected; and though a fowl we had for dinner – roasted, boiled, and then browned over, and which collapsed on being touched – roused him to make some jokes about the effect of snow on hens, all his fun vanished when we got into beds with a single thin blanket each in a room with the fine snow drifting in through the badly fitting windows, and he spent the night tossing about and moaning, thoroughly upset by the long journey and his anxiety about his old servant. Next day the gale had increased in force, and I became very anxious about my old friend's state, so I encouraged his disinclination to face the sea voyage, for I knew that he was a bad sailor. Finally it was decided that George and his son should go on to Corfû by themselves, and that we should go to Naples and Rome. So after seeing George off we started for Naples, which we reached early next morning in warm and brilliant sunshine, and Lear at once began to revive . . .

'We spent two days at Naples, visiting Baiae, Pompeii &c., Lear pointing out every object, each point of view, and dwelling on the historical or other associations with eager interest in my unrestrained delight at all we saw.

'We then went on to Rome, and the week we were there was one of the fullest and happiest we spent together. No one knew his Rome better than Lear, and in a week he had shown me more of the wonders and beauties of the old city and its surroundings than most people see in three months . . .

'We met in the evening in our hotel an old lady who greatly attracted Lear, and they had a long conversation on poetry and music; after dinner she mentioned Tennyson's song, "Home they brought her warrior dead". Lear at once went to the piano and sang his own setting of the words in a voice hollow with age, but with great style and deep feeling and accompanied with his favourite open chords, and he brought tears into the old lady's eyes. "Why!" she exclaimed, "that is the setting I referred to; do please tell me whose it is." "It is mine," replied Lear, and seeing the old lady's evident pleasure he sat down again and sang several of the Tennyson songs he had set to music, and the room filled with attentive listeners. As soon as he became aware of their presence he got up, and with an abrupt "Good-night" retired. A sudden change of feeling and manner to casual acquaintances was one of his characteristics . . .'[11]

When they reached San Remo, Lear knew that he must settle into long months of solitude. For twenty-one years Giorgio had organised his house, and latterly he had become a companion as well. Lear's anxiety about Giorgio's illness was exacerbated by his sense of guilt at having kept him away from home for months at a time. He had been an unusually thoughtful master, within the convention of those days when servants were often regarded as personal chattels, but he had grown to be so dependent upon his 'semi-=civilised Suliot . . . wild Rob Roy or Highlander',[12] that he had not thought of Giorgio's happiness as he should have done. Reproaching himself for his selfishness, Lear quoted over and over again Giorgio's last words to him. '"Padrone, so che non vi vedo più". 'O Earth! O Life! O Time!' he lamented. 'Useless it is to dwell on the past – useless to look ahead!'[13]

He moved into the hotel, going each day to the villa to work, taking with him a cold lunch which he shared 'with Poor old Foss, whose queer ways are in a manner touching'.[14] 'As yet – all this kind of life simply stupifies me,' he wrote, '& the cruel loneliness of every day drives me wild.'[15]

He had, however, one other companion and that was Hubert Congreve. Gradually, in the lonely, anxious months that followed, Lear's feeling for Hubert deepened. He had been a child when Lear came to San Remo, and Lear had given him and his brother Arny drawing lessons. 'These lessons were some of the most delightful experiences of my young days,' Hubert recalled, 'as they were accompanied with running comments on art, drawing, nature, scenery, and his travels mixed up with directions for our work. . . . I was frequently with him in his studio, and we also went sketching expeditions together, Lear plodding slowly along, old George following behind, laden with lunch and drawing materials. When we came to a good subject, Lear would sit down, and taking his block from George, would lift his spectacles, and gaze for several minutes at the scene through a monocular glass he always carried; then, laying down the glass, and adjusting his spectacles, he would put on paper the view before us, mountain range, villages and foreground, with a rapidity and accuracy that inspired me with awestruck admiration ... [The drawings] were always done in pencil on the ground, and then inked in in sepia and brush washed with colour in the winter evenings.'[16] Now he had grown up, and Lear found him 'a wonderfully delightful lad – free from all priggishness & vanity & yet full of knowledge'.[17]

Lear's relationship with Hubert's father had fared less well. Left a widower for a second time, Walter Congreve had become involved with his cook. She had become pregnant, and he had decided to marry 'that woman', as Lear called her. Uncharacteristically, Lear's reaction was stridently sanctimonious and aloof.

He took it upon himself to tell Hubert what had happened, and in order to give the boy the moral protection he now needed, he placed himself in loco parentis. He began to dream of the boy becoming an artist, and even conceived the idea of Hubert coming to live with him whilst he learnt to paint. Lear was at the end of his life, Hubert at the beginning, and the older man dreamt of seeing fulfilled in the boy some of the things that he himself had missed. He longed for companionship, and in Hubert he found both this and a charming, youthful enthusiasm. Hubert's visits lit up the days: alone, Lear became 'broken down with a hideous load of sorrow – the blinding accumulation of now nearly 60 years'.[18] One should not be naïve, but it would be doing Lear a disservice to suggest that he was an elderly man seeking a homosexual affair with a young boy. The longing that leaps from the diaries throughout this time is for some break in his interminable loneliness. The tenderness he expresses towards Hubert is that of a father towards an adored son, with all the dreams and longings that may involve.

He decided to spend the summer of 1877 in England, delivering his paintings and exhibiting his work. 'My brain is in so bewildered a condition from the contrast of this infernal place with the quiet of my dear Sanremo that I have nearly lost all ideas about my own identity,' he told Fortescue a few days after his arrival in London, '& if anybody should ask me suddenly if I am Lady Jane Grey, the apostle Paul, Julius Ceasar or Theodore Hook, I should say yes to every question.'[19]

He paid a happy visit to the Tennysons. Emily looked well, and the poet had lost much of his cantankerousness and become almost gentle. He went to see poor Ellen once or twice. She rambled on and on, reminiscing about the past, and he found it difficult to stay awake – but she was so pitifully blind and deaf that she did not notice.

Then, at the end of July, came news that shattered Lear. Hubert was leaving Italy and coming to King's College in the Strand. Lear had been told nothing of the plans, and this hurt him deeply. Beyond that, his dreams of companionship, of reciprocated affection and vicarious fulfilment were suddenly exploded. Time and again he had told himself that he must not care for anyone new, and now he had grown to love the boy.

'Is it better "to have loved and lost than never to have loved at all"? I don't know,' Lear had written years before. 'I think, as I can't help being alone it is perhaps best to be so altogether, jellyfish-fashion caring for nobody.'[20]

During August he came nearer to a mental breakdown than he had ever done. It was like the black winter of 1855, only then there had been a future. Now there was nothing. 'Tears, idle tears – always,' he wrote in his diary on 2 August. 'In vain I resolve & re-resolve: – gloom contracts & convulses me. But I am gradually getting to see that the past must be past, & buried: – yet I can by no means think of anything to put forward as the future. Meanwhile the present is a fearful blank – cutting off heart strings the only serious order of the day . . . In vain I work for an hour – tears blind me. In vain I play on the Piano, – I get convulsed: in vain I pace the large room – or try to sleep. True, all these symptoms happened also in 1855 – but then there was not the finality there is now: – then – there were unreal glimpses of light – : now – back returns the dark, "with *no more* hope of light". God help me. I was never nearer to utter & total madness than now. Yet, I don't mean to give way, & shall stave off worse things, if I can.'[21] 'How to "accommodate" a brain diseased?'[22] he asked as he turned inwards to the source of his isolation.

At the end of the summer he heard that Giorgio was worse,

and he decided to go to Corfu to see him. It was eleven years since he had been there, and coming round the point of S. Salvador into the canal & the Bay of Corfu was like a dream. 'No words can express the loveliness of what I saw, or the crowd of memories that overwhelmed me as I looked on the well known forms.'[23] He found his old servant better than he had expected, though still looking thin and ill. Giorgio now had to decide whether to come back to San Remo, or to stay in Corfu with his sons. If he remained, he would need better rooms than the dreadful ones in which Lear had discovered him. He decided to stay, and Lear found rooms where the whole family could live. He made all the arrangements and paid the rent, then he helped them to move in. As soon as this was done he left the island.

But Giorgio preyed on his mind. It had shocked Lear to see the conditions in which he had been living after all the faithful service he had given, and he brooded on his lack of thought in taking him from his family and expecting him to travel so far.

Giorgio stayed in Corfu throughout the winter and spring; then in the early summer a letter arrived from his doctor saying that he was better and would benefit from a change of air. Lear cabled to him to come, and he went down to Genoa to meet the boat. Together they travelled up to Monte Generoso in Switzerland, and for six weeks soaked in the mountain air. When they left in August Giorgio was fit enough to carry Lear's folio along the shores of Lake Como – it was like the days of old. When Lambi, one of his sons, arrived from Corfu to help with the heavy work, life at Villa Emily was ordered again.

Then one day in the early autumn, Lear realised that there was activity on the piece of land that separated his house from the sea. In 1873 he had wanted to buy this land and had offered £800 for it, but the owner, Miss Kay Shuttleworth, had been bound by contract not to sell whilst the adjoining villa was let. Two years later, when he did have a chance to buy, Lear could no longer afford to do so. Instead, a written agreement was drawn up saying that nothing would be built there without his being told, and then only two-storey villas. Now the olive trees were being felled and the land cleared, and it was rumoured that a huge hotel was to be built. Still, he had the agreement, so he need not worry.

By now his Indian commissions had come to an end, and he turned again to the Tennyson illustrations. 'There are 250 in all,' he told Lady Wyatt, '& 35 are advanced to a 2^d stage of their existence. These – wh in their 3^d or complete state will be good sized finished water-color drawings, are only to be done leisurely, & will go on all the rest of my asinine life.'[24]

'Ah the Tennyson illustrations!' wrote Holman Hunt, 'how they take one back – twenty seven years by Jupiter! when we neither had a gray hair – and there seemed plenty of time for regenerating oneself and the world by display of powers yet unknown. I feel that I might have got nearer than I did – to speak of my own part only but there were the heavy weights to drag me back all the while my life had spring in it, and so the impossibility of thinking of anything but how to get my next quarter's rent. I often wonder that when a young man has done something to prove the possession of talent some of the many people who had more money than they know how to have with satisfaction do not endow him with a hundred or two per annum to give him a better chance of doing his best with his short life. It used to strike me as very preposterous that while I met scores of millionaires – male and female who rightly or wrongly glorified my works as a sort of revelation from Heaven I was at the time wearing away my powers in doing miserable pot boilers sitting up half the night scraping glittering copper to illustrate some rubbishing book.'[25] How exactly he echoed Lear's feelings.

Lear's thoughts were still on money when he wrote to tell Fortescue some sad news. 'The Akhond of Swāt would have left me all his ppproppprty, but he thought I was dead: so didn't,' he wrote. 'The mistake arose from someone officiously pointing out to him that King Lear died 7 centuries ago, & that the poem referred to one of the Akhond's predecessors.'[26]

On the whole Lear saw little of the people in San Remo, but there was a new family there that winter to whom he took a liking. Their name was Bevan, and one day in April Miss Bevan and Lear joined forces to write a new poem, 'How Pleasant to Know Mr Lear'. When Lear called on the family one afternoon he found the children having tea, so he sat down at the piano to entertain them with some of his Nonsense songs. He sang 'The Owl and the Pussy-cat' and then the 'Yonghy-Bonghy-Bò' – but half-way through he broke down in tears. 'I was sorry I could do no more to help the swarry,'[27] he wrote sadly.

Throughout the spring of 1879 the activity on the land next door had increased, and Lear discovered that indeed a huge, four-storey hotel was to be built there. This would completely block his view to the sea, and wreck his studio light – to him the most important feature of the house. Not only had the agreement been broken, but the transaction had been kept a secret until it was too late for him to do anything about it. Moreover, the hotel was being built by a German, a race whom Lear had always loathed, and San Remo would become even more 'bescattered with horrid Germen, Gerwomen, & Gerchildren'.[28]

For Lear it was a far greater tragedy than a vanished view or a ruined studio light. Ever since he had been a young man he had saved carefully to safeguard himself financially against the very real possibility of his sight going, and to avoid the financial collapse and misery that his parents had known. Most of this money had gone into the house and its improvements, and now its value had suddenly been cut away. All his life he had been wary of encumbering himself with a house, which experience told him could only lead to unhappiness, and now he knew that he was right. Then there was the waste of his precious time when he knew that he had little enough left, and so much that he wanted still to do. '. . . it is a dreadful thing to be obliged to stop all one's poetical life=work,'[29] he told Fortescue. But perhaps more distressing than anything was that he had been deceived. He, who had given so much pleasure to so many and done so little harm, had become the victim of another's malignity. In fact, had he not cut himself off so totally from San Remo society, he might have known what was being planned and been able to call upon the agreement that had been drawn up. Now it was too late. He felt it as a personal attack, and gradually it acquired a huge dimension in his mind.

In July he got away from the building and went up to Monte Generoso for his usual summer stay. On the way he stopped in Varese, and in the papers for Monday, 7 July, he saw that Fortescue had a far greater tragedy to bear – for Lady Walde-grave was dead. Lear knew how devotedly Fortescue had loved her, and how terrible he must be feeling now, and he sat down at once and wrote him a heartfelt little note:

'I have just seen the London & Paris papers of Monday – & know – to my great sorrow – what has happened.

At present I only write to say that I am thinking of you & grieving for you.

God bless you.
Your's affectionately,
Edward Lear'[30]

By the time he reached Monte Generoso he had worked out ways that Fortescue could travel out to be with him. He suggested routes, where he could meet him, what he should bring to wear in the cold mountain air . . . almost as soon as one letter was posted he began on another with different, better suggestions. For the first time in years he felt that he might really be needed; he had always been Fortescue's confidant, and he was in a better position than anyone to help him now. Somewhere in his mind was probably the thought, too, that he could reclaim Fortescue's friendship which had been mortgaged since his marriage.

But, though Lear always moved on when his life became unbearably saddened, Fortescue preferred to stay near the places that his wife had known. It was as well that he did not come, for Lear would not have been good company just then. Samuel Butler met him that summer and found no gaiety in the old man. Marianne North was luckier, for he made a real effort to be a bright companion for her. She was on her way back from India so they had a lot to talk about, and Lear travelled down to Lake Como to see her. They decided to have a day out, and went by rail up to Monza to visit a new hotel at Monte Civita still undiscovered by the English. Marianne had been ill, and the 'Laughing and sunshine did more than any doctor's physic.'[31]

But when she saw him in San Remo a month later he was no longer able to make the effort. 'The laughing humour was over, and he was very grave, but had promised to avoid his great grievance if I came, and did so, showing me all his wonderful sketches of India, making me eat pellucid periwinkle soup, mulberry jam, and every other luxury only Mr Lear could think of, till at last, as the train was moving off, he looked in at the window and moaned out lugubriously, "Hasn't somebody been good not to mention the Enemy all day?"'[32]

The Enemy had grown whilst he had been away, and he was heartbroken to see the size of it. Not only did it completely block his view to the sea, but it had been painted white so that the dazzling sun and sea light were reflected in glaring brilliance into his studio. Wilkie Collins had been asking him to finish the story of Mr and Mrs Discobbolos, and it was now that he wrote the second part:

Suddenly Mr Discobbolos
    Slid from the top of the wall;
  And beneath it he dug a dreadful trench,
  And filled it with dynamite, gunpowder gench,
    And aloud he began to call –
'Let the wild bee sing,
'And the blue bird hum!
'For the end of your lives has certainly come!'
    And Mrs Discobbolos said,
    'O, W! X! Y! Z!
    'We shall presently all be dead,
  'On this ancient runcible wall,
    'Terrible Mr Discobbolos!'
Pensively, Mr Discobbolos
    Sat with his back to the wall;
  He lighted a match, and fired the train,
  And the mortified mountain echoed again
    To the sound of an awful fall!
And all the Discobbolos family flew
In thousands of bits to the sky so blue,
    And no one was left to have said,
    'O, W! X! Y! Z!
    'Has it come into anyone's head
  'That the end has happened to all
  'Of the whole of the Clan Discobbolos?'

He sent a copy of the poem to Mr Fields of Boston, who had published his nonsense songs in *Young Folks*, and to it he attached a statement reminiscent of excerpts from the *Nonsense Gazette*, only this time there was no nonsense and it showed, all too pathetically, what he was feeling:

'We regret to learn that a serious misfortune has happened to the well known Artist & Author, Edward Lear, whose various works have for years been favourably noticed by the Press. Millions of English=speaking people have laughed over Mr Lear's "Books of Nonsense"; many have read his "Journals of a Landscape Painter" in Italy, Albania, & Corsica: & not a few delight in his Landscapes in numerous houses throughout England. A considerable portion of the public therefore, cannot but be interested in what affects a man who has been the cause of instruction & of infinite amusement to so many.

'Some 10 years back Mr Lear bought a piece of ground at Sanremo, on which he built a house, trusting to pass the rest of his life in quiet there, and to carry out a long=ago commenced series of Landscape Illustrations of the Laureate's Poems. But, – through the unworthy intrigues of a few heartless persons the Land immediately below that of Mr Lear has suddenly been sold; – and, – notwithstanding the written promise of its owner that no such outrage should be committed, an immense Hotel has been erected, which not only shuts out every particle of sea view and condemns the Garden of the unfortunate Artist to sunlessness in winter, – but – what is of far greater importance, – wholly destroys the Light of his Studio by the vast mass of glaring reflection thrown from the enormous whitewashed building opposite.

'Unable any longer to use his house for Artistic purposes, we hear that Mr Lear is preparing to abandon the place he has made so pleasant, and is about to leave Europe for New Zealand. It is sad that a person so well known & to whose talents so many are beholden should be thus cruelly treated. His departure from Sanremo will be greatly regretted; nor are the Sanremesi at all reticent in their remarks on the parties whose intrigues are about to cause it.'[33]

Unwisely, copies of his Statement were sent to some newspapers, and it was published in *The World* and *The Atheneum*, losing him the friendship of John Addington Symonds, who was Miss Kay Shuttleworth's nephew, and bringing rumbling threats of libel.

He wondered seriously if he should leave San Remo, and told Mr Fields of a suggestion, 'that I should stump all Europe & America & wherever the English Language is spoken, as the Writer of the Book of Nonsense, with a view to colect innumerable sixpences so as to raise 7 or 8 Thousand Pounds to buy new land & build another house! ! – So look out for me & my cat some fine day – by a Boston steamer, on my way to San Francisco.'[34]

His talk of going to New Zealand was not serious, for he knew that he could not leave his friends in Europe. In England his friends were worrying about him. At Knowsley Lord Derby and Lord Northbrook discussed how they could best help him. '(How extremely queer),' wrote Lear, '(2 Earls talking over this "d——d Landscape=painter's" affairs!)'[35] In October Northbrook wrote offering him an interest–free loan of £2000 towards building another house, whilst Lord Derby commissioned £500 worth of drawings, 'for loans are a mistake'.[36] 'I cannot understand how such an asinine beetle as myself could ever have made such friends as I have,'[37] Lear thought.

He must decide now if he should start again with a new piece of land and a new house. At the end of December 1879, whilst he was still uncertain what he should do and completely preoccupied with the whole affair, he heard that Fortescue was coming to the south of France for the wedding of Constance, Lady Waldegrave's niece, and that he planned to come on to San Remo to stay with Lear. It would be the first time he had been there. Lear had earlier encouraged him to come, but now he dreaded the visit, though he told Fortescue, 'as you have more trouble than I, I will try to be a good boy & as cheerful as possible'.[38]

Fortescue arrived on 24 January 1880, and found his old friend turned in on his troubles: they were two isolated men filled with thoughts of their own. Still, he stayed for two months and felt happier than he had done since Lady Waldegrave's death. Before Fortescue left Lear had bought a new piece of land, and this time he made sure that no one would spoil it for him.

21 Villa Tennyson
1880–1883

'My new land has only the road and the Railway between it & the sea, so unless the Fishes begin to build, or Noah's Ark comes to an Anchor below the site, the new Villa Oduardo cannot be spoiled,'[1] Lear told Emily Tennyson.

Buying the land meant that until he had sold Villa Emily he would have to live on £100 a year, plus anything he made from the sale of his paintings. Since he had come to San Remo ten years before it had become an accessible and profitable resort, and the price of houses had risen. Of course, he should get a good price for Villa Emily with its additions and improvements, and he was advised to ask £7000 for it. In a dreadful way he was going to repeat the mistake he had made when he priced the 'Cedars of Lebanon'.

The money from Northbrook and Lord Derby was only a beginning. He had to rely on other friends – Lord Aberdare, Clowes and Cross – to supplement the '"compassionate squash'd=villa restorative fund"'.[2] Meanwhile, he began to sort through his thousands of drawings, for he planned to send boxes of them to London to be sold. Generally, the work that Lear exhibited for sale were water-colours or oil paintings made from the drawings he collected on his travels. He rarely sold the drawings themselves, regarding them as the topographical capital on which he based his work.

It was a sad task choosing the first four hundred, and as he turned over his old drawings of Rome and Greece and Corfu and Palestine, he felt that he was parting with something of himself. Whilst he was sorting and arranging them in packing cases, Northbrook arrived to visit him. He was appalled at Lear selling his drawings, and at once offered to buy fifty for £500. Lear would not accept the offer from someone who had already done so much, but he was persuaded that it would be more sensible to take an exhibition of his other work to London for the summer. Lushington had invited him to stay at his home in Norfolk Square, and to exhibit his work there.

Lear was in London by the end of April 1880 and his exhibition opened a month later. It went well, but he found London bewildering: '... in the interval between possible ruin or prosperity & present worry & work, I walk daily in this mucilaginous Metropolis, handed over the streets by polite Policemen in mercy to my blindness, – but horribly exasperated by the quantity of respirators or refrigerators or percolators or perambulators or whatever those vehicles are called that bump your legs with babies' heads. There are also distressing Bycicles, & altogether the noise and confusion so bewilder me that I have little knowledge of my personal identity left ...'[3] 'Bricks & mortar do not agree with me,' he told Lord Derby, '& London life is of all punishments the most shocking.'[4] Altogether it was '... a frightful whirl of inconsequent life that makes me wish I were an octapod or a Jerusalem Artichoke, or a Hippopotamus'.[5]

He saw Hubert Congreve, and went to the end-of-year prize-giving at Kings. He recorded the occasion like a protective, anxious and unbearably proud parent: 'Hubert called up II times: great applause to him & some others – most to him: (He was the only one who "backed" properly. –) Well for me I was a good way off as it was no slight task to keep nerves straight.'[6]

He visited the Tennysons, Fortescue, Northbrook. He dined with Gussie and her husband. 'Adamson Parker's gentleness under complete privation is beautiful,' he wrote in his diary, '& so is Gussie's constant care of him ... What would not life have been with that woman! !'[7] He visited Holman Hunt who was working on his painting, 'Flight into Egypt', which Lear thought 'very unlovely'.[8] Increasingly, Lear had grown to dislike Hunt's subject matter. 'I would fain see somewhat of a truer & broader caste of poetry,'[9] he told him, than 'any subject connected with miraculous or mythical, or even traditional interest,' particularly where it 'tends to strengthen the hands of priests – of whatever creed – the race who have preyed for ages on the foolish & helpless.' 'So far as populous delight would make success sure,' he wrote, somewhat cheekily, 'Daniel &c – with Balaam's ass seen thro' a window – Jonah's whale on a distant shore – Elijah's ravens – & the Gadarene piggywiggies – would be a lovely subject.'[10]

In June Bush went bankrupt, so there would be no more editions of the Nonsense from him, nor any of the money he owed Lear. Worse than this, he had lost the blocks of the last three Nonsense books, and if Lear wanted more editions he would have to do all the drawings again.

He stayed in London for four months, and before he left he made a final visit into the past. One evening he took Hubert to have dinner at the Zoological Gardens. '"You are just beginning the battle of life," he said, "and we will spend the evening where I began it." It was a beautiful evening in July and we dined in the open and sat under the trees till the gardens closed, he telling me all the story of his boyhood and early struggles, and of the meeting with Lord Derby in those gardens, and the outcome of that meeting – the now famous book, *The Knowsley Menagerie*. I never spent a more enjoyable evening with him, and Lear, when at his best, was the most inspiring and delightful of companions. He was then absolutely natural and we were like youths together, despite the forty and more years that lay between us.'[11] How one longs for a record of that evening's conversation.

Lear left London at the end of August 1880. It was his last visit to England.

'"The new house he go on like one old Tortoise,"'[12] Giorgio had written, and it was only up to the second floor when Lear got back. It was still unpleasantly hot in San Remo, so he left the building and went up to Mendrisio for a few weeks. Hubert Congreve joined him there and they spent a week together. The Congreves had moved now from San Remo, and when they parted for the last time Lear broke down and wept.

His self-imposed isolation in San Remo was now almost total. 'It is not agreeable to be disliked,' he wrote in his diary, 'but one has grown to be so, from one's lonely habits, – misunderstood & misconstrued.'[13] He wished that his friends would come to visit him, and he wrote suggesting how this might be achieved. 'My fervent advice to you is that you sit out for 8 nights consecutive in the Wadham Coll: gardens, with your feet in a pan of cold water & without your hat,' he instructed one of them. 'You could hardly fail thus to get a bad cold & perhaps a little rheumatism, – whereby your Cambridge Doctor would give you a Certificate for leave of absence, & you would be required to come & stay at San Remo.'[14]

A few days after this he read, without comment, *Alice in Wonderland*.

He began to plan his winter's work, and decided to begin on a new group of three hundred Tennyson drawings, 'in their final or Butterfly Condition. For at Clive Vale Farm they were in the Egg state: & next I advanced them to a larger size which may be called their caterpillar life. Then came detailed monochrome outlines of the full size they are to be, & that is their Chrysalis condition – whence the next move is the last & present one.'[15] By now his sight had become horribly bad. His right eye, which had been troubling him ever since his fall, was now almost useless. In order to see what he was doing, he had first to lay in a heavy outline, which destroyed the quality of his work. The project would never be anything but a grandly conceived failure, yet he could still dream of its eventual success. 'When the 300 drawings are done, I shall sell them for 18,000£: with which I shall buy a chocolate coloured carriage speckled with gold, & driven by a Coachman in green vestments and silver spectacles, – wherein, sitting on a lofty cushion composed of muffins & volumes of the Apochryfa I shall disport myself all about the London parks, to the general satisfaction of all pious people.'[16]

By June the new villa was finished. He named it Villa Tennyson, and this time he could not claim that he was calling it after a relation in New Zealand: the names of his two houses complemented one another to make up all that was most beautiful in a home. In order that the move might be as easy as possible for Foss, the new house had been built as an exact replica of the old. From Balmoral, Fortescue wrote to wish him well: 'I write a line at once to send you at once my best and warmest wishes for the Villa Tennyson, & for your prosperity and happiness – at all events for your peace – within its walls,'[17] he said, realistically.

Lear went as usual into the Swiss mountains for the summer, and on 8 August he wrote in his diary: 'I am obliged to add that I have not felt so well or so cheery for a long long time. O! the difficulty of dovetailing the charm of early artistic life, with the formality of later days! The calm & brightness of the view, & the lovely sweetness of the air, bring back infinite days & years of outdoor delight; – & I am thankful for this blessing, – though it can only last a few minutes.'[18]

He came back after two months with one hundred and fifty Tennyson drawings, and an idea for an immense new oil painting of Enoch Arden's island. 'I am feeling as melancholy as Enoch Arden; the loneliness of Sanremo is becoming difficult to bear when I am unable to work,'[19] he had written as far back as 1873. Now he planned to escape into the fantasy island, where he would put all the exotic trees and flowers that he had seen in India. His study of nature and his world of fantasy were converging.

He continued to work hard when he got back to San Remo, for he wanted to fill the walls of his new gallery ready for his

open days. He was pulled up suddenly by a frightening attack of giddiness, and Giorgio told him that he was working too hard and drinking too much. He had been warned about over-drinking during the summer he had stayed with Fortescue in Ireland, but now it had become a more chronic state and he was drinking a good deal of Marsala and water, though by his own account he 'never gets tipsy at all'.[20] As for working too hard, 'I *cannot* be idle, even if I could get my living by idleness,'[21] he wrote in November. '. . . it is a part of my creed that folding one's arms & dropping all energy is the worst thing one can do as age comes on.'[22] Each year he copied into the front of his diary, 'Always have 10 years' work mapped out before you, if you wish to be happy.'

He did think that perhaps he would write fewer letters, and he told Hubert Congreve, 'I am about to make a new arrangement at the end of 1881, *i.e.*, to correspond only with those I have been in the habit of writing to since 1850.'[23] But this was an impossible threat, for his correspondence was such a joy to him. 'He really *lived* upon the letters of his distant friends more than any man I have ever known,'[24] Lushington wrote after his death.

So he carried on with both his letters and his work, and by the end of November his gallery was ready. Constance Strachey, Lady Waldegrave's niece, later recalled Lear on his open days: 'He was by way of showing his studio on one afternoon in the week,' she wrote. 'On this day he sometimes sent his servant out and opened the door himself. This procedure was resorted to in order that he might keep out Germans, whose presence, for some unknown reason filled him with dread. If he did not like the appearance of a visitor, with a long face and woe in his voice he would explain that he never showed his pictures now, being much too ill. He would then shut the door, and his cheerfulness would return.'[25] Generally the visitors were allowed in, in fact his Wednesdays were usually very busy, but though his picture prices were modest enough – £9, £12 and £14 for drawings and 40 and 50 guineas for oil paintings – he sold very little.

That winter Constance Strachey found that although Lear was 'much aged and broken by worries and health, still the same sad whimsical personality and undefinable charm of the man attracted as ever'.[26] Not everyone would have agreed. 'About 11 came a ring at the bell,' he grumbled in the spring, 'a servant of Miss Lockharts with a large Bouquet & a card "with Miss M.L.'s kind regards, on Easter Day." – So I said I "didn't like presents", & sent it back. Possibly rather brutal, but better than re=entangling oneself with the Pharisee flunky folk.'[27] He found not 'a single creature here for whom I care the 999th part of the eight thousand-five-hundred-&-sixty-fifth fraction of a hog's bristle'.[28]

His attitude, though extreme, was not entirely surprising, for as he told Fortescue in March, 'My former income of over 100£ a year from 3500£ in the 3 percents, is now gone, & the worry of getting money to pay weekly bills is not pleasant at 70 aet – when one had thought to be high & dry above all bothers of the kind.'[29] Responsibility for his predicament rested on those who had allowed the hotel to be built, and he wanted nothing more to do with any of them.

He had to be more careful with some visitors though. That spring Queen Victoria came to stay at Mentone, and it was rumoured that she was coming to see Lear. In fact, word went round San Remo that Giorgio had been working for two days and nights making quantities of maccaroons for 'it is known that the Q of England eats maccaroōn cakes continually, & also insists on her suite doing the same. And there is no one in all Sanremo who can make maccaroōn cakes except Sig.r Giorgio Kokali,'[30] they said. Lord Spencer, the President of the Council, came over to lunch, and Lear tells us that more than a hundred people gathered outside the gate hoping that the Queen, too, would come.

'I dislike contact with Royalty as you know,' Lear wrote contentedly to Fortescue, 'being a dirty Landscape painter apt only to speak his thoughts & not to conceal them. The other day when some one said, "why do you keep your garden locked?" – says I,

– "to keep out beastly German bands, & odious wandering Germans in general." – Says my friend, – "if the Q. comes to your gallery, you had better not say that sort of thing." Says I, I won't if I can help it.'[31] 'The protocol involved in crossing the frontier prevented the Queen from coming, but she had not forgotten her one-time drawing master.

Nor, indeed, had her daughter. Lear spent the summer of 1882 in the Swiss mountains, and sitting at dinner one evening he saw a little woman peering at him through the dining-room door. Eventually, the man beside her pushed open the door and walked over to him. '"My wife wishes to know if you are Mr Lear, & she would be glad to make your acquaintance again – the Princess Royal of England."'[32]

Lear took the Tennyson drawings with him to Switzerland, hoping 'by making copies of them in black & white, – to reproduce them by Autotype – with a view to some separate publication'.[33] He had decided that they were to be his Liber Studiorum: published as a set they would represent his life's work as a painter.

In September he went back to San Remo, the pockets of his loosely fitting clothes crammed with Alpine plants. 'I was glad to get home again,' he wrote to Laura Coombe, '& to have the fun of gardening once more, which is really the only unchangeable pleasure now left in life.'[34]

And this is certain; if so be
You could just now my garden see,
The aspic of my flowers so bright
Would make you shudder with delight.

And if you voz to see my roziz
As is a boon to all men's noziz, –
You'd fall upon your back & scream –
'O Lawk! O criky! it's a dream!'[35]

Occasionally, of course, it brought problems. 'There have been deluges of rain lately,' he wrote in October, '& my garden was all overbeflowed, otters & salmon swimming all over the Virginia Stock, Walrusses walking about the Geranium cuttings, & an obese Hippopotamus sitting on the giant Anemone.'[36]

During the winter he decided to have no more open days. Little was bought, and the interminable chatter bewildered him. Henceforth he would deal only through the London gallery, sending over 'various small works to Foords – 129 Wardour Street, – which may eventually Wardoorff tin=difficulties.'[37]

In January Lord Derby wrote saying: 'Come over this spring and bring a room full of work with you. There is space still at Knowsley for a few more of your drawings, though I have a pretty good stock already.'[38] But Lear felt too old to take up this offer from a family that had never allowed him to be forgotten.

Then, in the spring of 1883, Gussie arrived in San Remo. Her husband had died a few months earlier and she was free again. 'What will now happen, who can tell?'[39] Lear had pondered when he heard the news. Would he, even now, think of marrying her? 'I wish I were not so "dam old",'[40] he wrote. She came to the Villa Tennyson every day during her stay, but he did not propose. 'Had her husband died 10 years ago, I might even then have hoped to have a good woman to nurse me at the last – but now it is too late,'[41] wrote Lear. On the morning she left he went into his garden and picked three nosegays – one for Gussie, and one for each of her nieces who were travelling with her, and he took them up to the hotel. Whilst he was with them he was composed; as he left he wept.

22 The End
1883–1888

One by one Giorgio's sons had moved into Villa Tennyson. Lambi had been joined by thirteen-year-old Dmitri, and soon Nicola, who found work in the local trattoria, became part of the household as well. Now that Giorgio was with his family Lear was seeing a different, less attractive, man. There were frequent noisy rows which Lear, who hated quarrels, was called upon to umpire. Then Giorgio began to turn against him, and early in 1882 Lear realised that his old servant was drinking heavily. One day in June he disappeared, and was found, days later, wandering on the hills above Toulon. He had lost his memory and was in a pitiable state. All that Lear could discover was that Giorgio had cabled to Lushington that he needed money, and was apparently on his way to England. Nicola went to collect him, and together they travelled up to Monte Generoso so that Giorgio could rest in the mountains. 'I scout the notion of treating domestics less kindly than horses or dogs – & even when they are eversomuch in fault I think it is wiser to try to keep them from total ruin, than to be indifferent to their welfare. And if I am laughed at for these ideas & acts, – vy, – I don't care for that the 999th part of a spider's nose.'[1]

Lear joined them in July, and from Monte Generoso he wrote to Fortescue: 'His health has gained greatly . . . but the brain is affected to a miserable extent, & I see no prospect but of a gradually increasing idiotcy or softening of the brain. The poor fellow is generally quiet enough, but has become melancholy & semi=savage, – sometimes not speaking all day long, or bitterly angry when he speaks at all.'[2]

Despite his worries, Lear was typically philosophical. 'I must be thankful that I am not blind & paralytic,' he wrote, 'nor have dropsy, smallpox, typhus, rheumatism, or any similar obsquash-tulous nuisance. When the infuriated beetle bit off 73 of the Centipede's legs, what did that philosophical but unpleasant animal remark? – "Let me be thankful that I have still seven legs left!"'[3]

They spent a quiet winter in San Remo, but as the summer of 1883 came on there was more trouble, for Lambi was discovered stealing wine. Then Lear discovered that the boy had a wife and two children in Corfu. Giorgio endorsed Lear's decision to send Lambi home, but the fuss did him little good and his health became gradually worse. In June Lear sent him to Monte Generoso again, but when he followed shortly after he saw that Giorgio was really ill. For a month he watched his old servant becoming tireder and weaker, and he could do nothing to help. As Giorgio weakened his belligerence disappeared, and he became as Lear had always known him.

Early on the morning of 8 August 1883, he died quietly. Lear wrote at once to Fortescue:

'This is to say, my dear good servant & friend George died, quite calmly, an hour ago.

'He is to be buried at Mendrisio, by the Milan English Protestant Chaplain.

'Please write to me.'[4]

'I hold it truth with him who sang
To one clear harp in divers tones
That men may rise on stepping stones
Of their dead selves to higher things'

he wrote to Emily Tennyson, misquoting from *In Memoriam*. 'It is well for foolish people to say, – how can a mere servant be such a stepping stone? – but to one who for 30 years knew George's constant fidelity, activity, humility, goodness of disposition, – endless cheerfulness – honesty, – patience, & untold other virtues, it is plain since his death, that as a 'stepping stone' he is ever of more value to my life now than in all the 30 years of his unbroken kindness & service.

'I wish I could think that I had merited such a friend, & that I had never been hasty or cross; but if *anything* is known to those separated from us, then *all* may be known, & more allowance may be made for faults than self accusing memory may imagine.'[5]

The idea that friends who died could be stepping stones into his own eternity appealed to Lear as his thoughts turned more and more to the purpose of life and death. It was positive, a continuing act of human kindness, and he made lists of the people who had become his stepping stones, from Ann to Giuseppe, his little gardener who had died of fever after working on in the cold rain.

As soon as Giorgio had been buried Lear wanted to be on the move again. 'I feel that the only thing that can mitigate this sorrow, & give a thorough change to the direction of my thoughts, will be to try the novelty of some place hitherto unvisited, say Madeira, or S. America, or Japan, or Java. But neither my 72 years nor my general health would allow of this relief.'[6] Instead, with little Dmitri to carry his folio as Giorgio had always done, he walked through Florence and Perugia, Spezia and Genoa and reached San Remo in September.

The first thing he did there was to choose a site for his own grave, and then he arranged for a stone to be placed alongside to commemorate his old servant. He thought a great deal about death that winter. '. . . the Grasshopper has become a burden, & the quick=pace downhill transit to indifference & final apathy is more & more discernible as month follows month,'[7] he wrote to Fortescue. 'The longer I live the more I think I perceive the spaces of this life to be inexpressibly trivial & small, – & that, if there be a life beyond this, our present existence is merely a trifle in comparison to what may be beyond. And that there *is* a life beyond this, it seems to me the greatest of absurdities to deny, or even to doubt of.'[8] 'That all this trouble=whirl of sorrow & worry – all these entangled & dumb feelings are nil – I cannot believe.'[9]

He spent some time sorting through his possessions and deciding what he would leave to each of his friends, but he could not finally settle his affairs until the Villa Emily was sold. The previous autumn it had been let to two women as a school for young ladies, but they had disappeared without paying the rent and now he had bills for insurance and tax and repairs for more than £100: '. . . you will perceive,' he wrote to Fortescue, who like some of his other friends was getting a little tired of hearing about Villa Emily and the hotel, 'that "*the hotel*" is *not* a mere bugbear, but a matter that *may* eventually drive me mad, & which in the meanwhile prevents my working & makes me ill.'[10] He had earlier reduced the price from £7000 to £3000 but now in desperation he was prepared to take whatever he could get. In February, at last, the house was sold for £1600. This was £400 less than he had paid for it fourteen years before, but at last he was freed from the preoccupying worry.

But the strain and worry had told on him. Within a few days he had collapsed with pleurisy. For several days he was really ill, and he recovered only slowly. As he lay in bed his mind turned back to the past. 'I think a great deal in these latter days of all my life,' he wrote, '*every particle* of which from the time I was 4 years old, I – strange to say, – can perfectly remember . . . And, thinking over all – I have long since come to the conclusion that we are *not wholly* responsible for our lives ie – our acts, *in so far as* congenital circumstances, physical or psychical over which we have no absolute control, prevent our being so. Partial control we assuredly have; but in many cases we do not come to know our real responsibilities or our nonresponsibilities – till long after it has become too late to change the lines we have early begun to trace & follow.'[11]

As the hot weather came on, he left San Remo to convalesce, but as soon as it was cool enough he was back in the 'Paradise quietness' of his home. 'As for ıny elth, it ain't elth particularly –but rather pheebleness, & I can now hardly doddlewaddle as far as the pestilential po-stoffis,'[12] he wrote.

In London his work had not been selling, and 'I am beginning to do like old Simon Stylites – i.e. to live "on my Capital" – wh. may (or may knot) last my time out.'[13] He told Foord & Dickenson to halve the price of the Corsican pictures, but paintings are not like strips of carpet, and reducing their price can make them even less attractive than before. Then they tried advertising them for 'wedding or birthday presents . . . of most sizes and prices', but still no one wanted them.

That winter saw the final unhappy break-up of Giorgio's family. In October little Dmitri too began to steal. It was hard for Lear to see this happening, for he had looked after the boy for five years and had taught him to read and write. But he was dismissed and sent back to Corfu. Now there was just Nicola, and he was dying of consumption. As the winter went on he became weaker, and by February he was more or less confined to his room. He was the last person to whom Lear could repay his debt to Giorgio, and he spent a great deal of time with him. Nicola wanted to talk, but what he had to say was not happy. He looked back to his childhood in Corfu. Each summer, said Nicola, when Lear had gone back to England and Giorgio had returned home, they had dreaded his coming. He drank and kept another woman, he gave his wife practically no money and he bullied them all. Nicola probably exaggerated what had happened but, unpleasant as it must have been for Lear to see this picture of his old servant, perhaps it did help to settle his worried conscience.

Nicola died on 4 March 1885, aged 34. Less than a fortnight later Ellen died at her home in Leatherhead. This was the final break with his immediate family – now there were just nephews and nieces in New Zealand and North America. 'The "stage" is indeed fast becoming vacant,'[14] he wrote sadly.

Yet, in spite of everything, he continued to work hard, 'unwilling to subside into muffinlike & mucilaginous monotony'.[15] In April, Foord & Dickenson mounted an exhibition of his Egyptian water-colour drawings which he was offering for sale at only £5 each. The exhibition was reviewed in the *Academy Magazine* by Amelia Edwards, who had recently published an account of her journeys up the Nile. This set Lear wondering, and he brought out his own unpublished journals, then wrote asking if she could advise him about placing them with a publisher. 'I don't say – mind, – that my "Nile Diaries of a Landscapepainter" would be worth the 99th part of a grasshoppers eyelash,' he wrote to her, 'but they might be so if considered as a part of this child's art life, & also if orbemented by good yet small would=cuts.'[16] '. . . there is & must be a great drawback in *my* writing wh. your's on a similar subject would not have: – & that is, that whatever *I* write would be *Edward Lear* – egotistical & unmitigated – fanciful – individual – correct or what not – but nevertheless always *Edward Lear*: – whereas what *you* write might be written by Mrs Tompkins, or Queen Boadicea, or Lady Jane Grey, or Rizpah of Gibeah, Joan of Arc or anybody else – because "A.B.Edwards" never appears at all.'[17] She offered to arrange an introduction to Harpers, but then Lear seems to have decided that they were after all not good enough, and since he did not feel up to re-working them the idea was dropped.

He was still working at the Tennyson drawings, 'vainly hitherto seeking a method of doing them by which I can eventually multiply my 200 designs by photograph or autograph, or sneezigraph or any other graph',[18] for the Autotype reproductions had not been successful. He wondered if he would ever see the project complete, though 'directly I die, they will (all the 200) be recognised as sublime, poetical, & unique: they will all be exquisitely engraved, & endless beastly booksellers & pestiferous publishers will be enriched thereby'.[19]

Nevertheless, he felt that the project was far enough advanced for him to prepare the text for the lengthy Dedication to Emily Tennyson. He was thinking now of using lithography and publishing them 'in a series of 10 or 12, but to be had separately – as the centipede said of his 100 legs when they kept dropping off as he walked through the raspberry jam dish'.[20]

In 1863 a young artist called Underhill had helped Lear with the lithographs for the Ionian Islands book, and now Lear wrote asking him to come out to San Remo to help him again. He had just made arrangements for the visit, when Fortescue wrote to say that he would like to come out to stay. In 1881 he had been appointed Lord Privy Seal in Gladstone's administration, but now they were out of office he had decided to have a holiday. 'I am so glad to think of you as quiet, & out of the miserable mumbling of governmental gluepots,'[21] Lear wrote to him. Lear's dislike of 'Polly Titians' had taken over from his dislike of priests, and Fortescue had grown weary of hearing him ranting against Gladstone in particular.

For months Lear had been trying to persuade Fortescue to come and stay, offering him a bedroom 'looking out on the sounding syllabub sea and the obvious octagonal ocean',[22] but now, since Underhill would be at Villa Tennyson, Lear booked a room for Fortescue at the Hotel de Londres.

Both men were shocked at how the other had aged. Fortescue was still overwhelmed with his responsibility for his wife's death, and after a hard term of office he was feeling tired and low. One evening, about a week after his arrival, he sat out on the promenade watching the sun go down, and when he arrived back at the hotel he was thoroughly cold and shivery. Within a few hours he had a high temperature. It was the first time he had broken down since his wife's death, and he succumbed completely.

Perhaps it would be unfair to say that Lear resented his friend's illness, but possibly it would be true. In fact,

Fortescue's illness seems almost to have weakened Lear's own formidable resolve. Lady Waldegrave's death, for which he felt some responsibility, had left Fortescue shattered with grief, and he became morbidly depressed. 'I am & have been quite alone – living with my dead love, wh. yet lives more than anything else within me,'[23] he had told Lear earlier. In his sad loneliness he would sleep with her glove in his hand, or cover her clothes with his tears and kisses. He had worked on in demanding public office, though a part of him was dead. He probably never expressed the real depth of his distress, and it is doubtful if Lear appreciated how he really felt.

Though dependent on his friends in many ways, Lear's whole life had been a lonely struggle against difficulties which he could share with nobody. 'The wonder is, things are as well as they are through constant fighting,'[24] he had written. Yet here was Fortescue, who still had so much – indeed Lady Waldegrave had left him a very rich man – giving in so apparently easily under the one burden of her death. Nowhere does Lear criticise his old and dear friend, yet a note of increasing weariness and irritation now creeps into his letters to Fortescue, and his own determination seems to falter.

They dined together on Christmas evening, and Fortescue wrote in his diary: '. . . he came at 6, & has just gone at 9. He had felt very unwell, & said he wd. not have come for anyone else "except Frank Lushington". Last night he said he felt as if he were dying. He was the better for his dinner, & we had a great deal of talk.'[25]

Within a few days Lear was bedridden with bronchitis; he was thoroughly weary and ready to give up the fight. Emily Tennyson wrote to cheer him: 'However solitary your life has, for many years been, you must not forget that to you is given the precious gift of peopling the lives of many not only of this generation but of generations to come with good & beautiful things & thoughts, to say nothing of your own life of which so many think with a loving admiration very precious to them.'[26]

Lying in bed he completed his obituary which he had begun when he was ill with pleurisy in 1884, then he copied it out and sent it to his closest friends. It was called 'Incidents in the Life of my Uncle Arly'. He described his youth when he lived by teaching, and 'by selling Propter's Nicodemus Pills' – his 'uncommon queer shop sketches'. Then came his introduction into society, which gave him his 'First Class Railway ticket'. And the pea-green cricket

'Clinging as a constant treasure, –
Chirping with a cheerious measure, –
Wholly to my uncle's pleasure, – '

Was this his Nonsense, his real means of self-expression? Then
he wandered for 'three-and-forty winters' – from 1827 when
Bowman's Lodge was sold until 1870 when he bought Villa
Emily –

'Sometimes silent; – sometimes yelling: –
Till he came to Borley-Melling,
Near his old ancestral dwelling; –
(But his shoes were far too tight.)'

What a strange phrase – and he had written on it before:

'O dear! how disgusting is life!
To improve it O what can we do?
Most disgusting is hustle & strife,
& of all things an ill fitting shoe –
    shoe,
O bother an ill fitting shoe!'[27]

Is he talking about the constraints that he felt had crippled his
life – the epilepsy, the homosexuality, the deep, inexpressible
realisation of the sadness of life that had grown from the depths
of his own unhappiness? Yet, perhaps even he knew that from
this very perception of sadness had grown a compassion, an
understanding and a pity for man's suffering, and it was this
compassion that made him the loved and loving man he was. It
was from this too that Lear's humour had come – as Carlyle said,
'The essence of humour is sensibility, warm, tender fellow feeling with all forms of existence.'[28]

This was the last piece of Nonsense he wrote: Prospero's wand
was broken. But as he snapped it, he knew that it had been worth
while, for in February 1886 Ruskin wrote in the *Pall Mall
Magazine*: 'I really don't know any author to whom I am half so
grateful, for my idle self, as Edward Lear. I shall put him first of
my hundred authors.'[29] It was a moment of rare pride for Lear –
and he made one more copy of 'Uncle Arly' and sent it to
Ruskin.

In March he was able to settle the final payment of his debt to
Northbrook. 'It is impossible to say what a relief this has been to
me,'[30] he wrote. It was six years since he had borrowed the
money, and now he was old and ill and tired.

It was not until April that Lear was well enough to be out of bed again. He had been ill for four months, and he never really picked up. He tried Brianza once more for the summer, but it was too hot and he went on to Mendrisio. Coming home through Lucerne in September he was taken ill. '. . . my health . . . is quite broken,' he wrote to his nephew, 'though I am thankful that my sight & intellent are all they ever were.'[31]

Lushington came to stay in November, and from San Remo he wrote to Hallam Tennyson:

'I won't leave this place without sending you an account of my dear old Lear – He is much better than he was in the summer, and his Dr (Hassall) who at Lucerne thought very ill indeed of his chances of recovery, now says that he may be considered as having "taken out a new lease" subject to various conditions which always make his life 'more or less precarious. But he is sadly aged and feeble – very crippled at times with rheumatism – totters about within the house – hardly goes out at all even on his terrace just outside the windows – has to be dressed and un-dressed by his manservant Luigi – and goes to bed by 6 o'clock. A great deal of the day he passes on the sofa – and all that he does do is only done by short fits and starts. He still occupies himself mainly with his series of illustrations of your father's poems – always trying some new schemes for getting them properly reproduced in autotype with a view to publication. I am afraid it will turn out an expensive hobby to him, even if it is successfully done – I doubt if he is likely ever to do much more work as a painter . . . The only point in which he is quite his old self is his intense interest in all his friends and his pleasure in hearing from them.'[32]

He only said, 'I'm very weary. The rheumatiz
he said. He said, it's awful dull & dreary – I
think I'll go to bed.'[33]

wrote Lear to Fortescue on 10 December.

In the spring he felt better and tried again to work through a full day, but by the evening he had collapsed.

Then in March he wrote asking Gussie to come out to San Remo. She stayed in the hotel, and each day she sat with him, talking and looking over his drawings or occasionally reading to him, and on 4 April he wondered 'more or less perplexed as to if I shall or shall not ask Gussie to marry me. Once or twice the crisis nearly came off, yet she went at 5 & nothing occurred beyond her very decidedly showing me how much she cared for me . . . This I think was the day of the death of all hope.'[34] And so at seventy-four, when he was almost a complete invalid, he had come nearer to proposing to her than he had ever done. The fears he had had about marriage were unimportant now, and if she had accepted him he would have been nursed lovingly out of life.

His friends did not forget him, and a few weeks after Gussie left the Northbrooks came to stay. In England Lushington was arranging the purchase of his oil painting of Argos by members of Trinity College, Cambridge. The Tennysons were thinking of him too, for in April Hallam wrote to say that an American publisher called Estes was bringing out a new edition of his father's poems, and would like to see Lear's drawings. The proofs of Underhill's lithographs had been 'absolutely good for nothing',[35] but, undefeated, Lear had been struggling on, considering reproduction by photography or even Platnatype, though he knew that any such method was bound to fail. 'I fear I have only the alternative before me of beginning & executing the whole 200 over again,' he told Fortescue, 'or of giving up my 40 years work altogether, a disgust & humiliation I shrink from, as the snail said when they showed him the salt cellar.'[36] 'The work will never be what I intended it to be,' he wrote apologetically to Hallam, 'for I did not set out properly at the first to make the drawings really fit for reproduction; but at that time I had not the experience I now have as to the immense difficulty in the way of photography, Autotype, or any of the many "graphies". I have tried with so much patience – such great expense – & such continual failure . . .'[37]

Mr Estes arrived on 7 May 1887, and later told Hallam: 'Upon inquiry for Villa Tennyson I was warned not to visit it, unless I was a friend of its inmate. I found Mr Lear sitting up for the first time for several weeks, and he insisted upon showing Mrs Estes & I not only all the Tennyson drawings but all his other drawings & paintings one of the latter of which I bought to his evident satisfaction. He assured us that our call had enlivened him and done him a world of good. The 200 drawings are very interesting and would add greatly to the interest of our proposed Edition, but some portions are unfinished in details, and would require *very artistic treatment* at the hands of an engraver or etcher. It is very evident that their reproduction and publication are the dearest wish of the old gentleman's heart, but that he almost despairs of this result . . . I fear a sensation of pleasure is a rare thing to him in his sad old age.'[38]

But the idea came to nothing, and it was only after Lear's death that a small book was published, limited to one hundred copies signed by Tennyson, containing three poems – 'To E.L. on his Travels in Greece', 'The Palace of Art' and 'The Daisy' – and using some of his two hundred illustrations.

And so he sat, sometimes reading the Greek Testament or *In Memoriam*, sometimes just looking out of the window. The terrace was 'one complete bower of full blown roses – little cluster flowers',[39] and eleven pigeons, nurtured by the cook, had hatched and fluttered busily around outside. 'No bird is more beautiful than a pigeon,'[40] he wrote as he watched them, and he was ending where he had begun.

He managed to get to Adorno in the mountains for the three summer months. 'It seems all very like a dream,' he wrote, '& indeed reality & dream seem to approach each other in an undefined way.'[41] He was back in San Remo in September. A few days later Foss, his last faithful companion, died.[42] As the winter progressed he grew gradually weaker. Each day he lay on the sofa and took occasional walks on the terrace, but by the beginning of January he no longer tried to get out of bed. One day he seemed a little better, but all at once he became really ill. 'For a month and a half he was never tired of talking of his nearest and dearest, his good friends,' his servant Giuseppe Orsini wrote to Lushington. 'But on the 29th, half an hour after midnight, with the greatest grief I act as interpreter of his last words – they are these precise and holy words – "My good Giuseppe, I feel that I am dying. You will render me a sacred service in telling my friends and relations that my last thought was for them, especially the Judge and Lord Northbrook and Lord Carlingford. I cannot find words sufficient to thank my good friends for the good they have always done me. I did not answer their letters because I could not write, as no sooner did I take a pen in my hand than I felt as if I were dying."[43]

At about 2.20 a.m. on the morning of Sunday, 29 January 1888, Lear died peacefully.

'We went of course to the funeral. I have never forgotten it, it was all so sad, so lonely. After such a life as Mr Lear's had been and the immense number of friends he had, there was not one of them able to be with him at the end.'[44]

On a little heap of Barley
Died my agèd uncle Arly,
    And they buried him one night; –
Close beside the leafy thicket; –
There, – his hat and Railway-Ticket; –
There, his ever faithful Cricket; –
    (But his shoes were far too tight.)[45]

A Brief Chronological Table
of Lear's Travels

1831 or 1832   Amsterdam, Rotterdam, Berne, Berlin.
1835   *July–August*, Ireland.
1836   *August–October*, Lake District.
1837   *June–July*, Devon and Cornwall. *July–December*, Belgium, Luxembourg, Germany, Switzerland, Italy, Rome.
1838   Rome. *May–August*, Bay of Naples.
1839   Rome. *Summer*, walking tour towards Florence.
1840   Rome. *Summer*, Subiaco.
1841   Rome. *Spring*, England, *September*, Scotland. *December*, Rome.
1842   Rome. *April–May*, Sicily.
1843   Rome. *July–October*, Abruzzi.
1844   Rome. *September–October*, Abruzzi.
1845   Rome. *May*, England.
1846   England. *December*, Rome.
1847   Rome. *May–June*, Sicily. *July–October*, Southern Calabria and the Kingdom of Naples.
1848   Rome. *April–June*, via Malta to Corfu, Ionian Islands. *June*, Greece: Athens, Marathon, Thermopylae, Thebes. *August*, Constantinople. *September–December*, tour of Greece and Albania. *December*, Malta.
1849   *January–February*, Cairo, Suez, Sinai. *February*, Malta. *March–June*, tour of southern Greece, Yannina, Vale of Tempe, Mount Olympus. *July*, England.
1850   London, Royal Academy Schools.
1851   London, Royal Academy Schools. *July–August*, Devon.
1852   London. *July–December*, Hastings.
1853   *January–February*, Hastings, London. *December*, Egypt.
1854   *January–March*, Egypt. *April*, Malta, Marseilles, England. *August–October*, Switzerland, England.
1855   England. *October*, Corfu.
1856   Corfu. *April*, Albania. *August–October*, Greece, Mount Athos, Dardanelles, Troy, Corfu.

1857   Corfu. *April*, Albania. *May*, via Venice to London. *November*, Corfu.

1858   Corfu. *March*, Alexandria, Jaffa, Jerusalem. *April*, Bethlehem, Hebron, Petra, Dead Sea. *May*, Beirut. *June*, Corfu. *August*, England. *November*, Rome.

1859   Rome. *May*, England. *July–November*, St Leonards. *December*, Rome.

1860   Rome. *May*, Bay of Spezia, England. *October–December*, Weybridge.

1861   Weybridge. *January*, London. *May–August*, Florence, Switzerland, England. *November*, Corfu.

1862   Corfu. *May*, via Malta to England. *November*, Corfu.

1863   Corfu. *April–May*, Ionian Islands. *June*, via Italy to England.

1864   *January*, Corfu. *April*, Athens, Crete. *June*, England. *November*, Nice. *December*, Corniche walk.

1865   Nice. *April*, England. *November*, Venice. *December*, Malta.

1866   Malta. *April*, via Corfu, Dalmatian coast, Trieste to England. *December*, Egypt.

1867   Egypt. *April*, Palestine. *May*, northern Italy. *June*, England. *November*, Cannes.

1868   Cannes. *May–June*, Corsica, England. *December*, Cannes.

1869   Cannes. *June*, Paris. *July*, London. *December*, Cannes.

1870   Cannes. *March*, San Remo (briefly). *June*, San Remo. *Summer*, Certosa del Pesio.

1871   *March*, moves into Villa Emily, San Remo. *Autumn*, Genoa, Rome, Frascati, Bologna, Padua.

1872   Villa Emily. *June–October*, England. *October*, sets out to India, but turns back at Suez.

1873   Villa Emily. *October*, to India. *November*, arrives Bombay.

1874   India. *November*, Ceylon. *December*, leaves for San Remo.

1875   Villa Emily. *June–September*, England.

1876   Villa Emily.

1877   Villa Emily. *February*, Brindisi, Rome. *May–September*, England. *September*, Corfu, San Remo.

1878   Villa Emily. *Summer*, Monte Generoso, Switzerland.

1879   Villa Emily. *Summer*, Monte Generoso.

1880   Villa Emily. *April–August*, England. *September–October*, Varese, Monte Generoso.

1881   Villa Emily. *May*, moves out of Villa Emily. *Summer*, Monte Generoso. *October*, moves into Villa Tennyson, San Remo.

1882   Villa Tennyson. *Summer*, Monte Generoso.

1883 Villa Tennyson. *Summer*, Monte Generoso. *September*, Perugia, Florence, Pisa, Spezia, Genoa.
1884 Villa Tennyson. *Summer*, Recoaro, Milan.
1885 Villa Tennyson. *Summer*, Brianza.
1886 Villa Tennyson. *Summer*, Brianza.
1887 Villa Tennyson. *Summer*, Adorno.
1888 Dies on 29 January at Villa Tennyson.

Bibliography

Books are published in London, unless otherwise stated.

Works by Edward Lear

A Book of Nonsense, by Derry Down Derry. Thomas McLean. 1846, 1855.

A Book of Nonsense. Routledge, Warne and Routledge. New and enlarged edition, 1861.

Nonsense Songs, Stories, Botany and Alphabets. Robert Bush, 1871.

More Nonsense, Pictures, Rhymes, Botany, etc. Robert Bush, 1872.

Laughable Lyrics, A Fourth Book of Nonsense Poems, Songs, Botany, Music, &c. Robert Bush, 1877.

Illustrations of the Family of Psittacidae, or Parrots. Pub. R. Ackermann and E. Lear, 1832.

Gleanings from the Menagerie and Aviary at Knowsley Hall, ed. J. E. Gray. Privately printed, 1846.

Views in Rome and its Environs. Thomas McLean, 1841.

Illustrated Excursions In Italy, 2 vols. Thomas McLean, 1846.

Journals of a Landscape Painter in Albania, &c. Richard Bentley, 1851.

Journals of a Landscape Painter in Southern Calabria, &c. Richard Bentley, 1852

Views in the Seven Ionian Islands. Pub. Edward Lear, 1863.

Journal of a Landscape Painter in Corsica. Robert Bush, 1870.

Poems of Alfred, Lord Tennyson. Illustrated by Edward Lear. Boussod, Valadon & Co., 1889.

Natural History Books to which Lear contributed

The Gardens and Menagerie of the Zoological Society Delineated, ed. E. T. Bennett, vol. II, 1831.

A Century of Birds from the Himalayan Mountains, J. Gould. 1831.

Illustrations of Ornithology, Sir William Jardine, Bart, and Prideaux Selby, John, vols. III and IV, 1834.

A Monograph of the Ramphastidae, or Family of Toucans, J. Gould. 1834.

The Transactions of the Zoological Society, Vol. I, 1835, and Vol. II 1841.

A History of British Quadrupeds, Thomas Bell. 1837.

Birds of Europe, J. Gould. 1837.

A Monograph on the Anatidae, or Duck Tribe, T. C. Eyton. 1838.

The Zoology of Captain Beechey's Voyage, 1839.

The Zoology of the Voyage of HMS Beagle, ed. Charles Darwin. 1841.

The Naturalists Library, ed. Sir William Jardine, Bart, Vol. II Monkeys, Vol. IV Felines, Vol. IX Pigeons, and Vol. XVIII Parrots. 1843.

The Genera of Birds, G. R. Gray, vol. II, 1849.

Tortoises, Terrapins and Turtles, drawn from Life by James de Carle Sowerby FLS and Edward Lear. 1872.

Letters
Letters of Edward Lear, ed. Lady Strachey. T. Fisher Unwin. 1907.

Later Letters of Edward Lear, ed. Lady Strachey. T. Fisher Unwin. 1911.

A selection from the many books of Lear's nonsense published since his death
Queery Leary Nonsense, ed. Lady Strachey. Mills & Boon, 1911.

The Lear Coloured Bird Book for Children, Foreword by J. St Loe Strachey. Mills & Boon, 1912.

The Complete Nonsense Book, ed. Lady Strachey. New York, Duffield & Company, 1912.

Lear in Sicily, Introduction by Granville Proby. Duckworth, 1938.

The Complete Nonsense of Edward Lear, ed. Holbrook Jackson. Faber and Faber, 1947.

Teapots and Quails, ed. Angus Davidson and Philip Hofer. John Murray, 1953.

Lear in the Original, ed. Herman W. Liebert. New York, H. P. Kraus, 1975.

A Book of Bosh, chosen by Brian Alderson. Kestrel Books, 1975.

Bosh and Nonsense. Allen Lane, 1982.

Posthumous publication of Lear's travel journals
Murphy, Ray, ed. *Edward Lear's Indian Journal*. Jarrolds, 1953.

Fowler, Rowena, ed. *Edward Lear. The Cretan Journal*. Denise Harvey & Co., Athens and Dedham, 1984.

Books about Edward Lear

Slade, Bertha C., ed. *Edward Lear on my Shelves* (for William B. Osgood Field), New York, 1933.

Davidson, Angus. *Edward Lear: Landscape Painter and Nonsense Poet.* John Murray, 1938. Second edition, 1968.

Reade, Brian. *Edward Lear's Parrots.* Duckworth, 1949.

Richardson, Joanna. *Edward Lear.* Writers and their Work series, No. 184, Longmans, Green, 1965.

Hofer, Philip. *Edward Lear as Landscape Draughtsman.* Oxford University Press, 1968.

Noakes, Vivien. *Edward Lear: the life of a wanderer.* Collins, 1968.

Noakes, Vivien. *Edward Lear 1812–88: Catalogue of the Royal Academy of Arts Exhibition 1985.* Weidenfeld and Nicolson, 1985.

Byrom, Thomas. *Nonsense and Wonder: The Poems and Cartoons of Edward Lear.* E. P. Dutton, New York, 1977.

Thorpe, Adrian, ed. and introduced. *The Birds of Edward Lear.* The Ariel Press, 1975.

Hyman, Susan. *Edward Lear's Birds.* Weidenfeld and Nicolson, 1980.

Notes to the Text

Abbreviations used in the Notes

EL	Edward Lear.
d	Edward Lear's diary.
Ann	Transcriptions of the letters which Lear wrote to his sister Ann.
F	Chichester Fortescue.
Ly.W	Lady Waldegrave.
ET	Emily Tennyson.
HH	Holman Hunt.
LEL	*The Letters of Edward Lear.*
LLEL	*The Later Letters of Edward Lear.*
A &c	*The Journal of a Landscape Painter in Albania &c.*
Carl. ms.	Carlingford manuscripts in the Somerset Record Office, Taunton.
IJ	The *Indian Journal* at the Houghton Library, Harvard.
OF	William B. Osgood Field – *Edward Lear on my Shelves.*
AD	*Edward Lear*, by Angus Davidson.
BP	By way of Preface, *Nonsense Songs and Stories*, sixth edition.

1 Childhood 1812–1828

1 Edward Lear's recently discovered birth certificate gives his date of birth as 13 May 1812. Lear himself kept this date as his birthday until at least 1848. Some time between then and 1859, however, he began to keep it on 12 May. In a letter of 12 May 1882 he writes: 'I ain't 70 till 11.30 tonight.' He was not a superstitious man: most likely, the late hour of his birth led to a mis-dating, a fact which he discovered some time before 1859.

2 EL–Hubert Congreve, 31.12.82, quoted LLEL 18.

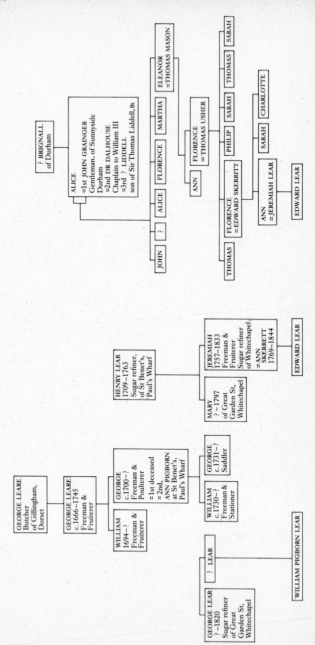

THE BRIGNALL/BRIGNELL FAMILY
(Edward's mother)

THE LEARE/LEAR FAMILY

Lushington repeats this story in his Introduction to *Poems of Alfred, Lord Tennyson*, illustrated by Edward Lear, 1889. It was probably, therefore, a story Lear told to all his friends. Whether it was his own invention, or that of his father, we do not know, but see Chapter 20[37] for further fanciful reference by Lear to his family, and Chapter 21[2] for an example of expedient fibbing. These were not the only occasions where I have felt that Lear is elaborating a little on the truth. Whilst he was in Rome, Lear came to know well a group of Danish painters. Possibly the Danish version of his name came from them: certainly it is typical of his enjoyment of analysing sounds and spelling. One other use of this word has survived. In a letter to F of 25.12.85, he says: 'Lör, I am sorry to say that foot swelling came on yesterday.'

3 The statements about Lear's ancestors have been built up from the following documents:

a the wills of George Lear, 1745; Henry Lear, 1763 (administration); Margaret Lear, 1795, and Florence Brignall Usher, 1802; all in Somerset House;

b London Directories from 1763;

c the records of the Corporation of London in the Guildhall Library;

d the records of the Chamberlain's office in the Guildhall;

e the parish records of St Mary's Whitechapel in County Hall, Westminster;

f Boyd's Marriage Register, and the parish records of All Hallow's, London Wall, in the Guildhall Library.

Despite a search of all the possible relevant documents other than these, I have been unable to trace Henry Lear's parentage: he may have been a son of George Leare who, like Jeremiah, was a Freeman of the City of London and a Livery Member of the Fruiterers' Company. There are sufficient circumstantial linkages to show that they were members of the same family, but whether Henry was of direct or collateral descent from George Leare I do not know.

4 Wanstead Parish Church Marriage Register. The banns of marriage between Jeremiah Lear, bachelor, and Ann Clark Skerrett, spinster, were published on 27 July, 3 August and 10

August 1788. 'Jeremiah Lear of this Parish, bachelor, and Ann Clark Skerr[e]tt of this parish, spinster, married in this church by Banns this 24 day of August, 1788 by me, Thomas Lyttetton, Curate. This marriage was solemnised between us

Jeremiah Lear
Ann Clarke Skerrett

in the presence of

Emma Lawrence
Thomas Barker (parish clerk).'

5   The Fruiterers' Company Minute Book, 1764–91, ms. 5401/2 in the Guildhall Library. 'At the Dolphin Inn, Bishopsgate St, on 12 April 1790, Mr Jeremiah Lear of Pinners Court Broad Street, Sugar Refiner was admitted into the Freedom of this company (by Purchase) & took the oath for that purpose Prescribed and paid his ffees – at the same time the said Jeremiah Lear took upon himself the Livery or Cloathing of this company and paid his ffine and the usual fees.'

He was admitted to the Freedom of the City of London on 27 April 1790, by redemption in the Fruiterers' Company. (Records in the Chamberlain's Court, Guildhall.)

6   The Fruiterers' Company Minute Book, 1764–91: 25 January 1797 – Jeremiah Lear elected Renter Warden; 25 January 1798 – Jeremiah Lear elected Upper Warden; 25 January 1799 – Jeremiah Lear elected Master, a post that he held for two years as his successor was unable to take up his post.

Records of the Corporation of London, Guildhall – 'Jeremiah Lear of 21 Hermes Street, Pentonville, and later of Pinners Court, Old Broad Street, was admitted and sworn a broker on 12 March 1799.'

7   List of Proprietors of the New Stock-Exchange anno 1801 in the Guildhall Library. Certificate in the possession of the Stock Exchange for one share.

8   Islington Rate Books Poor L–D to Michaelmas 1806, Upper Side, in the Central Library, Islington. The house was empty for the Midsummer Quarter: Jeremiah Lear began to pay in the Michaelmas Quarter. He paid £80 rent for the house and £20 for an adjoining piece of land.

9   Death registered in St James's district of Dover, Kent, on 31 May 1844, and recorded at Somerset House.

10 Records of the Official
    Assignees Office, Stock
    Exchange, London –
    Register of Defaulters.
    His account was settled for
    him by William Smith Jr.

11 AD 4. This was based on
    written family tradition
    formerly in the possession
    of the late Mrs Bowen.
    Although the ms is lost, a
    typed copy of these
    recollections has recently
    been rediscovered. In this
    Mrs Bowen states: 'The
    following notes were told
    to me by my grandmother
    Sophie Street, and written
    down by me at the time –
    about 1907.' Sophie Street
    was the wife of Lear's
    nephew Charles who was
    Sarah's son. The
    remoteness of the
    relationship to Jeremiah
    Lear and the lapse in time
    between the incidents and
    their telling – nearly 100
    years – accounts for their
    unreliability. Since,
    however, they have formed
    the basis of much that has
    been written about Lear –
    and indeed much that
    continues to be written – it
    is worth quoting from
    them. 'Jeremiah Lear a
    Dane by birth, but an
    English stockbroker by
    profession fell in love with
    Ann Clarke Skerritt, a girl
    of good birth and
    belonging to wealthy

people, whilst she was yet a
girl at school. She eloped
with him . . . Jeremiah was
himself a wealthy man, but
his wife had also £800 a
year in her own right. The
daughters often told Gram
– as we always called my
grandmother – that they
had 12 men servants, and
their Mother kept 12
carriages. When Edward
was quite a small boy (5) a
financial crash came (said
to have been the South Sea
Bubble) and while
Jeremiah was in the city
the bailiff put in his
appearance at Holloway.
Jeremiah was lodged in the
King's Bench Prison, and
resided there for 4 years.
In the meantime, his wife
who was a very plucky
woman, sold Holloway
and with it many of her
possessions, sent her
daughters out into the
world as companions and
governesses, and did
everything she could to pay
her husband's debts,
which she succeeded in
doing at the end of 4 years,
when every claim was
settled. But in the mean
time several of her
daughters had succumb-
ed, 4 are said to have died
in 4 months . . . The 4
eldest sons who before the
crash, had lived gay lives,
and never worked at all,

were so crushed that they declared they could not remain in England where they were so well known, and leaving their Mother and sisters to help the father, they departed (Henry and Frederick) to America, Charles to West Africa. Uncle Edward never forgave them for this . . . The Lears were a very handsome well educated family, they were all tall, save Mary and Harriett, but the girls were exceptionally handsome. Every night at Holloway they had to dress for dinner in white evening dresses with blue bows. Jeremiah had a hobby. He had a work shop with forge etc etc right at the top of the house, and he used to spend Sundays from 4 in the morning working there, the girls were never allowed in. He dressed beautifully in the evenings . . . Whilst in the King's Bench Prison Mrs Lear who had gone to live in Graves End – took him every day a full course dinner with the delicacies of the season . . . The 18th son Charles had an interesting story, he became medical Mission-ary and went to the West coast of Africa, was a great favourite of the Chiefs,

and when he nearly died of malaria, was put on board a ship for England. The Captain would not take him without a nurse, so Adjouah the native girl who nursed him went too, Charles insisted upon marrying her first. He took her to his sister Eleanor Newsome who had no children, and lived with her husband at Leather-head, Surrey. The story goes that the first day after her arrival she poured the jug of water in her bedroom over her head. They became very fond of Adjouah, she was sent to school for three years, and Charles returned to the Mission field, where he died. Afterwards she became a Missionary and returned to work amongst her own people.' In d, 27.4.81, Lear gives us the more likely reason for his brothers' departure: '2 of my Brothers suffered for deserting the Army, & for Forgery.'

12   The Fruiterers' Company Minute Book 1764–91 in the Guildhall Library. Jeremiah Lear remained on the livery of the Company until his death.
    Jeremiah Lear's name is not to be found in the surviving records of all the debtors' prisons preserved

in the Public Record Office, Chancery Lane, though the records of the Clink, Milbank, and the New Gaol, Southwark, have not survived. He was definitely not bankrupt: his name does not appear on the list of bankrupts published by the *London Gazette* throughout all the years of his business life. In fact, the whole thing is odd, as there is no break in his membership of the Stock Exchange from 1799 until 1828 as there should have been when he became a defaulter – but there is no doubt at all that he was a defaulter.

13 IJ, 13.1.74.

14 Quoted Ellen–Fanny, 15.2.7[3].

15 El–Ann, 15.12.56.

16 Ann–Frederick, 10.9.47.

17 El–Ann, 10.2.56.

18 d, 17.1.65.

19 Edward's recorded memories of Highgate jump from 1815 to 1819 or 1820. The Islington Rate Books give Jeremiah or J. Lear's name throughout these years. It is interesting to note that in the entry for 1819–20 Jeremiah Lear's name is given as Jh. Lear. In the next entry this becomes Josiah Lear until 1825 when Josiah Lear is crossed out and Jeremiah

Lear written over the top. This could mean that the house was taken by a relative during this time: but I believe that it was a clerk's error in substituting Josiah for Jh. as the family was certainly at Bowman's Lodge during the years the entry reads Josiah.

20 d, 27.9.62. OF 17.

21 d, 24.3.77.

22 d, 21.8.73.

23 d, 14.2.80, '. . . it is wonderful that these fits have never been discovered – except that partly apprehending them beforehand, I go to my room.' Also d, 21.8.73, 10.6.71. It is possible that some of Lear's Sussex friends knew of his attacks, e.g. d, 31.1.64 '. . . as Bern says, at 50 odd these bouts are not as when one was 30.' See also EL–Fanny Coombe, 15.7.32, Houghton Library.

24 d, 17.2.87, 'X reappearance of the Demon, after several weeks absence, a longer period than for years past. As yet it seems, the "self-control" is not worth much.' d, 12.4.87, 'X – it does not seem that "self control" has much to do with the matter.' See also d, 13.5.59, and 25.5.59, and Chapter 19, note 41.

25 d, 15.8.66.

26 *Sanditon*, Jane Austen, p. 25

27 EL–Ann, 9.9.48.

28 EL–F, 2.9.59, LEL, 148.

29 d, 18.9.61. No explanation is given of where '———' was.

30 Preserved at the Houghton Library, Harvard, and in the National Library of Scotland, Edinburgh.

31 AD 5. I have been unable to trace the source of this.

32 *Pickwick Papers*. 'See Mr Blackmore Engages an Office Boy' by Wm. J. Carlton, in *The Dickensian*, vol, 48, The Dickensian Fellowship, 1952.

33 EL–Fanny Coombe, about 15 July 1832.

34 EL–C. Empson, 1.10.31.

35 Both these poems are in the Houghton Library.

36 Talk of these introductions is found in Lear's diaries, e.g. 11.8.73, and in letters, e.g. EL–F, 12.6.74, LLEL 174.

37 Sir Edward Strachey's Introduction to *Nonsense Songs and Stories*, where he talks of Lear having heard Turner sing at a party, and d, 28.4.71. At this party, in Hullmandel's studio, the only occasion Lear mentions of having been with Turner, Lear heard Turner sing 'And the world goes round a-bound, a-bound'.

38 Florence Brignall Usher's will (given in 1792 and proved in 1802) states that her property was to be put in trust for her daughter, Florence Skerrett, and then for her granddaughter, Ann Clarke Lear, not subject to the debts of her husband. The trust was then to benefit the children of Ann Lear, that is Edward's generation, free of marital control. In 1869, Edward's sister Ellen spoke of her grandmother's money which she wished to settle on her nephews. Since this was not inherited from her paternal grandmother, it looks as though some at least of Florence Brignall Usher's money did come through her daughter to her great grandchildren. When Edward's sister Ann died in 1861, he inherited from her an annual income of £50. This must also have been part of her great-grandmother's bequest, for Ann inherited nothing from either her father or her mother. It is strange, and probably of considerable significance in Lear's attitude to money, that he apparently inherited none of this money directly. His constant reference to being 'thrown out into the

world without a penny' (or
a halfpenny, or a farthing)
may have come from his
sense of injustice that the
share of the inheritance
that was his in fact never
came to him.

39 d, 29.3.68.

2 **The Family of Parrots
    1828–1832**

1 Uncle Arly.
2 BP, p. 6.
3 Fowler autobiography.
4 EL–F, 21.1.62, LEL 222.
   Lear met Jardine a little
   later. 'I was introduced to
   him as a young artist by *N.
   A. Vigors*, then Secy. Z.S.'
   (El–Sir Joseph Hooker,
   3.6.78.) Several plates –
   e.g. CXLVII and CXLIX
   (1835) – are signed by Lear.
5 BP, p. 6.
6 Minutes of the meeting of
   the Zoological Society for
   16 June 1830.
7 Page 125. See *Edward
   Lear's Parrots* by Brian
   Reade, p. 10. I am indebted
   to Brian Reade for his
   book, from which a
   number of points made in
   this chapter have been
   culled.
8 The Houghton Library
   possesses a splendid
   collection of drawings,
   water-colour drawings and
   lithographs, and there is a
   further collection in the
   Wood Library of McGill
   University, Montreal.

9 Lear was proposed for
   Associateship on 2
   November 1830, and
   elected on 18 January 1831.
10 EL–C. Empson, 1.10.31.
11 ibid.
12 W. Swainson–EL, 26.11.31.
   Edward Lear's Parrots,
   p. 16.
13 EL–W. Jardine [c. 23.1.34]
   ibid.
      On 16 January 1834,
   John Gould wrote to Sir
   William Jardine: 'Mr
   Lear's Parrots stopped at
   the 12th number. I have
   purchased from him the
   whole of his stock so that if
   you are not complete as far
   as published I can make
   them so – I have some idea
   of finishing them myself.'
14 EL–Baring, 11.10.67.
15 EL–C. Empson, 1.10.31.
   Lear often spoke of
   himself as ugly, yet all
   drawings and photographs
   show him as a pleasant-
   looking man of sensibility.
   The burden of his epilepsy
   made him feel that his
   whole body carried an
   ugliness, however; e.g. d,
   8.1.67: 'I am coming to the
   conclusion that my small
   brain is better able to
   manage my ugly body.'
16 Fowler autobiography.
17 d, 20.2.85, 'Considering
   that I myself in 1833 had
   every sort of syphilitic
   disease, who am I to blame
   others, who have had less

education & more
temptation?'

18 National Library of
Scotland. Published in
Poetry Review, London,
April 1950. This is
subscribed *Bury Hill, E. L.
Novr. 1829.*

19 'The Pelican Chorus'.

20 d, 20.9.62.

21 d, 26.9.69. Quoted in
Nonsense and Wonder by
Thomas Byrom, p. 34.

22 These drawings are
ascribed to Mrs Gould but
Lear almost certainly
helped her. The drawings
by Lear in the Trans-
actions of the Zoological
Society are all animals.

23 Vol. XIX *Pigeons*, and
vol. XVIII *Parrots*.

24 Several drawings though
not attributed to Lear, are
inscribed 'Drawn by me.
Edward Lear', in his own
copy. Houghton.

25 See for example *Birds of
Europe* – Barn Owl and
Cinerous Vulture, both in
vol. 1

26 d, 7.2.81.

27 *Journal of a Landscape
Painter in Corsica*, 21.5.68.

3 The Knowsley
Menagerie 1832–1837

1 Uncle Arly. CN 276.

2 *Creevey Papers*, vol. II,
p. 57.

3 *The Diary of Frances, Lady
Shelley 1787–1817*, p. 13.

4 AD 15. I have been unable
to trace this story.

5 Fowler autobiography.

6 EL–C. Empson, 1.10.31.

7 LEL xix–xx.

8 EL–F, 1.5.84.

9 AD 17. EL–Miss Coombe.
I have been unable to trace
this letter.

10 Introduction to *More
Nonsense.*

11 LEL xix.

12 One of Lear's fellow
students was William
Frith.

13 EL–Gould, 31.10.36.

14 EL–Ann, 15.12.56.

4 Italy 1837–1845

1 EL–Ann, 3.11.37.

2 ibid.

3 ibid.

4 EL–Ann, 14.12.37.

5 EL–Ann, 3.11.37.

6 EL–Ann, 14.12.37.

7 ibid.

8 ibid.

9 ibid.

10 EL–Ann, 27.1.38.

11 EL–Ann, 28.5.38.

12 EL–Ann, 10.6.38.

13 EL–Ann, 26.9.38.

14 ibid.

15 EL–John Gould, 17.10.39.

16 ibid.

17 EL–John Gould, 27.2.41.

18 ibid.

19 EL–Ann, 29.10.38.

20 EL–Gould, 28.8.41.

21 EL–Lord Derby, 5.6.42.

22 EL–Gould, 12.8.44.

23 EL–Ann, 27.8.44.

24 *Illustrated Excursions in*

Italy, vol. I, 28.9.44.

25 Carlingford diary, 1.5.45, quoted LEL xxiii.

26 ibid., n.d., quoted LEL xxv.

27 ibid., Sunday, quoted LEL xxv.

5 A Queen and a Revolution 1845–1848

1 For material in this paragraph I am indebted to Muriel Jaeger for her book *Before Victoria*, Chapter V, 'The Model Child'.

2 *The Butterfly's Ball* started a spate of similar books, and during 1807 and 1808 appeared *The Peacock at Home, The Lion's Masquerade, The Lioness's Ball, The Elephant's Ball, The Jackdaw at Home, The Fishes' Grand Gala*, and *The Water-King's Levee*.

3 Lear himself never used the word 'limerick' and preferred to call the rhymes 'nonsenses'.

4 Mrs Hugh Fraser, *A Diplomat's Wife in Many Lands*, vol. II, Chapter XX.

5 Lear said that Madame de Bunsen 'would never allow her grandchildren to look at my books, inasmuch as their distorted figures would injure the children's sense of the beautiful'.

6 Review of 1861 edition on undated newspaper cutting.

7 An edited transcript of Queen Victoria's diary preserved in the Royal Archives.

8 EL–F, LEL 214.

9 LEL xx–xxi. Introduction written by Lady Strachey.

10 EL–Ann, 31.12.46.

11 EL–Ann, 6.2.47. In August 1846, Queen Victoria and Prince Albert visited Mount Edgcumbe, and the Queen wrote: 'We walked about the garden near the house and then drove to the "Kiosk", by beautiful stone pines and pinasters, which interested Albert very much and put me so much in mind of Mr Lear's drawings.' (*Leaves from the Journal of our Life in the Highlands*, Smith, Elder & Co., 1868, p. 286.)

12 ibid.

13 ibid.

14 EL–Ann, 8.1.47.

15 EL–Ann, 27.3.47.

16 Cicero. *Against Verres*, II, iv.

17 EL–Ann, 11.7.47.

18 EL–Ann, 24.7.47.

19 See AD, p. 47. I have been unable to trace the source of this story.

20 *Journal of a Landscape Painter in Southern Calabria*, 31.7.47.

21 ibid., 20.8.47.

22 ibid., 16.8.47.

23 ibid., 1.9.47.

24 ibid., 2.9.47.

25 ibid., 5.9.47.
26 EL–Ann, 16.10.47.
27 EL–Ann, 25.1.48.
28 EL–F, 12.2.48, LEL 8–9.
29 EL–Ann, 15.11.47.
30 EL–F, 12.2.48, LEL 6.

6 The Mediterranean 1848
1 EL–Ann, 19.4.48.
2 EL–Ann, 14.5.48.
3 EL–Ann, 19.4.48.
4 EL–Ann, 3.6.48.
5 ibid.
6 EL–Ann, 19.7.48. The length of his letters to Ann is truly remarkable. At the end of days of travelling he would settle down to write pages describing in detail the places he had visited and the things that had happened to him. One letter, written from quarantine on 8.10.57, is nearly 8000 words long. He asked Ann to keep his letters and he used them when he wrote up his journals for publication.
7 EL–F, 19.7.48, LEL 10.
8 EL–Ann, 19.7.48.
9 ibid.
10 EL–Ann, 12.8.48.
11 EL–F, 25.8.48, LEL 13.
12 ibid., LEL 13.
13 ibid., quoted LEL 12.
14 EL–Ann, 27.8.48.
15 A &c, 13.9.48.
16 A &c, 19.9.48.
17 EL–Ann, 13.11.48.
18 EL–Ann, 21.10.48.
19 A &c, 22.10.48.
20 ibid.

7 Franklin Lushington 1848–1849
1 EL–Ann, 24.2.49.
2 EL–F, 26.8.48.
3 EL–Ann, 8.3.49.
4 *Joint Compositions – A Rural Ride.*
5 ibid. – *Swing.*
6 EL–Ann, 21.4.49.
7 ibid.
8 d, 29.1.62.
9 d, 1.6.70.
10 d, 10.5.62.

8 Pre-Raphaelite 1849–1853
1 EL–F, 1.8.49, LEL 16.
2 ibid., LEL 15.
3 Mary–Frederick, [c. May 1850].
4 d, 25.9.58.
5 EL–F, 20.1.[50], LEL 23–5.
6 EL–Henry Catt, 11.4.51.
7 EL–ET, 2.12.51.
8 ET–EL, 4.12.[51].
9 *Household Words*, 15.6.50.
10 EL–Lord Derby, 28.11.50.
11 EL–Lord Derby, 3.3.51.
12 d, 30.1.61.
13 d, 6.7.64.
14 *Early Victorian England*, Oxford University Press, 1934, vol. 1, p. 177.
15 d, 14.3.68.
16 Ann–Fanny, 22.9.51.
17 EL–ET (n.d.).
18 F, 19.7.51, LEL 18.
19 EL–F, 26.8.51, LEL 21.
20 *Pre-Raphaelitism and the Pre-Raphaelite Brotherhood* by William Holman Hunt, vol. 1, p. 239.

21 ibid., vol. 1, p. 241.
22 Hunt–F. G. Stephens, Bodleian Library, MS. Don. e. 66, fol. 10v. Later during that stay Hunt told Stephens: 'I shall be glad when I can get back to town – everything tries my patience here, even good natured Lear who, being older than myself, I am obliged to humour.' (fol. 16v.)
23 EL–ET, 5.10.52.
24 EL–ET, 12.10.52.
25 ibid.
26 HH–EL, 24 April n.y.
27 d, 27.5.65.
28 EL–HH, 19.12.52. The painting of Reggio hangs now in the Tate Gallery.
29 EL–F, 23.1.53, LEL 28–30.
30 *Recollections of a Happy Life*, Marianne North, vol. 1, p. 29.
31 See *Alfred Tennyson* by Sir Charles Tennyson, p. 441. The other poems in this first publication were 'Edward Gray', 'A Farewell', and 'Sweet and low'. See also Chapter 12[27].
32 EL–F, 9.12.82, LLEL 279.
33 EL–F, 16.8.85.
34 *John Everett Millais* by John Guille Millais, vol. 2, p. 142.
35 EL–ET, 18.11.52.
36 EL–HH, 9.2.53.
37 F. G. Stephens–T. Woolner, 21.4.53, quoted in *Thomas Woolner R.A.*, by Amy Woolner, pp. 58–9.

38 EL–HH [June 1853].
39 EL–HH, 11.7.53.
40 EL–Lord Derby, 15.6.53.
41 EL–HH, 26.7.[53].
42 EL–HH, 11.7.53.
43 EL–HH, 12.10.[53].
44 EL–ET, 8.10.53.
45 HH–EL, 8.12.52.
46 EL–ET, n.d.
47 d, 8.12.60.

9 **The Morbids, 1853–1855**
1 EL–Ann, 7.12.53.
2 EL–Ann, 19.12.53.
3 Thomas Seddon to his brother, 30.12.53, quoted in *Thomas Seddon* by his brother, p. 32.
4 EL–Ann, 21.12.53.
5 EL–Ann, 23.12.53.
6 EL–Ann, 4.1.54.
7 EL–Ann, 17.1.54.
8 EL–Ann, 7.2.54.
9 EL–Ann, 15.2.54.
10 ibid.
11 ibid.
12 EL–Ann, 17.3.54.
13 EL–William Rossetti, 6.5.54.
14 EL–HH, 7.7.54.
15 EL–HH, 11.9.54.
16 EL–Mrs Ford, 19.2.[55].
17 EL–HH, 22.2.55.
18 Carlingford diary, 18.3.55. Carl. ms.
19 EL–AT, 9.6.[55].
20 ibid.
21 *Alfred Tennyson* by Sir Charles Tennyson, Macmillan, p. 286.
22 EL–ET, 27.7.55.
23 ET–EL, 13.11.55.
24 ET–EL, 17.8.55.

25 ET–EL, 30.8.55.
26 ET–EL, n.d. [Sept. 1855]
27 ET–EL, 27.10.[55?]
28 EL–ET, 29.10.55.
29 EL–ET, 28.10.55.
30 ibid.
31 Carl. diary, 16.9.55. Carl ms.

10 Corfu, 1855–1857
1 EL–Ann, 29.11.55.
2 Lear had been painting large canvases as far back as 1844 when he was working on one 6 feet long. See EL–Ann, 24.9.44.
3 When he lived in Rome Lear had known the Danish painter called Wilhelm Marstrand. On 18 October 1873, Lear wrote: 'Wilhelm Marstrand died 2 months ago. He was the F.L. of those days & I cannot dare to think of them.' See also, d, 7.10.61.
4 EL–Ann, 13.12.55.
5 EL–Ann, 26.1.56.
6 Quoted in F–EL, 17.9.56, LEL 37.
7 EL–ET, 15.12.61.
8 EL–Ann, 19.6.56.
9 Franklin Lushington – ET, 13.4.56.
10 EL–Ann, 13 & 3.4.56.
11 EL–Ann, 26.1.56.
12 EL–Ann, 27.4.56.
13 EL–ET, 9.10.56.
14 ibid.
15 EL–HH, 11.5.56.
16 EL–Ann, 8.10.56.
17 EL–Ann, 31.5.56.
18 EL–Ann, 15.7.56.

19 EL–Ann, 21.8.56.
20 EL–Ann, 23.8.56.
21 'The Story of the Four Little Children who went round the World'.
22 I am indebted to that most enjoyable book, *Mount Athos* by John Julius Norwich, Reresby Sitwell and A. Costa, for many of the facts about Mount Athos contained in this chapter.
23 EL–Ann, 8.10.56.
24 ibid.
25 ibid.
26 ibid.
27 ibid.
28 EL–F, 9.10.56, LEL 41–2.
29 EL–F, 11.1.57, LEL 49.
30 EL–F, 9.10.56, LEL 38.
31 EL–F, 11.1.57, LEL 45 & 47
32 EL–ET, 9.10.56.
33 Franklin Lushington – ET, 20.6.56.
34 EL–Ann, 15.12.56.
35 EL–HH, 7.2.57.
36 EL–Ann, 22.3.57. See Tennyson's poem to Christopher North.
37 EL–Ann, 18.1.57.
38 EL–Ann, 15.12.56.
39 d, 29.9.64.
40 EL–Ann, 9.11.56.
41 EL–Ann, 25.12.56.
42 EL–F, 11.1.57, LEL 45.
43 EL–Ann, 22.3.57.
44 EL–Ann, 15.3.57.
45 EL–F, 1.5.57, LEL 49–50.

11 The Holy Land 1857–1858
1 Thomas Woolner – ET,

25.6.57. Quoted in *Thomas Woolner* by Amy Woolner, p. 134.

2 EL–Ann [Aug. 57].

3 Lady Waldegrave retained this name after her third and fourth marriages. Lady Waldegrave's first husband, John, was illegitimate, so that she was legally able to marry her deceased husband's brother.

4 Carl. diary, 8.8.57. Carl. ms.

5 EL–Ann, 31.8.57.

6 Carl. diary, 9.8.57. Carl. ms.

7 EL–F, 6.12.57, LEL 64.

8 EL–Ann, 6.9.57.

9 ET–EL, 17.11.57.

10 EL–F, 6.12.57, LEL 65–8.

11 d, 28.2.58.

12 EL–F, 27.12.57.

13 EL–Ann, 1.1.58. This was in fact the Marchioness of Headfort.

14 EL–F, 27.2.58, LEL 88.

15 EL–F, 9.3.58, LEL 92–3.

16 EL–Ann, 29.3.58.

17 ibid.

18 EL–Ann, 30.3.58.

19 ibid.

20 d, 28.3.58.

21 d, 29.3.58.

22 EL–Ann, 29.3.58.

23 'The Journey to Petra – A Leaf from the Journals of a Landscape Painter.' First published in *Macmillans Magazine* in April 1897, and subsequently in *Edward Lear's Journals*, ed. Herbert Van Thal, Arthur Baker, 1952, p. 236. 10.4.58.

24 ibid., 13.4.58, pp. 244–5.

25 ibid., 14.4.58, p. 253.

26 EL–Ly. W, 27.5.58, LEL 106–7.

27 ibid., LEL 110.

12 Rome 1858–1860

1 d, 21.6.58.

2 EL–F, 5.7.58, LEL 112.

3 d, 22.10.58.

4 d, 1.10.58.

5 d, 12.10.58.

6 Woolner – ET, 22.10.[58]. Quoted in *Thomas Woolner* by Amy Woolner, p. 154.

7 d, 16.11.58.

8 EL–F, 10.11.[58]

9 EL–F, 13.12.58, LEL 123.

10 EL–F, 5.1.59, LEL 124.

11 EL–F, 13.12.58, LEL 123.

12 EL–Ann, 1.1.59.

13 EL–Ann, 20.1.59.

14 EL–F, 5.1.59, LEL 128.

15 d, 29.3.59.

16 EL–Ann, 10.4.59.

17 d, 7.6.59.

18 EL–F, 12.6.59, LEL 138.

19 d, 8.6.59.

20 EL–F, 12.6.59, LEL 139.

21 EL–F, 7.9.59, LEL 151–2.

22 EL–F, 31.7.59, LEL 145–6.

23 EL–F, 2.9.59, LEL 148.

24 d, 13.10.59.

25 EL–F, 4.11.59, LEL 155–6.

26 EL–HH, 9.12.59.

27 The five new settings were, 'Home they brought her warrior dead', 'As through the land at eve we went', 'Come not, when I am dead', 'O let the solid

ground not fail', and 'The time draws near'. Those from the Idylls of the King, whose publication was delayed until after Lear's return from Rome in 1860, were 'Turn, fortune, turn', 'Sweet is true love', and 'Late, late, so late'. Lear set at least nine other Tennyson poems to music, but these were not published. See *Edward Lear Sings Tennyson Songs* by Anne Henry Ehrenpreis, Harvard Library Bulletin, Vol. XVII, No. 1, Jan. 1979. See also Chapter 8[31].

28 d, 29.1.60.
29 EL–Ann, 16.2.60.
30 EL–ET [1860].
31 d, 11.3.60.
32 EL–ET [1860].
33 EL–F, 29.4.60.
34 EL–F, 21.9.61.
35 EL–F, 1.5.59, LEL 135–6.
36 EL–F, July 1859, LEL 141.

13 **Landscape Painter 1860–1863**
1 d, 17.2.61.
2 d, 16.6.60.
3 d, 17.6.60.
4 Ly. W–EL, 26.5.59.
5 EL–F, 9.7.[60], LEL 143. This is wrongly dated in LEL.
6 EL–ET, 19.7.60.
7 *Saturday Review*, p. 770, 15.12.60.
8 EL–F, 30.9.60, LEL 175.
9 ibid.
10 d, 30.9.60.

11 EL–F, 30.9.60, LEL 175.
12 EL–ET, 14.1.61.
13 EL–Ly. W, 23.10.60, LEL 180.
14 EL–Drummond, 10.10.61.
15 EL–ET, 30.12.60.
16 diary of 15th Earl of Derby, 15.2.61.
17 EL–Ly. W, 8.5.61.
18 EL–ET, 6.3.61.
19 ibid.
20 EL–F, 7.3.61, LEL 183.
21 d, 9.3.61.
22 d, 10.3.61.
23 d, 11.3.61.
24 EL–F [11.3.61].
25 d, 17.1.65.
26 ET–EL, 15.3.61.
27 d, 5.4.61.
28 EL–F [2.5.61].
29 d, 13.6.61.
30 d, 22.4.61.
31 d, 23.4.61.
32 EL–F, 24.6.61.
33 d, 27.5.61.
34 EL–HH, June 1861.
35 EL–F, 8.6.61.
36 EL–F, 29.8.61, LEL 189.
37 F–EL, 3.9.61.
38 EL–F, 5.9.61, LEL 194.
39 EL–HH [Nov. 64].
40 d, 31.7.62.
41 EL–Aberdare, 23.8.77.
42 EL–F, 5.9.61, LEL 194.
43 EL–HH [1861].
44 d, 24.12.61.
45 EL–F, 21.1.62, LEL 222.
46 *Saturday Review*, 21.12.61.
47 EL–F, 21.1.62, LEL 219 and 222.
48 EL–F, 17.12.61, LEL 212.
49 EL–Ly. W, 15.3.63, LEL 276–7.

50 EL–Ly. W, 13.4.66, LLEL 76.

51 EL–F, 21.10.62, LEL 252.

52 EL–F, 18.10.75, LLEL 187.

53 EL–F, 20.4.62, LEL 234–6.

54 d, 12.5.62.

55 EL–F, 20.4.62.

56 EL–ET, 18.7.62.

57 In his diary, 10.7.62, Lear noted for tax that his average annual income was £250.

58 EL–HH, 22.10.62.

59 EL–F, 7.5.62.

60 EL–ET, 18.7.62.

61 EL–F, 16.8.69, LLEL 107.

62 d, 24.2.61.

63 d, 20.12.67.

64 EL–F, 11.10.61, LEL 198.

65 EL–ET, 6.3.61.

66 EL–Aberdare, 23.8.77.

67 EL–F, 4.10.62, LEL 249–250.

68 EL–Ly. W, 4.11.62, LEL 255.

69 d, 1.11.62.

70 EL–F, 22.8.68, LLEL 105.

71 EL–F, 23.3.63, LEL 280.

72 d, 7.11.62.

73 Sir Edward Strachey, Introduction to fourth edition of NSS.

74 d, 10.1.63.

75 EL–Ly. W, 1.1.63, LEL 261.

76 d, 31.12.62.

77 EL–F, 25.11.58, LEL 119.

78 EL–F, 5.9.61, LEL 193. It has been said of Lear (AD33) that he sometimes wrote 35 letters before breakfast. HH tells us that 'sometimes he would write as many as thirty letters before breakfast'. Yet Lear tells us that a quick letter might take him twenty minutes. The only occasion on which he might write so many was when he was appealing for subscribers to his books.

79 EL–F, 17.10.62, LEL 250.

80 EL–F, 26.5.72, LLEL 150.

81 Franklin Lushington. Introduction to Petra Journal. See 11[23].

82 d, 31.1.63.

83 EL–Ly. W, 1.1.63.

84 EL–F, 1.3.63, LEL 274.

85 Reproduced in *Queery Leary Nonsense*, p. 6.

86 d, 13.4.62.

87 d, 15.1.63.

88 d, 6.3.63.

89 d, 30.3.63.

90 EL–F, 14.9.63.

91 EL–Drummond, 23.3.63.

92 EL–Aberdare, 31.7.63.

93 EL–F, 9.8.63.

94 ibid., LEL 284.

95 d, 4.9.63.

96 EL–F, 14.9.63, LEL 285.

97 d, 10.9.63.

98 EL–Drummond, 22.10.63.

99 EL–F, 31.3.64, LEL 304.

100 d, 17.12.63.

101 d, 22.12.63.

102 EL–F, 1.1.64, LEL 296.

14 Wanderer 1864–1866

1 EL–F, 6.9.63, LEL 289.

2 d, 12.5.63.

3 EL–F, 31.3.64, LEL 308.

4 d, 4.4.64.

5 ibid.
6 d, 10.4.64.
7 Homer, *The Odyssey*, Book XIX.
8 d, 15.4.64.
9 d, 22.4.64.
10 d, 18.4.64.
11 d, 15.5.64.
12 d, 15.6.64.
13 d, 24.1.65.
14 d, 11.12.64.
15 EL–HH [January 1865].
16 d, 11.2.65.
17 EL–F, 24.2.65, LLEL 59.
18 EL–Mrs Bruce, 10.1.65.
19 EL–F, 8.2.63, LEL 270–1.
20 EL–HH, January 1865.
21 EL–F, 21.4.65, LLEL 61.
22 EL–ET, 10.5.65.
23 d, 4.5.65.
24 EL–ET, 10.5.65.
25 d, 8. & 9.7.65.
26 d, 10.7.65.
27 d, 23.9.65.
28 d, 11.1.66.
29 EL–Ly. W, 24.11.65, LLEL 63–4.
30 EL–F, 13.4.66, LLEL 77.
31 ibid.
32 EL–Ly. W, 13.2.66, LLEL 69.
33 ibid.
34 d, 18.4.66.

15 A Proposal of Marriage? 1866–1867

1 d, 29.5.66.
2 d, 1.6.66. Tennyson's *Maud*, IX.
3 d, 2.6.66.
4 'The Courtship of the Yonghy-Bonghy-Bò'. Gussie too was a writer of children's books, including *Echoes of an Old Bell, and other tales of fairylore* (1865), and *Stories from the Realms of Fancy* (1874).
5 d, 23.8.66.
6 d, 4.10.66.
7 EL–Gussie Bethell, 7.8.66.
8 d, 25.8.66.
9 EL–Ly. W, 17.10.66, LLEL 78–9.
10 EL–F, 11.12.66, LLEL 81.
11 'Once-a-Week', 5.1.67.
12 d, 17.12.66.
13 d, 23.12.66.
14 Lord Derby's diaries, 18.3.84.
15 Lord Derby's diaries, 14.1.80.
16 d, 25.12.66.
17 d, 16.1.67.
18 d, 9.1.67.
19 d, 5.1.67.
20 'The Pelican Chorus'.
21 d, 30.1.67.
22 d, 28.1.67.
23 d, 6.2.67.
24 d, 8.2.67.
25 d, 24.1.67.
26 EL–Ly. W, 9.3.67, LLEL 83.
27 d, 7.2.67.
28 d, 8.2.67.
29 EL–ET, 22.3.67.
30 d, 25.3.67.
31 d, 14.4.67.
32 EL–F, 9.8.67, LLEL 86.
33 d, 22.7.67.
34 d, 23.8.67.
35 d, 26.7.67.
36 d, 2.11.67.
37 d, 3.11.67.
38 d, 20.10.79.

39 EL–ET, 10.5.65.
40 EL–F, 26.8.51, LEL 20.
41 d, 5.11.67.
42 'The Story of the Four Little Children who went round the World'.
43 'The Courtship of the Yonghy-Bonghy-Bò'.

16 **The Greatest Nonsense 1867**
 1 EL–F, 26.12.67, LLEL 89.
 2 d, 10.12.67.
 3 'Eclogue'.
 4 d, 2.5.87. Some of the ideas expressed in this chapter have been published in *Twentieth-Century Children's Writers* (St James's Press, 1977), in my contribution on Edward Lear. I am grateful to St James's Press for permission to publish them here.
 5 J. St Loe Strachey, foreword to *The Lear Coloured Bird Book for Children*.
 6 EL–F [1855], LEL 295.
 7 I am indebted to Elizabeth Sewell for her thought-provoking book, *The Field of Nonsense*, the most extensive and convincing book I have seen on this subject.
 8 'How Pleasant to know Mr Lear'.
 9 d, 29.11.67.
10 EL–F, 26.12.67, LLEL 88.
11 EL–Aberdare [spring 1855].

17 **Last Travel Book 1867–1869**
 1 EL–Ly. W, 9.1.68, LLEL 91.
 2 *Journal of a Landscape Painter in Corsica*, 10.4.68.
 3 EL–Ann, 14.5.58.
 4 EL–Ly. W, 6.5.68, LLEL 104.
 5 *Journal of a Landscape Painter in Corsica*, 3.5.68.
 6 ibid., 28.4.68.
 7 ibid., 28. and 29.4.68.
 8 d, 11.7.68.
 9 EL–F, 22.8.68, LLEL 105.
10 d, 11.12.68.
11 d, 22.12.68.
12 d, 11.2.69.
13 EL–HH, 6.7.69.
14 EL–Fields, 18.1.80.
15 EL–F, 12.9.73.
16 EL–Lord Derby, 13.4.81.
17 EL–HH, 6.7.69.
18 EL–Wyatt, 27.6.69.
19 d, 17.11.70.
20 EL–F, 11.1.57, LEL 44.
21 diary of Marian Bradley, 21.1.68.
22 d, 11.7.68.
23 d, 22.9.61.
24 d, 29.8.69.
25 d, 2.9.69.
26 d, 7.9.69.
27 F–EL, 25.8.69. Lear's own copy of *Alice in Wonderland* is now in the USA.
28 EL–Fields, 18.11.69.
29 EL–F, 16.8.69, LLEL 106–7.
30 d, 18.8.69.
31 EL–F, 19.8.69, LLEL 108.
32 d, 27.9.69.
33 d, 11.7.65.

34 *Tennyson*, by F. L. Lucas, p. 24.
35 d, 11.7.65.
36 d, 17.10.64.
37 The price to non-subscribers was £1.50.

18 **Villa Emily 1869–1871**
1 d, 29.3.68.
2 EL–F, 24.11.67.
3 EL–F, 1.1.70.
4 EL–Wyatt, 15.1.70.
5 EL–F, 1.1.70.
6 d, 8.2.70.
7 d, 9.1.69.
8 d, 18.3.70.
9 EL–F, 1.1.70, LLEL 111.
10 d, 4.4.70.
11 EL–Thomas Woolner, 1.5.70, quoted in *Thomas Woolner, R.A.* by Amy Woolner, p. 284.
12 EL–F, 31.7.70, LLEL 122.
13 *Roman Spring* by Mrs Winthrop Chanler, pp. 29–30.
14 EL–HH, 7.7.70.
15 ibid.
16 d, 26.7.70.
17 EL–F, 31.7.70, LLEL 124.
18 Lord Derby's diaries, 14.7.70.
19 Lord Derby's diaries, 18.10.71.
20 EL–F, 21.12.70.
21 EL–Wyatt, 29.9.70.
22 d, 21.11.70.
23 Some people remember Lear as a small man, but those who knew him best recall a tall, large man.
24 Preface to LLEL, pp. 17–18.
25 EL–Morier, 12.1.71.
26 EL–Wyatt, 11.12.70.
27 EL–Mrs Bruce, 24.12.70.
28 Charles Kingsley – Tom Taylor, 16.3.71.
29 EL–Morier, 12.1.71.
30 EL–Mrs Bruce, 24.12.70.
31 EL–F, 21.12.70.
32 EL–Ly. W, 22.1.71, LLEL 129.
33 EL–F and Ly. W, 24.4.71, LLEL 133.
34 d, 7.4.71.
35 EL–F and Ly. W, 24.4.71, LLEL 131.
36 EL–Drummond, 30.12.71.
37 d, 3.6.71.
38 d, 19.6.71. Frederick Harding made the drawing of Lear's father reproduced in this book.
39 Preface to LLEL by Hubert Congreve, LLEL 19–20.
40 EL–Prescott, 26.5.71.
41 EL–F, 28.2.72, LLEL 145.
42 d, 22.5.71.
43 EL–F, 13.9.71, LLEL 139.
44 EL–F & Ly. W, 25.12.71, LLEL 142.

19 **Coast of Coromandel 1872–1875**
1 EL–F, 26.5.72 LLEL 149.
2 EL–F, 28.2.72, LLEL 145. It is usually assumed, wrongly, that this statement refers to Foss.
3 'The Quangle Wangle's Hat'.
4 EL–F, 26.5.72, LLEL 147–8 and 150.
5 d, 14.7.72.

6 EL–Aberdare, 11.9.72.
7 EL–Wyatt, 31.7.72.
8 EL–Sir Edward Strachey, 25.8.72, Carl. mss.
9 EL–Aberdare, 4.9.72.
10 ibid.
11 d, 21.10.72.
12 d, 22.10.71.
13 d, 5.11.72.
14 d, 31.1.73. Had Lear not turned back from India he would not have bought the famous Foss.
15 d, 23.2.73.
16 EL–F, 28.2.72, LLEL 146.
17 d, 17.2.73.
18 EL–Ly. W, 6.7.73, LLEL 153–4.
19 d, 16.6.73.
20 d, 20.9.73.
21 EL–F, 15.10.73.
22 EL–F, 12.9.73, LLEL 155–6.
23 EL–Charles Street, 7.2.79.
24 EL–HH, 7.2.57.
25 EL–F, 19.10.64, LLEL 46.
26 Lushington – Hallam Tennyson, 4.2.88.
27 Lushington – Mrs Charles Street, 12.5.88.
28 Henry Strachey. Introduction to fourth edition of More Nonsense.
29 d, 1.5.60.
30 F–EL, 21.8.79, LLEL 223–4.
31 LLEL 37.
32 EL–F, 12.9.73, LLEL 156–7.
33 EL–F, 15.10.73, LLEL 166.
34 IJ, 22.11.73.
35 IJ, 4.12.73.
36 IJ, 11.12.73.
37 IJ, 12.12.73.

38 IJ, 14.12.73.
39 IJ, 2.1.74.
40 EL–Drummond, 15.10.73.
41 IJ, 17.1.74.
42 IJ, 18.1.74.
43 IJ, 19.1.74.
44 IJ, 10.2.74.
45 IJ, 13.2.74.
46 IJ, 16.2.74.
47 EL–F, 24.4.74, LLEL 171.
48 IJ, 20.4.74.
49 EL–F, 24.4.74, LLEL 170.
50 IJ, 28.4.74.
51 EL–F, 12.6.74, LLEL 172.
52 IJ, 6.2.74.
53 'The Cummerbund'. An Indian Poem.
54 'Jabberwocky', from Through the Looking Glass by Lewis Carroll.
55 IJ, 1.8.74.
56 IJ, 25.8.74.

20 The Cruel Shore 1875–1880

1 EL–Aberdare, 13.2.75.
2 d, 23.3.75.
3 EL–F, 28.3.75.
4 d, 6.6.75.
5 EL–Drummond, 29.6.73.
6 EL–Mrs Scrivens, 27.7.75.
7 EL–F, 7.5.76, LLEL 195–6.
8 d, 17.12.75.
9 EL–F, 7.5.76, LLEL 195.
10 The Standard, 14.12.76.
11 Introduction to LLEL by Hubert Congreve, LLEL 27–31.
12 d, 18.11.83.
13 d, 3.3.77.
14 d, 20.5.77.
15 d, 27.3.77.

16 LLEL 22–3.
17 d, 17.12.76.
18 d, 9.4.77.
19 EL–F, 28.5.77, LLEL 204.
20 EL–Ly. W, 10.2.70, LLEL 114.
21 d, 2.8.77.
22 d, 25.8.77.
23 d, 15.9.77.
24 EL–Wyatt, August 1878.
25 HH–EL, 22.8.78.
26 EL–F, 28.10.78, LLEL 213.
27 d, 26.4.79. Henry Strachey, who stayed with Lear in 1882, recalled 'In the evenings he often sang; the "Yonghy Bonghy Bò" was inimitable. His voice had gone, but the refinement and expression was remarkable.'
28 EL–F, 12.9.73, LLEL 159.
29 EL–F, 30.11.79.
30 EL–F, 9.7.79, LLEL 218.
31 *Recollections of a Happy Life*, by Marianne North, vol. II, p. 83.
32 ibid., p. 85.
33 EL–Mr Fields, 15.10.79, Henry E. Huntington.
34 ibid.
35 d, 30.10.79.
36 Lord Derby's diaries, 5.9.79.
37 EL–F, 25.3.84, LLEL 307. In his diary for 5.11.79 Lord Derby notes: 'Lord Northbrook, with whom he stayed in India, says that Lear has no expensive tastes, but an immense family of brothers & sisters, who live upon him & keep him poor.' Lear implied a similar story when he wrote to Gould from Rome as a young man.
38 EL–F, 21.12.79, LLEL 227.

21 **Villa Tennyson 1880–1883**

1 EL–ET, 16.2.80.
2 EL–Fields, 18.1.80. It is interesting that Lear claimed that Fortescue lent him money towards the house: in fact, he declined to do so, though he did offer to pay the interest if Lear could raise the money through a bank.
3 EL–F, 19.5.80, LLEL 234.
4 EL–Lord Derby, 23.7.80.
5 EL–F, 27.6.80.
6 d, 3.7.80.
7 d, 12 & 26.6.80.
8 d, 19.7.80.
9 EL–HH, January 65.
10 ibid.
11 LLEL 35–6.
12 Quoted in EL–F, 27.6.80, LLEL 234.
13 d, 14.10.80.
14 EL–Selwyn, 20.10.80.
15 EL–HH, 27.10.80.
16 EL–F, 24.10.80.
17 EL–F, 7.6.81, LLEL 241.
18 d, 8.8.81.
19 d, 31.8.73.
20 'How Pleasant to Know Mr Lear'.
21 EL–Charles Street, 27.11.81.
22 EL–F, 22.8.81.
23 EL–Hubert Congreve,

28.9.81, LLEL 34.

24 Franklin Lushington–
    Hallam Tennyson, 7.3.88.

25 Introduction to LEL by
    Constance Strachey, LEL
    xxxiii.

26 ibid., LEL xv.

27 d, 9.4.82.

28 EL–F, 12.2.82.

29 EL–F, 30.2.82.

30 EL–F, 10.4.82, LLEL 262.

31 EL–F, 30.3.82, LLEL 258.

32 d, 2.8.82.

33 EL–F [July/August 1882].

34 EL–Laura Coombe,
    22.10.82.

35 EL–F, 30.4.85, LLEL 336.

36 EL–Selwyn, 15.10.82.

37 EL–Selwyn, 14.2.83.

38 quoted OF 96.

39 d, 5.8.82.

40 EL–F, 31.8.82, LLEL
    268–9.

41 EL–F, 8.4.83.

22 The End 1883–1888

1 EL–F, 21.12.84, LLEL 325.

2 EL–F [July/August 82].

3 EL–Selwyn, 29.7.82.
   Whilst Lear's philosophy
   was undoubtedly correct,
   his arithmetic was not.

4 EL–F, 8.8.83, LLEL 288.

5 EL–ET, 18.8.83.

6 d, 12.8.83.

7 EL–F, 7.1.84, LLEL 295.

8 EL–F, 21.1.84, LLEL
   229–230

9 d. 21.5.76.

10 EL–F, 27.1.84.

11 EL–F, 27.6.84, LLEL 311.

12 EL–Selwyn, 29.12.84.

13 EL–Selwyn, 19.5.86.

14 d, 28.2.87.

15 EL–Edwards, 18.10.85.

16 ibid.

17 EL–Edwards, 26.10.85.

18 EL–Hubert Congreve,
    1883, LLEL 25.

19 EL–ET, 20.12.83.

20 EL–Miss Mundella,
    27.10.85. Quoted in *Call
    Back Yesterday* by Lady
    Charnwood, p. 287.

21 EL–F, 17.7.85.

22 EL–F, 21.1.84, LLEL 298.

23 F–EL, 27.12.83.

24 d, 24.12.61.

25 Carl. diary, 25.12.85, Carl.
    ms.

26 ET–EL, 22.1.86.

27 d, 3.1.79.

28 Carlyle. *Jean Paul Frederick
    Richter. Critical and
    Miscellaneous Essays II.*

29 *Pall Mall Magazine*,
    15.2.86.

30 EL–F, 2.4.86, LLEL 351.

31 EL–Charles Street, 1.8.86.

32 Franklin Lushington–
    Hallam Tennyson,
    14.11.86.

33 EL–F, 10.12.86, LLEL 353.

34 d, 4.4.87.

35 d, 1.4.86.

36 EL–F, 22.5.87.

37 EL–Hallam Tennyson,
    27.4.87.

38 Mr Este–Hallam Tenny-
    son, 8.5.87.

39 EL–F, 22.5.87.

40 ibid.

41 EL–F, 1.8.87.

42 Lear buried Foss in his
    garden and put up a stone
    claiming that the cat was 31

years old – in fact he had bought him as a kitten in 1872.

43 Franklin Lushington–Fortescue, 6.2.88; quoted LLEL 362. Lear spoke these last words in Italian.

44 Madame Philipp, widow of Dr Hassall who had attended Lear. Lady Strachey, 21.1.1911, LLEL 361. Lear is buried in the British Cemetery in San Remo.

45 'Uncle Arly'.

Portrait of Foss: – in tä dictäne, Foss master –

Notes to Illustrations

Line drawings
All the line illustrations reproduced in the book are by Edward Lear. The following are taken from books published in his lifetime:
A Book of Nonsense 1846, 1855, enlarged edition 1816: pages 25, 28, 54, 193
Nonsense Songs, Stories, Botany and Alphabets, 1871: pages 21, 50, 90, 112, 126, 135, 183, 184
More Nonsense, Pictures, Rhymes, Botany etc., 1872: pages 30, 35, 37
Laughable Lyrics, A Fourth Book of Nonsense Poems, Songs, Botany, Music &c, 1877: pages 172, 177, 181, 189, 211

Six illustrations have been reproduced from *Queery Leary Nonsense*, 1911: pages 69, 78, 98, 100, 109, 290

The remainder of the illustrations have been taken from Lear's letters and nonsense writing unpublished in his lifetime. Acknowledgement is due to the following for permission to reproduce them:
British Library: page 32
British Museum: pages 9, 42
Cornell University Library, Department of Rare books, page 240
Christie's Fine Art Ltd., page 222
James Farquharson Esq., pages 129, 162, 165
Mrs Hornby, page 47
Houghton Library, Harvard, pages 64, 74, 104, 207, 227, 254
Henry E Huntington Library and Art Gallery, San Marino, California, page 235
David Magee, Esq., page 82
Pierpont Morgan Library, New York, page 83
National Portrait Gallery, page 157
Somerset Record Office, Taunton, pages 79, 170, 196, 197, 209, 217, 230

Tennyson Research Centre, Lincoln, pages 139, 143, 149, 199, 258
Victoria and Albert Museum, London, page 243

The following additional notes may be of interest:

42 'Scene in the Campagna of Rome, 1842.'

47 'The musicians emerge simultaneously from the bale of wool and play the 'Unting chorus in a perspicacious manner.'

79 '. . . I can place my canvas on a lofty easel, I myself standing on the green seat, thus:' Letter to Lady Waldegrave c. 1860.

82 Lear at the Royal Academy Schools. From a letter to Fortescue of January 1850.

83 Ye poppular author & traveller in Albania & Calabria, keepinge his feete warme. 1. ye traveller: 2. ye Railewaie rugge: 3. ye author his vestmentes: 4. his hatteboxe: 5. ye cheste of draweres: 6. ye chaire: 7. ye large cheste: 8. ye washingtable: 9. ye drying table: 10. ye traveller his bootes: 11. ye sparkling looking glasse: 12. ye table: 13. ye tinne tubbe: 14. ye china tub: 15. ye matting rolled uppe: 16. ye quadrangular pin-cushione: 17. ye jugge: 18. ye flaskes of gunnepowder: 19. ye picklejarres: 20. ye beautiful chaire made of wickerworke: 21. ye peaceful cherubbes that appeared to ye author when he fell asleepe.

143 Lear feeding 'the unfortunate birds at Oatlands Park Hotel'. Dated 14 January 1861.

165 'The Landscape painter perceives the Moufflons on the top of the Mountains in Crete'. Dated 5 July 1864.

170 'General appearance of a distinguished Landscape painter at Malta'. Letter to Fortescue dated 29 May 1862.

197 'If the sea is very rough I mean to hire a prudent & pusillanimous porpus, & cross on his bak.' Letter to Fortescue dated 26 September 1875.

209 '. . . I think of marrying some domestic henbird and then of building a nest in one of my own olive trees where I should only descend at remote intervals during the rest of my life.'

235 'Lear and Foss arriving in Boston'. Letter to Fields dated 15 October 1879.

Photographs

Plate	Name
1	Dr David Michell
2	Earl of Derby (photo Walker Art Gallery, Liverpool)
3	BBC Hulton Picture Library
4	'Illustrations of the Family of Psittacidae'
5	National Portrait Gallery
6 & 7	Dr David Michell
8	Islington Public Library
9	Mrs M. B. Coe
10	'Gleanings from the Menagerie at Knowsley Hall' (photo Houghton Library, Harvard)
11	Mrs M. Fowler
12	'Illustrated Excursions in Italy' 1st Series 1846
13	Houghton Library, Harvard
14	Tate Gallery, London
15	Houghton Library, Harvard
16 & 17	BBC Hulton Picture Library
18	Vivien Noakes
19	BBC Hulton Picture Library
20	Private Collection (photo Courtauld Institue of Art)
21	Fitzwilliam Museum, Cambridge
22	W. Leonard Congreve
23	Humphrey Nevill
24	BBC Hulton Picture Library
25	Mansell Collection
26	Private Collection
27	Houghton Library, Harvard (photo Worcester Art Museum)
28	Roger Musgrave
29	'The Later Letters of Edward Lear'

Acknowledgements

I would like to extend my warm personal thanks to: Mr Philip Hofer, Dr William Bond and Miss Eleanor Garvey of the Houghton Library, Harvard University, for their kindness and help before, during and after my stay at Harvard; Mr and Mrs Mitchell for the loan of their copy of Lear's letters to his sister Ann, and for family photographs and drawings; William Hornby for his endless trouble; Colonel and Miss Prescott for their hospitality and help; Mr Laurence Elvin; Mr Angus Davidson; Mrs Burt; Lady Marjorie Gillies for the loan of books and family papers; Professor Richard Harrison; Mr William Carlton for details of the family of Jeremiah Lear of Batsworth Park; the late Dr Edelsten and Mrs Edelsten; Lord Strachie; Mr Lyonson and Mrs Kay at Knowsley; Mr Herbert Cahoon of the Pierpont Morgan Library, New York; Mr John Naimaster, Managing Director, The Fine Art Society, New Bond Street; Mr Handasyde Buchanan, and Professor R. B. Martin.

I would also like to thank: Sir Charles Tennyson; Miss Constance-Ann Parker of the Royal Academy Library; Mr Osbert Wyndham Hewett; Susan, Lady Tweedsmuir; Miss Elisabeth Davidson of the Arts Council; Mr Christopher Hollis; Mr Bakhurst, Secretary of the Stock Exchange, London, and Mr Thompson of the Public Assignees Office of the Stock Exchange; Dame Janet Vaughan, and Mrs Russell, Librarian of Somerville College, Oxford; Mr J. R. Cuthbertson, Manager of Drummonds Bank; F. T. Baker of the City of Lincoln Libraries, Museum and Art Gallery; the Rev. A. J. Adams, Vicar of Wanstead Parish Church; Lord Derby; Lord Cromer; Lord Stanley of Alderley; Lord Tennyson; Lord Northbrook; Mr Robert North; Mr Godfrey Lushington and Mrs Marie Fowler; Major G. G. W. Horton-Fawkes; Mr F. D. Martineau; Lady Mander; Colonel G. Phipps Hornby; Major Sir Richard Proby; Miss Ingrid Barr; Miss Rebecca

Hornby; Mr Hugh Bedford; Mrs Frances K. Smith; Mrs Irvin Ehrenpreis; Dr Cope; Mr Roger Musgrave; Miss Elizabeth S. Henry, of the Worcester Art Museum, Worcester, Mass., Mr John Griffin; Messrs Walker Martineau; Messrs Bernard Quaritch Ltd.

The staff of the following also kindly helped me: Somerset Record Office, Taunton; The Tennyson Research Centre, Lincoln; The John Rylands Library, Manchester; the Linnean Society; The Zoological Society of London; the Chamberlain's Court, Guildhall; the Guildhall Library; the Department of Literary Enquiry, Principal Probate Registry, Somerset House; the Public Record Office; the Bodleian Library; Reigate Public Library; the Reading Room of the British Museum; the Victoria and Albert Museum; the New York Public Library; the Liverpool Record Office; the Glamorgan Record Office.

For quotations from Queen Victoria's diary I am indebted to the gracious permission of Her Majesty the Queen.

For permission to quote from unpublished work or to reproduce drawings and paintings I would like to thank: Harvard College Library; Lord Strachie; Mr William Hornby; Colonel Prescott; Mr Mitchell; Sir Charles Tennyson; Mrs Cuthbert and Mrs Burt; Susan, Lady Tweedsmuir; Lord Aberdare; Mr Maldwin Drummond; Dr B. W. Paine; Mr Robert Donnell III; Mr Edward Selwyn; Lord Derby; Mr Frederick R. Koch; Mr H. Nevill of Palmerston, New Zealand; and the trustees of the following: The Pierpont Morgan Library, New York; the Henry E. Huntington Library and Art Gallery, San Marino, California; the National Library of Scotland; the John Rylands Library, Manchester; the Beinecke Rare Book and Manuscript Library, Yale University; the University of British Columbia; the Bodleian Library; the Royal Botanical Gardens, Kew; the Agnes Etherington Art Centre, Queen's University, Kingston, Canada; Robert Manning Shozier Library, Florida State University, Tallahassee; the Victoria & Albert Museum; Balliol College, Oxford; Princeton University.

For permission to quote from published works I wish to thank: John Murray, from *Edward Lear* by Angus Davidson; *The Diary of Frances*, Lady Shelley; *The Creevey Papers*; The British Council from *Tennyson* by F. L. Lucas; Macmillan from *Recollections of a Happy Life* by Marianne North; *Alfred Tennyson* by Sir Charles Tennyson; Chapman & Hall from

Thomas Woolner by Amy Woolner; George Rainbird Limited, and Harper & Row, Publishers, Inc., from *Mount Athos* by John Julius Norwich, Reresby Sitwell and A. Costa; Mrs Edward Pickmann from *Roman Spring* by Mrs Winthrop Chanler; Oxford University Press from *Early Victorian England*, and Jane Austen, *Minor Works* (ed. R. W. Chapman); Eyre & Spottiswoode, from *Call Back Yesterday*, by Lady Charnwood; St James's Press from *Twentieth Century Children's Writers*.

Finally, I would like to extend my particular personal thanks to: Charles Lewsen; Jonathan Field; Mrs Caroline da Costa; the Warden and staff of St Deiniol's Library, Hawarden; the staff of Oatlands Park Hotel, Weybridge; Miss Sheila Watson; Adrian House of Collins; and above and beyond all to my husband, Michael Noakes, both for his professional advice as a painter, and for his encouragement, enthusiasm and support without which I would neither have begun nor completed this book.

Index